THE THEORY AND PRACTICE OF SYSTEMATIC STAFF SELECTION

Also by Mike Smith

INTRODUCING ORGANIZATIONAL BEHAVIOUR
(*with others*)

A DEVELOPMENT PROGRAM FOR WOMEN IN
MANAGEMENT

THE BRITISH TELECOM SURVEY ITEM BANK (Vols I and II)

Also by Ivan T. Robertson

HUMAN BEHAVIOUR IN ORGANIZATIONS
(*with C. L. Cooper*)

THE THEORY AND PRACTICE OF SYSTEMATIC STAFF SELECTION

Mike Smith

Senior Lecturer in Industrial Psychology
University of Manchester Institute of Science and Technology

and

Ivan T. Robertson

Lecturer in Occupational Psychology
University of Manchester Institute of Science and Technology

MACMILLAN

First published 1986

Published by
THE MACMILLAN PRESS LTD
Houndmills, Basingstoke, Hampshire RG21 2XS
and London
Companies and representatives
throughout the world

Printed in Hong Kong

British Library Cataloguing in Publication Data
Smith, Mike, *1945–*
The theory and practice of systematic staff
selection.
1. Recruiting of employees
I. Title   II. Robertson, Ivan, T.
658.3'112   HF5549.5.R44
ISBN 0–333–36570–4

Contents

List of Figures

List of Tables

List of Abbreviations

APRE	Army Personnel Research Establishment
AT&T	American Telephone and Telegraph
CBS	Columbia Broadcasting System
CODOT	Classification of Occupations and Directory of Occupational Titles
CPOAT	Card Punch Operator Aptitude Test
CRAC	Careers Research and Advisory Centre
CSSB	Civil Service Selection Board
DBA	Doctor of Business Administration
EPI	Eysenck Personality Inventory
EWS	Efficient Worker Standard
GNP	Gross National Product
LGD	Leaderless Group Discussion
MCB	Management Centre Bradford
MMPI	Minnesota Multiphasic Personality Inventory
NFER	National Foundation for Education Research
NIIP	National Institute of Industrial Psychology
ONR	Office of Naval Research
PAQ	Position Analysis Questionnaire
RJP	Realistic Job Preview
SCII	Strong Campbell Interest Inventory
TAS	Task Abilities Scale
TAT	Thematic Apperception Test
ULMA	Ultra Low Modulation Amplifiers
VDU	Visual Display Unit
WAIS	Weschler Adult Intelligence Scale
WISC	Weschler Intelligence Scale for Children

Acknowledgements

The authors and publishers wish to thank the following who have kindly given permission for the use of copyright material:

The British Psychological Society for figure 'Aptitude profile for the job setter', Sparrow *et al.* (1982) *Journal of Occupational Psychology*.

IPM Personnel Management Services Ltd and British Institute of Management for tables from *Selecting Managers*.

McGraw-Hill Book Company for a figure from Ghiselli and Brown (1955) *Personnel and Industrial Psychology*.

Personnel Psychology for the table from Klimoski and Strickland (177) 'Assessment centers – valid or merely prescient?' *Personnel Psychology* 30, 353–61; for a figure from Asher (1972) 'The biographical item: can it be improved?', *Personnel Psychology*, 25, 252–69; and for tables from Lawshe, Bolda, Brune and Auclair (1958) 'Expectancy charts II: their theoretical development', *Personnel Psychology*, 11, 545–59.

Sidney A. Fine and The Johns Hopkins Press for the figure from *Performance Assessment*, ed Ronald Buk, chapter 1, Sidney A. Fine, 'Job Analysis', 1986, The Johns Hopkins Press, Baltimore, MD.

Saville & Holdsworth Ltd, for the figure 'Saville–Holdworth's Categorisation of the world of work'.

Every effort has been made to trace all copyright-holders, but if any have been inadvertently overlooked the publishers will be pleased to make the necessary arrangement at the first opportunity.

Part 1
Preparation

1 Introduction

THE CONTEXT OF SELECTION

Next time you are on a long haul flight, take a good look at your 300 or so fellow passengers. Without doubt they will differ in all sorts of ways: some will be tall and some will be short. Some will be thin, and some, probably those in the seat next to yours, will be very large indeed. It is not only their physical characteristics which will differ. Their personalities will vary too. Jobs differ too. The cabin staff need qualities to enable them to deal with demanding passengers. The navigator needs precise spatial reasoning. It is clear that selecting the right person for some jobs can be literally a matter of life or death.

Even in less hazardous situations, selecting the right person for the job can be of enormous importance. A company can be dragged to its knees by the weight of ineffectual staff which decades of ineffectual selection methods have allowed to accumulate.

As subsequent chapters will show, vast sums of money are involved. It is fairly easy to use selection to improve productivity by 6 per cent. Under very favourable circumstances selection can bring about gains of 20 per cent or more. Applied to whole economies, the huge potential of proper selection is apparent. Six per cent of the Gross National Product (GNP) of the United States is over $200 billion, 6 per cent of the United Kingdom's GNP is over £18 000 million and 6 per cent of Australia's GNP is over A$11 000 million.

Effective selection also brings benefits to the employing organisation and their employees. Companies who are able to ensure a match between job requirements and people's characteristics will obtain a competitive advantage. Good selection procedures should reduce the worry and pressure on employees in jobs where they are out of their depth.

THE ESSENTIALS OF A SELECTION SYSTEM

The need for selection arises from two indisputable facts. First, people differ in their characteristics such as ability, personality and interests. Secondly, jobs differ in the demands they make on workers. In essence, selection involves systematically matching people to jobs. The stages can be divided into three (see Figure 1.1).

First is the preparation stage. Preparation involves analysing the job to determine what is involved and what is needed from workers. Two things flow from the job analysis: a specification of the characteristics of the people who are best equipped to meet the demands of the job, and criteria which can be used to assess work performance. The development of the personnel specification and the development of criteria often take place simultaneously. The third aspect of preparation is to attract a reasonable number of people who might have the characteristics the job requires.

The selection stage follows preparation. The first and crucial decision is to decide upon the most appropriate method of selection. The choice of methods is wide and ranges from tests and interviews to graphology and astrology. Each of these methods have advantages and disadvantages. Comparing their rival claims involves comparing each method's merit and psychometric properties.

The final stage of a selection system concerns evaluation. A part of this evaluation involves establishing the validity of the system. However, evaluation of a system will also involve other aspects such as the absence of bias and the appropriateness to an organisation.

This book follows the basic selection process which has just been outlined. In each chapter both the practical and theoretical aspects are described.

SELECTION AND OTHER AREAS OF INDUSTRIAL PSYCHOLOGY

Selection is one of the main methods which an organisation can use to ensure it has an effective work force. Certainly it is fairly easy to obtain a 6 per cent increase in productivity by using better ways of choosing among candidates. However, the contribution of better selection must be assessed in perspective. Figure 1.2 shows the relationship of selection to other methods of ensuring an efficient workforce.

Producing an efficient worker starts with a careful analysis of the job and then producing a personnel specification describing the person who is suited to the job. Then the process can take three routes or a combination of three routes. Suppose the personnel

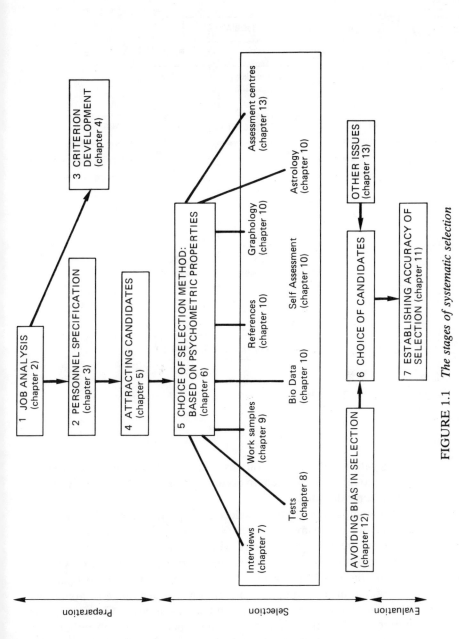

5

FIGURE 1.1 *The stages of systematic selection*

Preparation

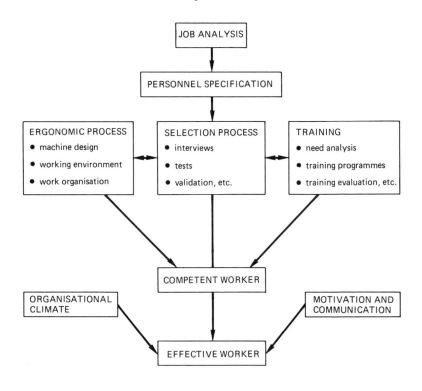

FIGURE 1.2   *The industrial psychology paradigm*

specification calls for operatives whose hand-eye co-ordination is good enough to allow them to accurately position the protective layer of a lazer video disc.

The company could try to select appropriate people. But, alternatively, the company could try the ergonomic approach. It could redesign the protective layers with a series of lugs which will fit together only when they are aligned correctly. Instead of trying to identify the top 10 per cent of applicants in terms of their hand-eye co-ordination, the company can employ a wider range of applicants and can save upon recruitment and selection costs. Generally, it is better to redesign equipment or other aspects of the job rather than try to select appropriate individuals: the result will be more precise and will last longer. However, there are many jobs which cannot be redesigned or where restructuring can only be achieved at inordinate expense.

Alternatively, the company could accept most applications and provide a training course in hand-eye co-ordination. Whilst this solution might be feasible, it is probably less effective than selecting applicants with the appropriate capabilities. The output of a training course can be uncertain and most training schemes cost far more than appropriate selection methods. Consequently the best general advice is that a company should first design a job so that it demands as few requirements as possible. Next, it should select workers on the remaining requirements. When it is impossible to select workers with the right abilities the company should invest in training facilities.

Of course, in practice the situation is rarely as clear cut, and ergonomics, selection and training interact and complement each other to produce a competent worker. To be effective, the organisation must also provide motivation, communication and an appropriate organisational climate.

2 Job Analysis

The first stage of filling any vacancy can be completed long before the vacancy ever arises: it consists of analysing the job. But the process of analysing a job is not solely concerned with selection. Accurate job analysis is an important part of the general management process and it can be used in many ways.

THE MANY USES OF JOB DESCRIPTIONS

One hosiery company maintains job descriptions for all its employees and ensures that they are kept up to date by a series of annual reviews. The company schedules the reviews to take place between the end of the financial year and the time when it recruits school leavers. The job analysis was originally undertaken in order to help their selection process, but once the job descriptions were available the company found that they were useful for many other purposes. To date the job descriptions have helped:

1   to reorganise the company workforce,
2   to produce a more rational and acceptable salary structure,
3   to identify training needs.

The reorganisation of the company structure arose out of the existence of job descriptions. Once the company had a clear statement of the contents of each job, it realised that it could structure its work force in a more efficient way by identifying bottlenecks etc. In the case of one employee the job descriptions helped to bring to light the fact that, due to past history, he was reporting to a director who was not in a position to exercise effective control over his work. The job descriptions also helped remove animosity between the canteen staff by ensuring that all tasks were allocated to specific individuals, and reducing the possibilities for misunderstanding.

In each of these instances the nature of the problem and their solutions were apparent from an accurate, clear, concise and *written* description of the jobs involved. In theory, the improvements could have been achieved without written descriptions. In practice, they were not. In practice, selection without a written job description is usually muddle-headed, capricious and incomplete.

METHODS OF ANALYSING JOBS

Standard textbooks in Industrial Psychology such as Blum and Naylor (1968), McCormick and Tiffin (1974) and Landy and Trumbo (1980) list several methods of analysing jobs. The method which is adopted will depend upon the exact situation and the intended use. In a situation where there are limited resources a fairly commonsense approach is called for. The selection process often requires only a straight forward analysis which identifies the six or seven most salient points. In large organisations such as the armed forces, or a large organisation in the telecommunications industry where there are hundreds of recruits each year, and where the consequences of mistakes are high, it is worthwhile undertaking a rigorous job analysis.

A Basic Five-Step Approach to Job Analysis

In most selection contexts a basic five-step approach is quite adequate and will bring about a notable improvement in efficiency:

Step one: collect together documents such as the training manual, which give information concerning the job.

Step two: ask the relevant manager about the job. Ask about the main purposes of the job, the activities involved and the personal relationships which must be maintained with others.

Step three: ask the job holder similar questions about their job. In some circumstances it may be possible to persuade the job holder to keep a detailed record of their work activities over a period of one or two weeks.

Step four: observe the job holder performing their work and make a note of the most important points. If possible, observe the job being performed on two separate days, at different times of the day.

Step five: attempt to do the job yourself. Of course, it will be impossible to follow this step for every job. It would be dangerous for anyone but a skilled worker to operate some types of machinery such as a drop forge. In other jobs the main activities are mental work which cannot be directly observed.

Step six: write the job description. When the information has been collected, the results are set out in the job description. There is no single format which is better than others. However, the format described in Table 2.1 (Checklist One) has been found to be very useful and can be used with little prior knowledge. It assembles the information about the job under six headings. In general, job descriptions should stick to specifying the results which should be achieved. Prescriptions of *how* the job is to be done should be avoided: working methods may change and individual workers may achieve their targets in different ways. Provided the targets are achieved, the method is usually of secondary importance. An Example of a job description produced using this six-stage method is given at the end of this chapter.

MORE INVOLVED APPROACHES TO JOB ANALYSIS

When to Use More Complex Methods

The basic six step approach is well within the competence of an intelligent manager or personnel specialist. It is cost effective and yields results which are quite adequate for most selection purposes. But, if the organisation intends to establish a complex and sophisticated selection system involving extended interviews, psychological tests and practical exercises, then the extra detail of a comprehensive job description can be usefully incorporated.

However, there are circumstances where more complex methods are fully justified. These circumstances usually involve three factors. First, more complex methods of jobs analysis are warranted when large numbers of recruits are involved. For example, if an electricity undertaking recruits more than 50 fitters per year and there is a good

TABLE 2.1 *Checklist One: Contents of job descriptions*

1 *Job Identification*
This section covers the job title, the location of the job (for example, press-shop, Longbridge works), the number of people in the job and the person to whom the job holder is responsible. It is worthwhile noting that the job description *does not* include the name of the person holding the job. It is a description of the job which needs to be performed irrespective of the person who is currently doing the job.

2 *Main Purposes of the Job*
A brief and unambiguous statement is all that is required under this heading.

3 *Responsibilities*
Often this section also contains a list of the key results which the job holder must achieve. It seeks to provide a record of the job holder's responsibilities for men, materials, money, tools and equipment. The responsibilities section is particularly important when describing management jobs and it is particularly important to identify the key results. Usually, the key results concern:

(a) a product produced to a previously agreed schedule (for example, 300 word processors per month from production line C),

(b) a specified standard of quality (for example, customer complaints less than 5% within 1 year of purchase, and costs of 'warranty repairs' less than ½% sales turnover),

(c) the efficient utilisation of resources (for example, value added per employee over £4000 and return on capital of 11%),

(d) the development of personnel, especially the development of subordinates (for example, to ensure that staff are trained in at least two skills and to ensure that the department provides at least one person per year who has sufficient potential and experience to warrant promotion to middle management).

In management job descriptions it may also be necessary to detail the control over subordinates: the numbers and level of people controlled, the responsibilities for their recruitment, supervision, development, discipline, dismissal and salary determination. Financial control is another area where detailed description may be necessary. For example, what responsibilities does the job holder have for budgetary control and cost control? What assets or stock fall under his jurisdiction? What are his obligations for sales, purchasing or investment? What role does he need to play in forecasting and planning. A final aspect which should be included in the responsibilities section of a job description is the amount of guidance and supervision the job holder should expect from his superior.

TABLE 2.1   *cont'd*

---

4   *Relationships with People*
The fourth section of a job description specifies the job holder's relationships with the people he works with. In addition to identifying the
people involved, it should also indicate the nature of the relationship, for
example, liaison, consults, directs, notifies. If the job holder needs to
work in a team or if he has to deal with different types of people, it is
usually specified in this section.

5   *Physical Conditions*
In job descriptions for operatives, the *fifth* section concerning *physical
conditions* may be the most important section. It specifies the place of
work, the hours and the possibilities for overtime working. The fifth
section should also state whether the work is active or sedentary and the
physical demands which are made on the job holder's senses or the
requirements for strength, physical endurance or skills. If the work
involves any risks, they are normally recorded in this section.

6   *Pay and Promotion*
The salary, increments, commissions, bonuses and perks such as lun-
cheon vouchers or company car should be clearly stated. Pension
schemes, absence and illness regulations and any bonus schemes should
also be included. Finally, the prospects for promotion or transfer should
be included in appropriate situations.

---

supply of candidates, the extra expense will be justified. A second
circumstance justifying the use of a more complex method is when
the consequences and costs of failure are very high. For example, the
costs of training a policeman are about £20 000, the cost of employing
an unsuitable refinery technician could, in an emergency, result in
millions of pounds of damage, and the cost of employing a zany chief
executive could spell disaster and bankruptcy. Thirdly, the extra
expense of sophisticated analysis may be acceptable if the job analysis
can be used for some other purpose such as the design of training or a
job salary grading exercise.

The Complex Methods of Job Analysis

Probably the most comprehensive list of job analysis techniques was
compiled by Blum and Naylor (1968) and it itemised ten different
methods. The main advantages and disadvantages of nine of the
methods is set out in Checklist Two.

TABLE 2.2 *Checklist Two: Advantages and disadvantages of ten methods of job analysis*

1. *Questionnaire Method*
   - *Advantages*   Good for producing quantitative information and can produce objective and generalizable results; cheap
   - *Disadvantages*   Substantial sample needed; Substantial fore knowledge needed to be able to construct questionnaire; respondents must be able and willing to give accurate replies

2. *Checklist Method*
   Similar to questionnaire method but since responses are either YES or NO the results may be 'cruder' or require larger sample. They tend to require fewer subjective judgements.

3. *Individual Interviews*
   - *Advantages*   Very flexible; can provide indepth information; easy to organise and prepare
   - *Disadvantages*   Time-consuming; expensive; difficult to analyse

4. *Observation Interviews*
   Similar to individual interview method but provides additional information, for example, visual or auditory information. The higher level of contextual cues make it more difficult for the analyst to be misled. The method may expose both the analyst and the worker to increased safety hazards.

5. *Group Interviews*
   Similar to the individual interview but they are less time-consuming for analyst and some claim that richer information is obtained since interviewees stimulate each other's thoughts. They are more difficult to organise and there is the danger that a group is over-influenced by one individual.

6. *Technical Conference Method*
   - *Advantages*   Quick, cheap and can be used for jobs that do not yet exist. Can avoid restrictive practices
   - *Disadvantages*   The 'experts' may not be true experts and an unrealistic analysis may result

7. *Diary Method*
   - *Advantages*   Cheap, flexible and requires little advance preparation. Useful for non-manual tasks where observation is of limited value. Can also be used in jobs involving a wide variety of tasks

cont'd

TABLE 2.2   *cont'd*

•	*Disadvantages*	Needs co-operation from respondents; tendency to keep incomplete logs – frequent but minor items often omitted

8. *Work Participation Method*

•	*Advantages*	Can produce very realistic analyses
•	*Disadvantages*	Expensive, time-consuming and can only be used for jobs requiring short training and no safety hazards

9. *Critical Incident Method*

•	*Advantages*	Focuses on the aspects of a job that are crucial to success
•	*Disadvantages*	Often produces incomplete data difficult to analyse

Observation Method

The most frequently used methods are observation, diaries and questionnaires. An excellent example of the *use of the observation method* is Mintzberg's study of the 'Nature of Managerial Work' (1973). He observed each of five chief executives over a week. Providing the observers are well trained, the observation method can provide high quality information, but it is labour intensive and costly. The observation method is most applicable to situations where there are a few people holding the jobs and where high quality information is needed. In principle, job analysis using the observation method is easy to conduct. All that is needed is a timepiece (usually with a digit to show seconds) and sheets of paper with the volunteer's name and other identification data, plus appropriate column headings such as time, activity, place. In practice, job analysis by observation methods encounters three main difficulties.

First, many jobs are not amenable to this type of analysis, some 'mental' jobs involve little observable activity, and some highly skilled manual jobs involve actions which are too speedy to analyse. Secondly, some 'volunteers' may not wish all their actions to be observed. This may arise when the job involves very confidential information or where work is done at non-traditional times in non-traditional settings – for example, when work is done in the evenings, at home. Thirdly, analysts may record their observations inaccurately, using words and concepts which are not in general use.

Functional Job Analysis was developed to mitigate the third problem (Fine and Wiley, 1977) and it was designed to control the language used to describe a job. Functional Job Analysis adopts the same conceptualisation of work as the United States Training and Employment Service which, essentially, maintains that work is done in relation to data, people or things. As Table 2.3 shows, each of these areas has a number of levels. Functional Job Analysis is relevant to many methods of job analysis, but it is particularly relevant to the observation method. However, it is a fairly complex system and minimum of four or five days' training is needed for observers.

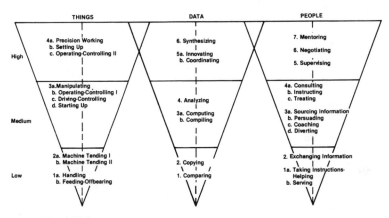

SOURCE Fine (1986).

Diaries

In principle, nothing could be easier than analysing a job using the diary method. All that is needed is a sheet of paper headed with the date and the volunteer's name. In practice, difficulties arise from five directions. First, not all jobs are suitable for this type of analysis – short cycle repetitive jobs, jobs involving speedy or delicate manual skills, and jobs occupied by employees unused to verbalising their activities present particular problems.

Secondly, there is the problem of controlling how and when the volunteers use the diary: some volunteers will ignore the diary for weeks and rely on their memories to make their entries in the ten minutes before the actual deadline for handing in their diaries. One variation which mitigates this problem is for the job analyst to telephone the volunteer at a prearranged time (for example, 4.30 p.m.) every day and ask what activities he has undertaken in the preceding 24 hours.

Thirdly, diaries are notoriously open to distortion according to the image the volunteer wishes to project. It is easy for him to record that he works longer hours on a wider variety of more important tasks than is objectively the case. Fourthly, it is difficult to maintain consistent reporting standards: some volunteers report in tedious, excruciating, graphic detail even the most minute work activity while others hardly give any information at all. Fifthly, there is the problem of analysis. The diary sheets have to be collated and the frequencies and duration of activities have to be extracted and tabulated. This time consuming process is inherently inaccurate. In addition, there may be an element of subjectivity because different volunteers may use different words to refer to the same activity, or even more confusingly, they may use the same words to refer to different activities. The analyst is often left with the subjective task of deciding what the volunteer means and *then* allotting it to an appropriate category.

One possible way of mitigating these problems is to abandon the idea of a blank piece of paper and to give a system of headings to guide the diary entries. Better still, all the possible entries can be listed and the volunteer is merely required to tick the appropriate boxes. For example, Hinricks (1964) designed a log sheet which he used in his study of the ways in which research staff communicate with each other. Each time there was communication involving a volunteer, the volunteer filled out a log sheet by ticking the appropriate boxes. This approach involves more preparation and there is the danger that something crucial is missed from the log sheet. However, it overcomes many problems and is much easier to analyse. An excellent example of the *use of diaries* is Rosemary Stewart's classic study of 'Managers and their jobs' (1967).

Questionnaire Methods

Many practitioners adopt the *questionnaire method*. The simplest type of job analysis questionnaire, or as they are sometimes called, a *job inventory*, is the checklist. *Checklists* usually contain over a hundred activities and job incumbents mark those activities which are included in their jobs. A classic example of a checklist is Morse and Archer's (1967) analysis of wire and antenna engineers in the USA Air Force. A more recent example of a checklist is Youngman, Ostoby, Monk and Heywood's (1978) checklist for engineering occupations.

Checklists require thorough preparation which should include wide consultation and a 'field trial' in order to ensure that no important activities have been omitted and that the instructions, wording, layout and method of responding are all correct. A distinctive feature of the checklist method is that it can be only used in situations where a large sample is available. In essence, the analysis will be based upon the proportion of people giving positive answers to an item. If the sample is below 30 the results will be both erratic and insensitive.

Rating Scales are an improvement upon the relatively crude and insensitive checklist. Like checklists, rating scales present the volunteer with a list of work activities but instead of simply asking him to mark those activities he performs in his job, a scale would ask him to give a rating between one, and typically, seven, according to the amount of time it involves. The following scale is typical of the seven-point scales in use.

1 It rarely occurs (less than 11 per cent of the job)
2 It occupies a small part of the job (between 11 and 24 per cent)
3 It occupies rather less than half the job (between 25 and 39 per cent)
4 It occupies about half of the job (between 40 and 59 per cent)
5 It occupies rather more than half of the job (between 60 and 74 per cent)
6 It occupies a large majority of the job (between 75 and 89 per cent)
7 It occupies practically the whole of the job (more than 90 per cent of the job)

The percentage bands need to be adjusted according to the complexity of the job since jobs with many component activities tend to produce lower percentage figures for each individual activity. Job rating scales are not necessarily restricted to estimates of time. Indeed, Morse and Archer's checklist also requested ratings of time spent and importance and their 1967 report contains a list of 17 variables which can be used in rating scales (see Table 2.4).

TABLE 2.4 *A typical job analysis questionnaire*

Listed below is a duty and the tasks it includes. Read the list and put a tick in the appropriate column if you perform the task as part of your job. Then rate the tasks you have ticked on the time you spend on the tasks and their importance. There is space at the bottom of the form for you to add any tasks which are not listed.	TICK THIS COLUMN IF TASK IS PER-FORMED	TIME SPENT	IMPORTANCE
		7. Very much above average 6. Above average 5. Slightly above average 4. About average 3. Slightly below average 2. Below average 1. Very much below average	7. Extremely important 6. Very important 5. Important 4. Average importance 3. Unimportant 2. Very unimportant 1. Extremely unimportant

NAME OF DUTY	INSTALLING AND REMOVING CABLE SYSTEMS		
1. Attach suspension strand to pole			
2. Change and splice lasher wire			
3. Deliver materials to lineman with snatch block and materials			
OTHER TASKS			

SOURCE Modified from Morse and Archer (1967).

Often a checklist will need to be designed for each type of job and guidelines for the development of checklists is given by McCormick (1976). However, several general purpose rating scales are available. The most widely used of the general inventories is the Position Analysis Questionnaire (PAQ) developed by McCormick, Jeanneret and Mecham (1972). The development of the PAQ was particularly rigorous and scientific – the studies involved collecting data for 3700 jobs and then using the statistical procedure of Principal Components Analysis to extract the recurrent trends in the data. There were six major trends concerning:

1 the input of information, for example, perceptual interpretation,
2 mental processes, for example, decision making,
3 work onput, for example, use of foot controls,
4 relationships with people, for example, serving/entertaining,
5 work environment, for example, hazardous physical environment,
6 other characteristics.

Within each of these headings scales were developed to measure more specific requirements. For example, the heading 'mental processes' included items concerning decision-making and information processing. In total there are scales for almost 200 job elements. Most of the scales share a particular advantage; they start with a thorough description of the aspect to be rated and then each point on the rating scale is accompanied by a benchmark – a specific standard which can be used for comparison. Examples of two of the scales are given in Table 2.5.

Thus the PAQ enjoys the advantages of being generally applicable, comprehensive and having benchmarks. However, it is time consuming to administer and requires some specialist knowledge.

AGREEMENT AND RESTRUCTURING

When the job description has been prepared it should be discussed with either the job holder or his union representative. In most circumstances a job description is prepared by the job holder's superior, but where it is prepared by someone else such as the Personnel Officer or Training Officer, the job description should be discussed with the job holder's superior. In the light of these

TABLE 2.5   *Two examples of benchmarked scales similar to those used by McCormick*

Near Visual Discrimination (visual discrimination of objects within arm's reach)

7   Inspects precision watch parts for defects
6   Proofreads newspaper articles before publishing
5   Reads electric house meters
4   Makes entries on sales tickets
3   Observes position of knife when carving beef
2   Paints house walls
1   Sweeps street with push broom
0   Makes no near visual discrimination

Finger Manipulation (Please check the activity below which involves about as much finger manipulation as the incumbent employs in his job)

7   Performs surgical operations on humans
6   Cuts ornamental designs in jewellery
5   Tunes auto engines
4   Adjusts camera settings to take commercial pictures
3   Packs cakes of soap in cardboard boxes
2   Pulls weeds by hand
1   Carries pieces of furniture
0   Job involves no finger manipulation

discussions the job description is amended until it is accepted by both the job holder and his boss. In some organisations agreement is formalised to the point where both parties are required to sign the final version.

THEORETICAL ASPECTS OF JOB ANALYSIS

Previous sections of this chapter have carefully avoided the theoretical and academic issues which concern job descriptions. But there are five issues that deserve some consideration: task- *v.* worker-oriented variables; reliability, validity; job families and comparisons between different methods.

Task-Oriented *v.* Worker-Oriented Variables

Job analysis can focus on two separate but related domains. The first, and probably the most traditional domain, focuses upon the *tasks* which the job holder performs, such as delivers lecture, counsels students, writes books. The second focuses upon the *activities* a worker has to perform such as oral communication, interpersonal empathy and written communication. Inventories use either of these approaches with a strong tendency for more recent inventories to concentrate upon the worker-oriented variables. In theory, the advantages of the two approaches are finely balanced. As Figure 2.1 shows, job analysis is itself an activity involving a number of stages. For both worker-oriented and task-oriented variables the process starts with the worker performing a job observed by the analyst, and in both cases the route leads to the same final output of attributes which are required to perform the job successfully. Furthermore, the two routes pass through the same three domains and involve equivalent sets of deductions and reports. The main difference lies in the positioning of the interim report. In following the *task-oriented* route there is first only a small inferential leap between the observation and the report of the task variables. This is followed by a large inferential leap to obtain the attributes. In following the *worker-oriented route* there is first a large inferential leap followed by a small one. According to this analysis there should be little difference in terms of the functioning of a selection system. However, opinion is more polarised and partisan. McCormick, Cunningham and Gordon (1967) suggest that the worker-oriented questionnaire yields results which are less vulnerable to technological constraints and that the technique is more inclusive of occupational areas. On the other hand Prien (1977) concludes that worker-oriented job analysis data 'is more vulnerable to contamination and ... more insufficient than task oriented job analysis'. Eventually this issue will probably be settled by reference to their psychometric properties of reliability and validity.

Reliability of Task Analyses

The concept of reliability is considered in detail in chapter 6. For the present purposes it is enough to note that it usually refers to the accuracy of a measurement and the degree to which it is uncontamin-

22

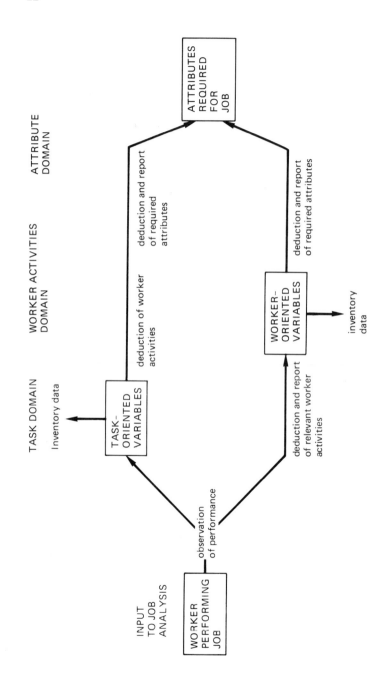

FIGURE 2.1 *A schematic analysis of job analysis*

ated by spurious artifacts such as random error. Often reliability can be equated with consistency. If the same measures are taken on two occasions and the same answer is obtained, the measures are perfectly reliable. Reliability is often the *sine qua non* of any measurement: without reliability there can be no validity, accuracy or sensitivity.

The question therefore arises 'How free are job analyses from artifacts such as random error'. This question rather resembles the question 'How long is a piece of string?' and it evokes the same answer: 'It depends'. Clearly, a rushed analysis by an untrained person will be subject to considerable error. So the question becomes 'How reliable can job analyses be?' Again, in reality, the question is more complex because there are three types of reliability.

Repeated measures reliability is obtained by one analyst performing a job analysis and then, reanalysing it after a period of, say, a week. The two analyses are then compared for consistency. It is difficult to guarantee that all investigators have used a pure 'test-retest' approach but the data in Table 2.6 is presented by McCormick (1976) and is based on three investigations.

It can be seen that there is a wide spread of correlations. McCormick notes that the lower coefficients were obtained by a study where the time interval was rather long (several weeks). However, the table shows that high test-retest reliability can be obtained. This conclusion is supported by an investigation by Birt (1968), who compared the consistency of replies to two inventories administered a week apart. He obtained correlations which ranged from 0.92 to 0.98,

TABLE 2.6 *Reliability of job analysis ratings*

Type of rating	Study 1	2	3
1 *Task occurence*	0.7 & 0.7	0.9	0.6, 0.6 & 0.7
2 *Time spent on task*	0.6	0.8	0.6
3 *Part of position*	–	0.8	0.6
4 *Importance of task*	–	–	0.6
5 *Difficulty of task*	0.5	–	0.4

SOURCE McCormick (1976).

with a median value of 0.96. A study by Brennecke (1961) obtained a correlation of 0.67.

There is more specific evidence concerning the second type of reliability: *inter-rater reliability*. In essence this is investigated by two analysts examining a job at the same time but arriving at independent conclusions. Their conclusions are then compared. It is rare for the strict requirements of this method to be met but a number of studies have approximated this design. For example, Wexley and Silverman (1978) administered an inventory to about 48 effective managers and to about 48 ineffective managers and their results indicated that effective store managers did not differ significantly from one another in their ratings of work activities and worker characteristics.

Schmitt and Fine (1983) summarise a number of studies using Functional Job Analysis, which uses a controlled language for the reporting of job analysis, and they note 'Data in unpublished technical reports do suggest high reliability. For example, in a Coast Guard study, Zepp, Belenky and Rosen (1977) reported that over 98% of 5754 FJA ratings made by independent raters were no more than one scale point different'. Schmitt and Fine go on to describe a study of graduate students who had attended only a four-day training programme. The six graduate students produced coefficients of 0.81, 0.97, 0.82, 0.97, and 0.79 depending upon the exact trait under analysis. This information supports Fine and Eisner's (1980) claim that when the language of a task statement has been structured and controlled levels can be reliably assigned. However, Algera (1983) obtained correlations ranging from 0.21 to 0.77 between ratings by three job holders and three people who were in supervisory or personnel positions. The significance of Algera's mixed results are, however, difficult to evaluate because the analysts had received no training and the judgements were not job analysis ratings in the usual sense of the word. Algera's results seem out of line with McCormick, Finn and Scheip's (1957) study and Madden, Hazel and Christal's (1964) study which both reported satisfactory inter-rater reliability. Indeed, Palmer and McCormick (1961) report a correlation of 0.75 between raters applying a 130-item checklist. Thus the overwhelming balance of evidence indicates that with properly constructed inventories and with analysts who have received at least minimal training, the inter-rater reliability of job analyses can be very good.

The third type of reliability concerns *inter-sample reliability*. In other words, do the results obtained from one sample correspond to the results obtained from another sample. The evidence on this question is relatively sparse and involves the assumption that two samples who are *said* to be performing identical jobs *are* in fact performing identical jobs. The study by Christal (1969) provides direct evidence. He took 35 samples representing ten career fields: the median correlation for estimates of whether a task was performed in the course of the job was 0.98 and the median correlation for estimates of the time spent on the task was 0.96.

Validity of Task Analyses

Validity is another topic which is discussed in much greater detail in chapter 6. Here it is sufficient to note that validity is concerned with how well job analyses measure what they claim to measure. Ideally, validity is assessed by comparing the measure in question against a measure which is known to be perfect. If they yield similar results, the measure in question is said to be valid. In practice, difficulties arise because it is hard to find any perfect measure against which to compare the job analysis. If the job analysis is compared against a suspect measure and there is disagreement, it is impossible to know whether the job analysis is at fault or whether the measure used for comparison is at fault.

Industrial psychologists have adopted four main approaches in attempts to establish the validity of job analyses.

The first approach involving *comparisons with objective data* is particularly concerned with job inventories which are filled in by workers themselves and it raises the question of whether the replies are an accurate reflection of the true position. Prien (1977) writes that, 'evidence concerning the first ... approach ... is limited and sometimes indirect'. Writing in the same year, Hartley, Brecht, Pagerey, Weeks and Hoecker (1977) comment 'we have been able to find only two studies relating to this question, and these have produced results that raise serious questions about the validity of self-report estimates'. They quote Burns's (1957) paper in which a comparison of diary methods and questionnaire responses revealed that workers over-estimate time spent on important activities and underestimate time spent on 'personal' activities. Klemmer and Snyder (1972) found that workers' estimates vary greatly in accuracy and that time spent in face to face communication is underestimated, whereas time spent reading and writing is overestimated. McCall, Morrison and Hannan's (1978) review of studies of managerial work also concludes that managers do not know how they spend their time. Against this uncertain background, the Hartley *et al*. data is relatively definitive! The highest levels of respondent accuracy was recorded when incumbents were asked *simply to identify* the activities they undertook: here accuracies of 82 per cent and 95 per cent were recorded for two organisations. When individuals were asked to *rank the order* of their activities, correlations of 0.66 and 0.58 were obtained. When individuals were asked to *estimate the absolute time spent*, a median correlation of only 0.31 was obtained.

The second approach to investigating the validity of job analyses such as the PAQ and the TAS (Task Abilities Scale by Fleishman) uses *comparisons with expert opinion*. This involves the difficulty of ensuring that expert opinion is correct. There is very little empirical evidence available. However, Prien (1977) writes, 'In general, the research results are clear and convincing. The PAQ and the TAS measure what they are supposed to measure.'

The third approach relies upon the ability of the analysis to *classify and differentiate between jobs*. Here the evidence is more plentiful. Prien (1977) notes, 'Task oriented questionnaires do differentiate within the jobs intended and the differences are consistent within the criterion group characteristics (chief executive officers have higher scores on 'long-range planning' than do middle management)'. This observation is supported by a study by Smith (1980) which used a novel 'Repertory Grid Technique' to analyse the jobs of a general manager, a factory manager and a product development manager, and found that the results indicated clear differences between the jobs. Prien (1977) refers specifically to the validity of the Position Analysis Questionnaire when he says, 'The validity of the PAQ ... has been established using ... an occupational classification criterion'. Presumably this refers to McCormick and Asquith's (1960) study of naval officers. They found that the PAQ responses varied much less when an individual filled out a form several times than when several different people responded to the PAQ. Meyerson, Prien and Vick (1965) also adopted this approach and found that Hemphill's Executive Position Description Questionnaire differentiated between company presidents, middle management and personnel department. Other studies indicating that analyses can differentiate between jobs have been conducted by Meyer (1961), Marshall (1964) and Rusmore (1967).

The final approach to establishing the validity of job analyses involves using them to *predict some other variable* such as salary or job evaluation rankings which could be expected to be related to job content. Typical studies are by Champagne and McCormick (1964), Prien, Barrett and Suwtlik (1965) and Mecham and McCormick (1969), who obtained correlations in the range of 0.83 to 0.90. Similarly, Boshoff (1969) found that Hemphill's Executive Position Description Questionnaire correlated 0.65 with conventional job evaluations.

Job Families

Job analysis is an essential first stage in the process of scientific selection of staff, yet it is a tedious, time consuming and expensive process. It is also wasteful because some jobs are very similar to each other. If the jobs which are very similar could be identified by a rudimentary examination they could be grouped into families. Then, when the situation arose, it would be unnecessary to perform a comprehensive and separate job analysis since the job analysis of the family could be used instead. Furthermore, as McCormick (1976, p. 678) notes, the jobs could be arranged in a hierarchical order, which would help us understand the relationships between jobs and job families, and would provide a useful tool for selection, placement, career guidance and training. Prien and Ronan (1971) review most of the studies of job taxonomies. For example, Coombs and Salter (1949) identified five dimensions on which jobs could vary. They were:

1 self responsible jobs,
2 routine entry occupations,
3 skilled machine operations,
4 clerical jobs,
5 a general factor.

Orr (1960) used a similar approach and obtained six job families, which were:

1 high-level technical supervisory and mechanical jobs,
2 low-level unskilled jobs,
3 high-level skilled mechanical jobs,
4 very high-level job with respect to intelligence,
5 clerical and supervisory level,
6 medium-level mechanical jobs.

Prien and Ronan (1971) offer a synthesis of Orr's and Coombs and Salter's results by offering a three-level classification: manual jobs, white-collar jobs and supervisory/technical/managerial jobs.

Pearlman (1980), in an excellent review of job families and their uses, points out that establishing job families would have three important benefits. First, it would help the development of better selection methods since it would be worthwhile devoting resources to a system that could be used for a larger number of vacancies. Secondly, the sizes of the samples used in validation studies could be increased because the occupants of several similar jobs could be aggregated. As a consequence of larger sample sizes, the results of these studies should be more accurate. Thirdly, a classification of jobs and job families would help determine whether results of studies were 'transportable' to other jobs within the same organisation and other organisations.

Comparison between Methods

A final issue on which to end this chapter is a comparison of the effectiveness of the different methods of job analysis (see Checklist Two). In view of the many methods and many research reports, it is surprising to find that few direct comparisons between methods have been attempted. Only two studies could be located. Boshoff (1969) compared three methods and, more recently, Levine, Ash and Bennett (1980) compared four methods. The methods were (1) Flanagan's (1954) critical incidents method; (2) Primoff's (1975) job elements method; (3) McCormick's PAQ and, (4) The US Department of Labor's system of task analysis. The results indicated that the PAQ was the cheapest method of analysis but some judges thought that the PAQ produced the poorest reports. The critical incident technique received the highest ratings but other differences were not large.

EXAMPLE OF JOB DESCRIPTION

Job Description – Wood Machinist

1. *Job Title*   WOOD MACHINIST (Trencher)
2. *Location*   MILL SHOP
3. *Number in Job*   8
4. *Purpose of Job*
   To take pre-cut and pre-planed wood and to cut trenches of specified dimensions at specified positions.
5. *Responsibilities*
   Responsible to the Mill Shop Foreman
6. *Relationships*
   Works largely on own, but has some contact with the operatives performing previous and subsequent operations. Sometimes required to train new operatives.
7. *Physical Conditions*
   The Mill Shop is dry, well lit and ventilated but there is no heating at any time of year. Noise levels can be high. Work is performed in standing position. Some lifting and carrying is involved.
8. *Outline of the Job*
   8.1 Transport batch of wood from previous process by pulling along trolley.
   8.2 Check with plan the position of the trenches, change cutters on trencher if necessary.
   8.3 Take small batches of wood to bench, place in position under trenching machine using pre-set guides. Pull cutters of trencher forward, keeping hands clear of cutters.
   8.4 Restack trenched wood neatly and safely.
   8.5 When batch is completed, pull cart to next operative.
   8.6 Complete simple forms.
9. *Safety Aspects*
   The work involves a number of serious potential hazards:
   9.1 Falling stacks of wood
   9.2 Injury from the cutters of the trenching machine
10. *Salary and Conditions of Service*
    Salary: Flat rate of £55.00 per week plus monthly group bonus.
    Holidays: Three weeks per year plus Bank Holidays
    Hours: Monday–Friday   9.00a.m. – 5.00p.m.
                      Saturdays – 8.30a.m. – 12.30p.m.
    Breaks: Afternoon and Morning breaks of 15 minutes. Lunch break of 1 hour.
    Overtime: Usually available.

3 Personnel Specifications

The previous chapter dealt with the first step of scientific personnel selection: job analysis which culminates in the first key document in the selection process – the job description. But before systematic selection can proceed a second key document must be produced – the personnel specification.

Job analyses are, essentially, a statement of the job to be done, either in terms of the *tasks* to be achieved or the *activities* which a worker must perform. However, the objective of any selection system is to choose the candidate who possesses the most suitable *characteristics*. It is this step, from tasks and activities to characteristics, which is undertaken when a personnel specification is produced. It is a step which is as important as any other. It is, therefore, quite amazing to discover that there has been very little research into the way that the inferences are made from statements of the job description to the statements of the personnel specification. There is little or no research on such obvious aspects as the cues that are used, the conventions adopted and the reliability and validity of the process. Because there is so little research, it is necessary to rely on experience and tradition or to rely upon intuitive methods derived from general psychological principles.

STRAIGHTFORWARD APPROACHES TO PERSONNEL SPECIFICATIONS

Experience and tradition lead towards a straightforward method of producing job descriptions based upon some type of plan: the most ubiquitous of which is the Seven Point Plan developed by Professor Alec Rodger. Often it is called 'Rodger's Seven Point Interview Plan' and this indicates a common confusion. The plan is not intended as a scheme or guide on how to conduct an interview. Indeed, if the plan is used as a basis for an interview, it often leads to a disjointed session in which the candidate is bemused by the need to 'backtrack' on his career in order to cover the categories of the plan. The plan is intended to provide a simple but scientifically defensible system for making judgements of occupational suitability.

The main points of the seven point plan are given in Table 3.1 and it can be seen that the plan is very practical.

Another well-known plan was devised by Munroe Frazer (1966) and consists of five points:

1. Impact on others,
2. Acquired knowledge,
3. Innate abilities,
4. Motivation,
5. Adjustment.

A personnel specification is usually produced by referring to the job description and systematically working through one of the plans noting the characteristics required under each heading. Of course the

TABLE 3.1 *Rodger's 'Seven Point Plan'*

1	*Physical make-up*	includes health, physique, appearance, grooming, demeanour, strength, speech.
2	*Attainments*	include educational qualifications, training successfully completed, licences, professional associations, offices held in clubs and societies, success in competitions, occupational experience, career progress.
3	*General intelligence*	involves the ability to identify the key aspects of a problem, deduce the relationships between these aspects and use logic to deduce the next step. It is sometimes useful to distinguish between the intelligence an individual *can* use and how much he *normally* uses.
4	*Special aptitudes*	includes numerical reasoning, verbal reasoning, memory, mechanical reasoning, spatial reasoning, musical aptitude, artistic aptitude, manual dexterity.
5	*Interests*	outdoor, mechanical, scientific, persuasive, artistic, literary, social service, clerical, practical, intellectual.
6	*Disposition*	cheerful, relates well to people, stable, easily thrown off balance, assertive, can handle difficult situations, independent, experimenting etc.
7	*Home circumstances*	include domestic commitments, mobility, family support, freedom to work certain hours.

Preparation

characteristics identified in this way will not be of equal importance. It may be useful to make a distinction between those characteristics which are *essential* to the performance of the job and those which are *desirable*. An example of a personnel specification drawn up in this way is given in Table 3.2.

When drawing up a personnel specification bear three extra points in mind. First, it may not be necessary to include every point. For example, if personality has no bearing on the ability to do the job then the section on 'Disposition' can be omitted. Secondly, it is important to avoid over-specifying requirements. Use the categorisation 'essential' sparingly and be aware than many physical disabilities do not impair job performance. Thirdly, ensure that the specification is fair to everyone, and does not imply any indirect discrimination. Be particularly careful to ensure that specifications under the heading 'home circumstances' do not offend particular subgroups or violate any equal opportunities legislation.

MORE COMPLEX METHODS OF PRODUCING PERSONNEL SPECIFICATIONS

In some circumstances a more rigorous and sophisticated approach will be justified. There are three main possibilities: job component analysis, repertory grid analysis and intuitive methods based upon a classification of human characteristics. In addition there are several less known methods, such as Fleishman's ability requirements approach (Fleishman and Hogan, 1978).

Job Component Analysis

The Position Analysis Questionnaire (PAQ) has the advantage that the job elements it identifies can be specifically linked to human characteristics. Shaw and McCormick (1976) and McCormick, Cunningham and Thornton (1972) describe how each rating can be given a weight which reflects its relevance to a particular characteristic. The weighted ratings are then added up to produce an estimate of the level of the characteristic needed. The process is then repeated for other characteristics.

In fact there are two methods of proceedings – the cross product approach and the critical behaviour approach.

TABLE 3.2 *Example of personnel specification*   33

Job Title:	*Upholsterer*	
Location:	*Silicon Valley, Whaley Bridge*	

1 *Physical characteristics*	Essential:	– Able to work in standing position – Able to bend at waist – Free movement of all limbs – Normal colour vision
	Desirable:	– Neat and clean appearance
2 *Attainments*	Essential:	– Time-served apprenticeship – Member of Trade Union
3 *Intelligence*	Desirable:	– Not in bottom third of population
4 *Special aptitudes*	Essential:	– Spatial ability and ability to work with patterned material – in top 20% of population – Manual dexterity
5 *Interests*	Desirable:	– Practical and manual interests, especially working with wood or fabric – interests requiring cleanliness, eye for detail and care over final presentation
6 *Disposition*	Desirable:	– Self-sufficient approach to life and willingness to work on their own with only infrequent social contact. Willingness to work at a job which offers only a minimum level of variety (that is, not suitable for strong extrovert)
7 *Home Circumstances*	Essential:	– Absence of commitments which could present difficulties to shift working
8 *Contra-indications*		– Medical history of rheumatic or muscular disease or back trouble – work history involving minor accidents

An excellent example of the use of job component analysis is given by Sparrow *et al.* (1982). They analysed the job of a machine setter for an injection-moulding machine. PAQ ratings were obtained from three setters, a senior setter and a training officer. The resulting profile is given in Figure 3.1.

Repertory Grid Methods

Repertory grids are derived from Kelly's personal construct theory (1955) and they are a flexible tool in many areas of industrial psychology (Smith and Stewart, 1977; Smith *et al.*, 1978; Smith, 1980). Kelly postulated that men behave like scientists, exploring their environments, and on the basis of these explorations they construct mental maps of their world. These maps consist of the elements – the objects and the constructs (the qualities which the objects have). Repertory grids are a procedure and a statistical technique which can be used to make the maps explicit.

Producing a personnal specification and a job analysis is analogous to producing these mental maps: the analyst is the scientist, the elements are the tasks from a conventional job analysis, and the constructs are the characteristics included in the personnel specification. An unpublished example by Smith concerned the production of a job specification for supervisors in the knitting and hosiery industry. The Industry Training Board had previously conducted a conventional job analysis from which 29 common 'supervisor' tasks could be identified. A sample of 34 supervisors were interviewed in order to obtain the characteristics which supervisors needed in order to perform these tasks.

The interview procedure followed the triadic method of elicitation commonly used in repertory grid methodology. Three of the tasks were chosen at random and the supervisor was asked to nominate which task was the odd man out in terms of the qualities and characteristics people need in order to do the tasks. Once they had nominated the odd man out they were asked to specify the quality or characteristic which made it the odd man out. This process was repeated until 10 to 12 different qualities had been elicited. This elicitation process has the advantages that the supervisor can answer in any terms he wishes, the investigator does not suggest any responses, yet the method samples the supervisor's ideas and forces him to make comparisons and contrasts. At the close of the interview

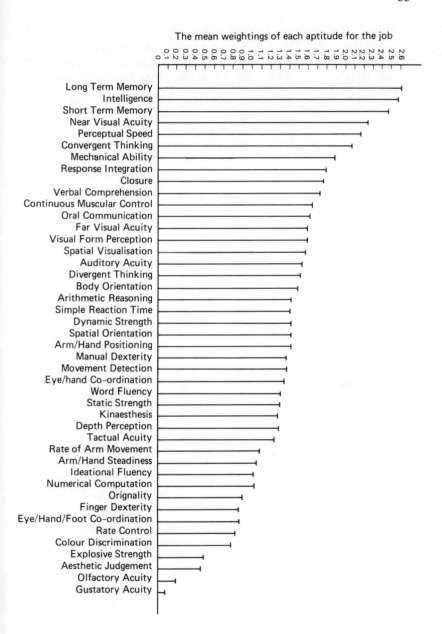

The mean weightings of each aptitude for the job

FIGURE 3.1 *Aptitude profile for the job of setter*

SOURCE Sparrow *et al.* (1982, p. 159).

the supervisor was asked to rate every task on every quality using a seven point scale. The data obtained from 34 supervisors could be cast into a 29 × 340 matrix which could be subjected to a principal component analysis. The results shown in Table 3.3 indicate that the job of supervisor required seven major characteristics.

TABLE 3.3   *Qualities required of supervisors in the knitting industry*

Qualities	% of variance
Sympathetic but firm personality	18
Ability to communicate clearly	13
Ability to plan and organise	8
Ability to solve problems	7
Knowledge of the industry and the firm	6
Ability to maintain safety and discipline	5
Trouble-shooting	5

SOURCE   Smith, J. M. (unpublished).

Intuitive Method based on Theory

If the job component approach, the repertory grid approach or perhaps the ability requirement approach (Fleishman and Hogan, 1978) are not appropriate for a particular situation, it becomes necessary to rely on a more 'intuitive' method. Clearly, however, the 'intuitions' should not be based upon guesswork, but they should be guided by knowledge and experience and by theories and classifications of human characteristics. Many classifications exist, but the following classification has many merits. Its broad outlines are implicitly accepted by most psychologists specialising in mental measurement (for example, Guion, 1965; Cronbach, 1970; Anastasi, 1982). It divides human characteristics into four main areas: mental abilities, manual abilities, temperament, and motivation and interests.

Mental Abilities

There is often an obvious need to select among applicants according to their mental ability, and consequently it is frequently included in personnel specifications. Often the term is used synonymously with 'intelligence' and many definitions exist. Perhaps the most specific, analytical and accepted definition is given by Spearman's (1927) three neogenetic laws:

The apprehension of reality is the extent to which an individual can identify, understand and absorb the different components of a problem.
The eduction of relationships is the extent to which an individual can identify the way in which the various components of problems are related to each other.
The eduction of correlates is the extent to which an individual can identify the logical consequence of the relationships and deduce the next step.

Thus, in a nutshell, intelligence is the ability to identify the constituent parts of a problem, to understand how they relate to each other and to be able to work out the next step. These basic mental operations underlie the tasks involved in many jobs such as research scientist, area manager, teacher, investment analyst, nurse or personnel officer.

There is, however, a complicating factor which arises from the question 'Does the type of question have any effect?'. For example, does it matter whether the problems involve numbers, words, shapes, or levers and pulleys? It is a debate which has now been largely settled. The main advocate of separate types of intelligence was Thurstone (1938), who administered 57 different tests to a large sample of *university students* and found that separate abilities existed depending upon the type of question he asked. He identified nine primary mental abilities as shown in Figure 3.2. An even more specific analysis was produced by Guilford (1967), who first noted that questions could differ on three main dimensions: their content, the mental operation required, and the nature of the final results. Each of these categories can be further subdivided. In principle there can be any combination of content, operation and product. So, according to Guilford, there can be 120 different types of intelligence!

In most circumstances Guilford's analysis is far too complex to be of practical use. Furthermore, both Guilford and Thurstone have been heavily criticised on theoretical grounds (Eysenck, 1973, Horn and Knapp, 1974). The most damaging criticisms relate to the way that their sampling methods biased their findings. For example,

THURSTONE'S PRIMARY MENTAL ABILITIES

S	spatial	M	memory
P	perceptual speed	I	induction
N	numerical facility	R	reasoning
V	verbal relations	D	deduction
W	word fluency		

GUILFORD'S TAXONOMY

CONTENT	OPERATIONS	PRODUCTS
● figures	● memorisation	● units
● symbols	● understanding	● classes
● words	● converging	● relations
● acts	● diverging	● systems
	● evaluating	● transformations
		● implications

FIGURE 3.2 *Structures of intellect*

SOURCE Thurstone (1938).

Thurstone's initial study was restricted to university students – the overwhelming majority of whom would have been highly intelligent. This was tantamount to controlling the influence of general intelligence and favouring less important aspects. An analogy should make the situation clearer. It is known that the most important factor determining a car's speed is the size of its engine and that other factors such as weight and aerodynamic styling have less importance. But, if we conducted an investigation only on cars with engine sizes over three litres, the importance of engine size would not have 'room' to show itself and consequently the secondary factors would be given undue importance. In fact, Thurstone and Thurstone (1941) repeated their study with relatively unselected primary school children and admitted the existence of a general intellectual factor.

Probably the most accepted analysis of the structure of intelligence is Vernon's (1960, 1969) hierarchical structure which is shown in Figure 3.3. According to Vernon's model, the most pervasive aspect of intelligence is 'g' but two domains, which largely overlap with 'g', can be distinguished: verbal-educational and practical. Subdomains which overlap with both 'g', 'v:ed' and 'k:m' can also be distinguished and indeed separate areas can even be found which overlap the subdomains.

In practical terms, these underlying theories of the structure of intellect imply that in most personnel specifications it will be adequate to refer only to 'general intelligence'. Sometimes, however, it will be necessary to refer to major group factors such as practical or v:ed. Minor group factors such as spatial or verbal will only need to be specified relatively infrequently. However, another argument points in the opposite direction and suggests that requirements should be as specific as possible in order not to rule out competent candidates. For example, if a garage specifies high general intelligence when it actually requires high mechanical ability, it will exclude people of average general ability who are particularly competent in mechanical matters.

One aspect of mental ability which was of considerable concern in the 1960s was *creative thinking*. The concern arose out of the belief that creativity was not the same thing as intelligence. Unfortunately, however, the evidence is not conclusive. Many different measures of creativity have been produced but they tend to correlate poorly with each other. This implies either that a single trait of 'creativity' does not exist or that our present techniques for measuring it are not

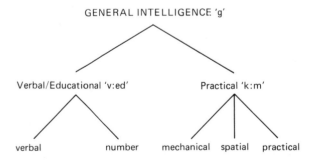

FIGURE 3.3 *Schematic representation of Vernon's model of intelligence*
SOURCE Vernon (1960, 1969).

adequate. Furthermore, some studies (for example, Getzels and Jackson, 1962) have shown that measures of creativity tests correlate as highly with measures of intelligence as they do among themselves – even though the design of the investigation has controlled the level of intelligence and therefore reduced the level of its correlations. In the light of these conceptual problems, it seems prudent to include creativity in a personnel specification only when it is a clear precondition to successful performance.

Psychomotor Abilities

Psychomotor abilities are 'physical' abilities which enable one to 'do' things and usually they involve muscular control and movement. Typical examples of psychomotor skills are: inserting an integrated circuit into a home computer, typing, standing to attention over a long period. In the same way that an attempt has been made to classify 'mental abilities', psychologists have attempted to classify psychomotor abilities. However, the outcome of these efforts has been rather different: a pervasive general factor has not emerged.

Perhaps the most authoritative analysis of motor skills has been the work of Fleishman (1966) who identified 11 factors in psychomotor skills and eight aspects of physical proficiency. The 11 factors in psychomotor skills were:

1. *Control precision* – fine control, rapid and precise actions.
2. *Multilimb co-ordination* – the simultaneous co-ordination of several limbs – especially the hands and feet.
3. *Response orientation* – involves directional actions made under speeded conditions in response to a stimulus (which is usually a visual stimulus).
4. *Reaction time*
5. *Speed of arm movement*
6. *Rate control* – involves making continuous adjustments to a moving target.
7. *Manual dexterity* – involves the manipulation of fairly large objects.
8. *Finger dexterity* – involves the manipulation of tiny objects.
9. *Arm/hand steadiness*
10. *Wrist and finger speed*
11. *Aiming* – placing an object in an area under highly speeded conditions.

Fleishman's eight factors of physical proficiency concern a separate but related area and were derived from studies of performance of 60 different physical fitness tests. The eight factors are:

1. *Flexibility of trunk and back muscles*
2. Ability of muscles to make *rapid flexing movements* and recover from strain or fatigue
3. Ability to *exert force over a brief period of time*
4. Ability to *exert force repeatedly* over a period of time
5. *Strength of trunk muscles*
6. Ability to *co-ordinate movements when moving the body*
7. Ability to *maintain balance*
8. *Stamina* and *endurance*

Personality

There are literally thousands of words which could be used in a personnel specification to describe the personality of an ideal applicant. To add to the difficulty of a superabundance of words, personality theorists often invent new, *ad hoc* terms which are ill-defined, overlap with existing theories and generally serve to obscure the situation. There is a statistical approach which does not rely upon any specific theory of personality and which performs the function of reducing a mass of data to a relatively small number of recurrent trends. The factor analytic approach has been applied to personality and four recurrent trends have emerged from the studies of independent investigators, such as Eysenck (1960) and Cattell (1965). They are: introversion-extroversion, stability, toughmindedness, and independence. Definitions of *extroversion* abound but it may be thought of as a general tendency of people to direct their energies outwards. It is the opposite of *introversion* where people direct their energies inwards towards their own thoughts and feelings. Extroverts seem suited to jobs which involve dealing with people and making quick, practical decisions. Extroverts also seem suited to jobs offering a wide variety of tasks or settings. Introverts, on the other hand, seem suited to jobs where they work on their own or in the company of a few long-term colleagues and where they work in a stable environment on one or two long-term projects. Extroversion can be subdivided in much the same way as intelligence. Catell, Eber and Tatsuoka (1970) suggest that extroversion is composed of warmheartedness, dominance, enthusiasm, adventurousness and group dependence. Eysenck (1970) suggests that extroversion is composed of sociability, impulsiveness, activity, liveliness and excitability.

A recent British analysis by Saville and Holdsworth (1984) does not use the term extroversion but it is clear that extroversion is similar to the handling people domain which is composed of influence, affiliation and empathy.

Instability refers to a 'brittleness' of temperament – the likelihood of 'snapping' under stress. Well-adjusted people can usually cope with distractions, do not ordinarily lack energy and they usually have a variety of interests. Cattell *et al.* (1970) calls the factor 'anxiety' which is composed of being easily affected by one's feelings, timidity, sensitivity, worrying, poor self sentiment and tension.

Toughness, or as Cattell calls it, 'tough poise', seems to be related in the activation level of the cerebral cortex. People who have tough poise can handle life's problems at an objective, logical level, whereas those low on this factor operate at a 'feeling' level. It seems to be composed of critical ability, practical realism, and a practical, down-to-earth approach.

The fourth major personality factor is concerned with *independence* and is high in people who are radical and something of a law unto themselves. According to Cattell *et al.* (1970), independence consists of dominance, suspiciousness, imagination, radicalism and self-sufficiency.

Interests

In many situations interests will be included on the personnel specification. For example, a personnel specification for a manager might specify administrative, persuasive and computational interests. Similarly, a personnel specification for a forestry worker might specify outdoor and scientific interests.

Unfortunately there is no agreed list of interests: each author seems to adopt his own list! But, as Table 3.4 shows, there is a considerable overlap among the lists adopted. The choice of interest categories has been made on largely pragmatic grounds except perhaps the categories used by Holland (1959), who structures his classification into a hexagon in clockwise order of intellectual, artistic, social, enterprising, conventional, realistic interests, on the basis of their closeness to each other.

TABLE 3.4 *Personal values and managerial interests*

Interest categories

. Outdoor
. Mechanical
. Computational
. Scientific
. Persuasive
. Artistic

. Literary
. Musical
. Social service
. Practical
. Medical

Personal values

. Theoretical
. Economic
. Aesthetic

. Social
. Political
. Power

Managerial interests (from Saville-Holdsworth)

Functions	*Skills*
. Production operations	. Information collecting
. Technical services	. Information processing
. Research and development	. Problem-solving
. Distribution	. Decision-making
. Purchasing	. Modelling
. Sales	. Oral communication
. Marketing support	. Written communication
. Personnel and training	. Organising things
. Data processing	. Persuading
. Finance	. Developing people
. Administration	. Representing

Of particular importance to those drawing up personnel specifications for management jobs is Saville and Holdsworth's (1983) list of managerial interests. As Table 3.4 also shows, they view management interests in terms of both management functions and management skills.

Motives

The inclusion of motives in a personnel specification is relatively infrequent and when it is included it is often in a general form such as

'the applicant must be keen'. However, in many situations it is clear
that motivation has a major influence on successful performance.
Unfortunately, psychological theory offers very little help in identifying the motivational *traits* which should be included in a personnel
specification.

The *locus of control* should, perhaps, be considered first. Rotter
(1966) suggested that people can have varying beliefs about the
degree of control they have over their lives. People with an *internal
locus of control* generally believe that their own characteristics and
their own behaviour determines the rewards and punishments they
receive. People with an *external locus of control* believe that a large
part of the rewards and punishments they receive are determined by
factors outside themselves such as luck, fate or more powerful
people. This approach has resulted in a great deal of research which
has been reviewed by Phares (1976) and Lefcourt (1976).

One of the most comprehensive list of needs was drawn up by
Murray *et al.* (1938), whose long list included three needs which are
particularly important in the occupational context: need for affiliation, power and achievement. A person who has a high *need for
affiliation* enjoys working with others and will make an effort to win
friendships and maintain associations. A person who has a high *need
for power* attempts to control the environment and to influence or
direct other people. He expresses opinions forcefully and enjoys
leadership roles. A person with a high *need for achievement* tries to
excel by maintaining high standards and achieving objectives by
faster, cheaper, better methods. Achievement motivation is probably
the most extensively reviewed human motive. Smith, Beck, Cooper,
Cox, Ottaway and Talbot (1982) review results gathered in many
countries which links high achievement motivation to economic
success. Achievement motivation is clearly relevant when producing
personnel specifications for jobs which involve entrepreneurial tasks.

THEORETICAL ISSUES

The theoretical issues underlying the production of a personnel
specification are probably the most ill-defined and unresearched
aspects of selection. Not only is there a dearth of research, but much
of that which is available confuses the production of a personnel
specification with the other stages of the selection process. The most
obvious theoretical issues are reliability and validity.

Reliability of Personnel Specifications

Reliability *is not* an important issue when the required characteristics are derived by objective procedures. For example, in job component analysis, the attributes required for a job are obtained by applying a predetermined set of weights to the results of an inventory such as the Position Analysis Questionnaire. In these circumstances coefficients of 0.99 or even 1.0 should be obtained provided the analyst is competent and careful.

However, reliability *is* an important issue when other methods such as the intuitive approach are used. In essence, reliability in the context of personnel specifications obtained by the intuitive approach will have two major components: 'repeated measure' reliability and 'inter-rater' reliability. *Repeated measure reliability* will arise when the same person is asked to read a job analysis and then specify the characteristics which a worker will need in order to perform the job. After a short delay of about one week, that process is repeated and the two specifications are compared. If the procedure is reliable, the two specifications should be very similar. Thus establishing the 'repeated measure' reliability is conceptually very straightforward and it is quite amazing that no empirical comparison of this type could be located in the literature. We simply do not know how consistent people are when they make judgements about the characteristics which workers need to be able to perform jobs.

Inter-rater reliability arises when separate analysts read a job description and then specify a list of required characteristics. If the procedure is reliable, there should be a strong relationship between the two lists. Fortunately there has been some research which suggests that separate raters can achieve a satisfactory level of agreement. For example, Schmitt and Fine (1983) obtained multiple ratings on requirements of jobs for reasoning, mathematics and language, and they obtained correlations of 0.86, 0.87 and 0.78 respectively. In a similar vein, Marquardt and McCormick (1972) obtained ratings by psychologists on 76 attributes and the median index of agreement was 0.90.

An earlier classic study by Trattner, Fine and Kubis (1955) adds an extra ingredient by comparing the way that the specifications were derived. One group of analysts rated the requirements for ten different jobs on the basis of a written job description. Another group of analysts made the same ratings on the basis of observing incumbents at work. The results were encouraging; the coefficients between the ratings of mental and perceptual requirements were good and in the range of 0.87 to 0.96. Slightly surprisingly, however, the coefficients for physical aptitudes, such as hand-eye co-ordination and manual dexterity were lower and ranged from a puny 0.08 to a very robust 0.87. Results of this kind are encouraging. It is probable, but not certain, that high inter-rater reliability implies high repeated measure reliability. In conclusion, the available evidence strongly suggests that the requirements contained in a personnel specification can be reliably deduced from the information contained in a job description.

Validity of Personnel Specifications

Reliability is important, but by itself it is not enough. Methods must also be valid. Validity is an involved and complex topic which is dealt with in much greater detail in chapter 6. For present purposes validity can be taken to mean 'are personnel specifications an accurate reflection of the human characteristics needed to perform a job?'.

Unfortunately there is no simple way of answering this question, since we do not have 'God-given' statements which can be used as a perfect standard against which personnel specifications can be measured. However, by using a 'boot-strapping' empirical approach some progress can be made. One of the most straightforward is by Sparrow *et al.* (1982). Using a tiny sample of only 14 tool setters, they first used the Position Analysis Questionnaire to analyse the job. Then they obtained an attribute profile. From the attribute profile they chose a battery of psychological tests. The scores on these tests produced a high multiple correlation of 0.92 with the manager's assessment of the performance of the 14 tool setters.

Trattner *et al.*'s (1955) study followed a similar rationale. They obtained the average test scores for workers in ten jobs. They also obtained estimates of the mean scores from analysts. Finally they compared the estimates with the actual scores. For tests of mental and perceptual characteristics they obtained acceptable correlations of 0.6 and 0.7. However, for tests of physical aptitudes the correlations were only 0.01 and 0.27.

Another investigation by Parry (1968) asked psychologists to estimate the validity of certain psychological tests and then he compared these estimates with the actual validities. The rationale behind the investigation was that if the psychologists believed that a test measured a characteristic which was not required by a job, they would estimate a low validity. On the other hand, if they thought that the characteristic was relevant, and might therefore be included in a personnel specification, they would estimate a high validity. Furthermore, the accuracy of the psychologists' intuitions could be checked by comparing the predicted validities with the actual validities. Unfortunately, however, Parry found only a moderate relationship.

Probably the most extensive and sophisticated attempts to determine the validity of personnel specifications were made by Mecham and McCormick (1969), Mecham (1970) and Marquardt and McCormick (1974). This series of studies was based on about 8000 questionnaires from 141 jobs. On the basis of these results it was therefore possible to deduce three separate indices for each job: the mean score, the potential cut-off scores and the validity coefficients. Each of these indices could, in turn, be correlated with the data on the personnel specification. In general, the correlation between the personnel specification and the mean test scores was good – about 0.73. The correlation for the potential cut-off score was also good – about 0.71. However, the correlation between the personnel specification and validity was distinctly mediocre – about 0.39. It must be remembered that these figures give a global view. When the correlations for individual subscores were examined it emerged that relationships involving mental abilities such as general intelligence, verbal intelligence, numerical intelligence and clerical perception was high. However, the relationships for *some* physical abilities, such as finger dexterity and manual dexterity, were lower. Fleishman and Berniger (1960) also attempt to investigate the validity of personnel specifications.

All of these studies, except Fleishman and Berniger's investigation, involve a comparison with either a test score, or a supervisor's rating. Unfortunately this involves a major problem. Neither tests nor superior's ratings are themselves perfect. The imperfections in the criteria will tend to reduce the correlations which are obtained. This reduction cannot be blamed upon the quality of the personnel specifications and consequently it is tempting to ask whether higher validities would be obtained if perfect criteria were available. The criteria problem is not restricted to investigations of the validity of personnel specifications. It is endemic to practically all research in personnel selection. It is a problem which must be faced squarely in the next chapter.

4 Criteria

Once a job description and personnel specifications have been prepared, there is a very strong impetus to proceed directly to placement of adverts and selection of candidates. However, *the stage which should follow the analysis of a job is the development of criteria.* To understand the reasoning behind this it is necessary to look forward to the time when the selection system is in operation. Sooner or later someone will ask whether the selection system works and whether it is valid. To answer these questions it will be necessary to compare the predictions of the selection system against a standard or, perhaps, several standards. These criteria *can* be produced at this later stage but there are two good reasons why they should be defined soon after the job analysis has been completed.

REASONS FOR CHOOSING CRITERIA AT AN EARLY STAGE

The first of these reasons is very prosaic: it may be too late to collect the information if a decision is delayed until criteria are actually needed. An example is a company involved in making cellular telephones. It installs a selection system for the inspectors in charge of the probe cards that are a vital component of the integrated circuits. The new selection system is installed. At the end of the six-month experimental period, it was decided that the number of service calls to customers to replace faulty probe cards would be an appropriate criterion. Had this decision been taken six months earlier it would have been easy to devise a simple system to collect the information. In the event, many tedious hours were spent scanning engineers' reports and collating the data. This particular company was in a relatively fortunate position. With effort it could retrieve the data at a later date. In many companies it would have been lost forever.

The second reason for determining the criteria immediately the job description has been prepared concerns intellectual honesty and professional integrity. If the choice of criteria is delayed until the selection methods are in use, the decision stands a greater chance of being biased in a favourable way. At its worst, a selector may choose the criteria which support the methods in use. More subtly, it can mean that the choice can be distorted at a subconscious level by the absorption of subsequent decisions and events. Intellectually, there is greater integrity in deciding in advance the standards by which the system will be evaluated.

IMPORTANCE OF CRITERIA

Not only should criteria be chosen at the right time, but they should also be chosen with great care. This care and effort is justified by the fact that an unwise choice of criteria can lead to conclusions which are severely misleading. For example, Albright, Smith and Glennon (1959) give details of a selection system for salesmen developed by the Standard Oil Company. Initially, the opinions of supervisors were used as criteria. When compared against these opinions, the selection method seemed to make inaccurate predictions. However, at a later date, other criteria were obtained. When judged against actual promotion decisions it was clear that the same selection methods were able to discriminate between good and poor salesmen. In this example, poor choice of criteria led to a misleadingly pessimistic view of the selection methods involved. Perhaps less frequently, poor choice of criteria could lead to a misleadingly optimisic view. For example, Smith (1981) suggested that the high validity obtained by the UK Civil Service Selection Board might be spuriously inflated because the criterion was influenced by a self-fulfilling prophecy. As a generalisation, it could be claimed that deficiencies in the criteria usually lead us to underestimate the value of our selection proce-dures. Fortunately, as shown by formulae in Appendix I, in certain circumstances, it is possible to apply statistical corrections in order to obtain more accurate estimates (see also Table 4.1).

Unfortunately, the importance of taking care in choosing a crite-rion is not always recognised. Jenkins (1946) wrote that inadequate criteria is at the heart of much poor prediction and that psychologists in general 'tended to accept the tacit assumption that criteria were either given of God or just to be found lying about', and that most textbooks and journal literature would lead to the conclusion that 'expediency dictated the choice of criteria and that convenient availability of criterion was more important than its adequacy'.

LEVELS OF CRITERIA

The most obvious starting place for a search for appropriate criteria is the job description, because it is almost certain to contain explanations of the behaviours and actions which a worker is expected to perform. These behaviours and actions are *immediate level criteria* and can be used to check whether the selection system is choosing the workers who do the expected things and behave in an appropriate way. However, the fact that a worker is smartly dressed, punctual and polite does not necessarily mean that he is a good worker.

So, perhaps a search for criteria should concentrate upon a *second level: the results which should be achieved*. A good job description should give clear clues to the location of criteria at the results level. For example, it may refer to a sales objective or it may refer to production output. Often conceptual problems arise. A worker may be doing the right things but achieving poor results through no fault of his own. He may have been issued with outdated equipment. He may have been given the hard jobs with short production runs and frequent changes in methods and design. Under these circumstances the criterion has become contaminated by other influences and it would be unreasonable to expect any selection system to identify, with total accuracy, those workers who are most productive.

The search for criteria does not stop at this second level. A worker might obtain prodigious levels of production. He might sustain an output each day of assembling 80 onboard computers for an 'up market' car. If, however, the production line which then uses the computers can only cope with 50 cars per day, the extra effort is wasted. The point of this slightly trite example is that there is an organisational aspect of choosing criteria. In Thorndike's (1949) terms, the *third level* is the level of *ultimate criteria* – how much the person contributes to the organisational goals. Typical indices of ultimate criteria in industrial companies are productivity levels, net profit, organisational growth and satisfactory accomplishment of obligations placed on it by higher authority. To locate these criteria it is often necessary to refer to company policy documents or even the policy documents of government agencies. Bass (1952) points out:

> Instead of evaluating the success of programs for improving selection ... in an industrial organisation solely in terms of the extent to which they serve to increase the company's productivity profits and efficiency, it has been proposed that they also be evaluated on the extent to which they increase the worth of the organisation to its members and society as a whole.

At this point the use of ultimate criteria becomes almost unbearably complex. Furthermore, there are several practical problems. First, data concerning ultimate criteria takes a very long time to accumulate. By the time conclusive data is available the company will be bankrupt! In any event, there is a high probability that the data will emerge too late to influence a selection system. Secondly, many ultimate criteria are too nebulous and ill defined to be measured within reasonable cost limits. Thirdly, there may be many contaminating influences caused by government policy, economic conditions or changes in the company's markets. Except perhaps at top executive level it would be unreasonable to expect the results of a selection system to be strongly related to ultimate criteria.

TYPES OF CRITERIA

Guion (1965) provides a useful classification of the many different criteria by dividing them into three major types: Production Data, Personnel Data and Judgemental Data.

Production Data

Production data has many attractions as a criteria, especially in manufacturing organisations where high levels of output are nearly always a part of the organisation's goals. Consequently, management are usually impressed when production data are used. Another advantage is that production data may be easy to quantify. For example, a pharmaceutical company can count the number of saline drips packaged by each operative for each shift and an aerospace company can count the number of heat resistant ceramic tiles which a technician can install each week. A final advantage of production data is, in many cases, their availability: often information already exists on time sheets or work schedules.

The exact nature of these criteria will vary from industry to industry and from occupation to occupation. Some general indices are listed in Table 4.1.

With some ingenuity, output statistics can be evolved for many non-production jobs such as sales, clerical jobs and service jobs, for example, a comedian could be evaluated on the laughs per audience member he evokes per minute!

In spite of this allure, production data suffer a number of disadvantages as criteria. First, they are usually *contaminated* by factors outside the worker's control. There are few situations where all

TABLE 4.1   *Some production indices used as criteria*

1 *Quantity indices*	– units of output per hour, day etc. – consistency of output – sales per month – new customers per month – time to locate faults (in inspection and trouble-shooting jobs) – enquiries dealt with per day – calls (salesmen) per day – commission earned – earnings based on piece rate
2 *Quality indices*	– percentage of rejects – percentage of waste materials – percentage of breakages – time required to detect and correct faults – complaints per week, month etc. – commendations per year – errors reported per day – average size of orders – response time to enquiry – customer satisfaction – repeat orders, or survey results
3 *Cost indices* (the dollar criterion?)	– cost per unit of production – value added per unit of production – cost per order – cost per enquiry

workers operate under exactly the same conditions. Even after heroic efforts some workers will only produce a mediocre performance because they work on old *machinery*. *Length of production run* and *product specification* can also make a difference. For example, in one carpet-manufacturing company, it was accepted that the best workers were usually asked to make the 'one off' carpets of difficult design, while the poorest workers were given long production runs of plain carpets, and this produced the paradox of higher output figures for the poorest workers. The *work situation* can also exert an influence: some good typists produce relatively little typescript because their desk is situated near a busy telephone and enquiry desk so that their work is subject to constant interruptions. The work situation is particularly important when assessing the output of salesmen: some have good territories and some have lousy territories. For example, Wietz and Nuckols (1953) illustrate that sales figures should be adjusted in some way for the sales potential of the territory.

In addition to these difficulties, in many jobs it is either *impossible* or even *dangerous* to use production data as criteria. At operative and senior management level it is relatively easy to identify key ratios which can be used to judge performance. However, in many staff positions and in many professional jobs, such indices are hard to identify or quantify. In some situations the use of production data as criteria can lead to a distortion of the organisation. For example, undue pressure for high monthly sales figures, can, on their own, lead to sales personnel pressuring customers, making false promises, and making impossible service commitments. In the short term these tactics can be successful and the salesperson is often promoted. In the long term, however, the rape of a sales territory in this way can lead to disaster. Similarly, pressure upon teachers for a high pass ratio can lead to a reduction in standards. Pressure on the courts to produce more decisions per day could lead to a collapse in the credibility of justice.

Personnel Data

Criteria can often be obtained from the records which a personnel department may maintain on an individual worker. They tend to be more global in nature than production data but they are still clearly linked to the objectives of an organisation. Again, they have the advantage of being fairly easy to collect – although it must always be remembered that some clerical errors are inevitable in making the original entries (see Table 4.2).

Several personnel criteria are concerned with job attendance. *Lateness* (or tardiness) is perhaps the most short-term aspect of job attendance and is difficult to measure unless mechanical 'clocking in' procedures are used – and even in these circumstances, collusion from colleagues can introduce additional error. The advent of electronically recorded 'flexi-time' systems produces added implications in defining lateness but data collection is facilitated. Unfortunately tardiness is influenced by short-term factors such as the weather. Mueser (1953) found that people tended to be late on sunny days!

TABLE 4.2   *Some personnel indices used as criteria*

1 *Job Attendance*	– number of times late
	– average number of minutes late
	– total absences
	– certified absences
	– uncertified absences
	– frequency of absences
	– average duration of absences
	– percentage labour turnover
	– half life of a cohort of recruits
	– percent dismissed
	– voluntary turnover
2 *Career progression*	– job level
	– number of promotions
	– number of times considered for promotion
	– number of times 'passed over'
	– speed of promotion
	– salary level
	– salary increase
	– difference between actual salary increase and increase expected from tenure
3 *Accidents*	– accidents per year
	– accidents per 'mile' covered
	– accidents per unit of production
4 *Training*	– weeks needed to reach standard
	– marks at 'end' of training

Absences are an important criteria since in most circumstances irregular and infrequent attendance will reduce the efficiency of an organisation. Unfortunately absenteeism is a fairly complex phenomenon. A major distinction lies between certified and uncertified absence: the presumption perhaps being that selectors should be particularly keen to reject candidates who are likely to be absent for no good cause. Another major distinction lies between the frequency and the duration of absences. Often there is a presumption that frequent, unpredicted absences are less desirable than a single protracted absence, even when the time of work is identical. Fox and Scott (1943) suggest that there are indications that the number of days absent is a more reliable criteria (Rosensteel, 1953). Many investigators (for example, Kerr, Koppelmeir and Sullivan, 1951; Locke, 1976) have noted that absences tend to be related to job satisfaction and that dissatisfied workers tend to be absent more often – although other factors such as the size of the organisation also have an influence. Perhaps the most dramatic form of non-attendance is *labour turnover*. If employees leave shortly after they have been engaged, the organisation has, in effect, wasted the resources they have devoted to their recruitment selection, training and providing a workstation and facilities. Also, termination of employment can often be viewed as clear evidence of a mismatch between the person and their job. Although labour turnover is a clear dichotomous act (people either leave or stay), its interpretation is often far from clear and the act is contaminated by other factors. Workers may be properly selected but their induction, training or supervision may be inadequate and cause them to leave. Generally, it is only reasonable to expect a selection process to predict labour turnover within the first few months of employment. After that period other influences may be much more important. It should also be noted that turnover is strongly influenced by possibilities of alternative employment (Behrend, 1953; Stark, 1959).

A set of personnel data which can also be used as criteria are indices of the individual's *career progression*. These criteria have the advantage that they are based on actual operational decisions which are usually carefully considered by the organisation and which reflect the organisation's values and its view of the individual's competence. The most commonly used indices of career progression are job level, speed of promotion and salary progression. In most circumstances *job level* and *speed of promotion* are synonymous, except that job level is used in samples equated for length of services whereas speed of promotion can also be used in samples whose cases have different periods of tenure. A good example of the use of job level as a criteria is Anstey's (1977) study. Anstey attempted to use the rank achieved in the Civil Service after a period of 30 years to validate the Service's selection procedure. Examples of the use of salary increase as a criteria are given by Hulin (1962), who compared the actual salary increase with the increase which would be expected for workers with the same length of service.

Unfortunately, measures of career progression are fraught with difficulties. First, there is a conceptual difficulty. A selection system may be superb for selecting staff at, say, operative level but poor at selecting at supervisory level. Thus, if the selection system is used to predict promotion to the third level in an organisation it will produce poor results. But this does not mean that the system should not be used for operatives. Thus the use of career progression usually involves comparisons outside the job for which the worker is initially selected. There are other difficulties. Promotion decisions may not be based on job competence. They may be based on social reputation or, as Wallace (1974) points out, the ability to get good ratings from the 'big shots'. Internal politics are rarely absent from the determinants of promotion decisions and in some organisations promotions are little more than long service awards. Furthermore, career progression may be heavily contaminated by external factors such as labour market conditions and chance factors. In many situations a mediocre 'performer' in the right place at the right time stand a better chance of promotion than a good 'performer' who is in the wrong place at the wrong time. It can be argued that these chance factors become more important as job level increases and where promotion decisions are relatively infrequent. At lower levels there are usually more promotions and chance factors may be able to cancel each other out.

Accidents are sometimes used as criteria because they have a major impact on the person concerned and may involve the organisation in disruption and litigation. Nevertheless, accidents are often poor criteria. One disadvantage from a scientific viewpoint is the narrowness of range. Most people have no accidents per year, a minority have one, and only a tiny proportion have more than one. Thus, effectively the range is from 0 to 1. A little extra discrimination can be improved by grading accidents according to their seriousness, but the essential problem remains. An additional problem arises from the instability of accident rates for individuals – the fact that a person has an accident this year does not mean that he will have an accident next year (Mintz and Blum, 1949; Ghiselli and Brown, 1955). Further difficulties in using accident statistics may arise from clerical errors in reporting accidents and from the fact that some workers are exposed to a greater risk of accidents than others. Perhaps one way of avoiding these difficulties is to change attention from actual accidents and instead observe the occurrence of unsafe practices (Whitlock, Clouse and Spencer, 1963).

Training information has many advantages as a criteria. In many well established training courses all trainees have similar tasks, tools and time tables. Organisational contaminants such as departmental politics and differential opportunities have less impact upon a trainee because they are more distant and because the relatively short periods involved in training do not allow them to work to maximum effect. In many training schemes there is an 'objective' pass standard and the 'marks' validated by an external body – which should reduce the possibility of the results being contaminated.

Thus training information, such as weeks needed to attain 'pass' standard or marks at end of course, may provide good criterion information. Ghiselli (1966) was able to show that training data provide criteria that are reliable. The main disadvantages may be the artificial nature of some training environments and the range of the information may be small. For example, most people in one company achieve efficient worker standard in either six or seven weeks and the criteria then becomes a crude two-point scale.

Judgemental Data: Person Making the Judgement

Because production data or personnel data are either unavailable, impractical or inappropriate, it may be necessary to utilise criteria which are drawn directly from judgements made by people. Usually these ratings are made by the individual's superiors, but they can also be made by peers, subordinates, the individual himself or herself and observers.

Judgements made by superiors are almost an automatic choice because there is a widespread belief that a superior knows a subordinate's job and the degree to which he is competent. Consequently this approach is acceptable to most organisations. It is also relatively easy data to collect – it often boils down to a simple process of identifying the correct superior and mailing some kind of rating scale in a confidential envelope.

However, a deeper examination raises a number of questions. First, to what extent does the superior know about the job being performed? It may be years since he did the job himself. Secondly, to what extent can he assess the competence of his subordinate. Analyses of managerial jobs (for example, Stewart, 1967; Mintzberg, 1973; McCall *et al.*, 1978) show that managers spend most of their time in meetings with managers at their own level and are able to devote only about 20 per cent of their time to their subordinates as a whole. Individual subordinates spend very little time with their boss. Consequently, the basis on which superiors make their ratings is often very slim. A filtering process also operates. Subordinates may actively manage the impressions they give to their boss by magnifying their successes and the difficulties they have overcome, while concealing their failures. All these factors may combine to make superiors' ratings very suspect criteria indeed. Other sources of judgements include ratings by peers, subordinates and self-assessments. These are discussed in greater detail in chapter 10. Chapter 10 discusses these methods as potential predictors but they may, nevertheless, be used as criteria.

Under some rather special circumstances, criteria can be based upon *judgements made by observers*. This can be achieved only when the job is fairly simple, short cycle and where motivational influences are likely to be small. It can also be used in artificial situations where special tasks are constructed and observable performance can be assessed against known criteria. The biggest theoretical advantage of rating by expert observers is that it becomes feasible to train a small cadre of experts to overcome the deficiencies usually involved in judgements. Also it becomes feasible for one or two people to make all the relevant judgements, thus reducing the error due to raters' differing standards. Unfortunately criteria from expert judgement can be obtained only in a narrow range of fairly artificial circumstances, and often generalising in the real world is suspect. Grant and Bray (1966) have shown that observer ratings are related to other criteria and Bray and Campbell (1968) have used these criteria to evaluate a selection system for salesmen.

Judgemental Data: Traditional Flaws

Most ratings, whether they are made by superiors, buddies, self or observers, suffer from a number of errors.

The *halo effect* refers to raters' lack of discrimination when describing the different aspects of the same employee. Thus Phil receives ratings of 7, 7, 6, 7 on intelligence, diligence, honesty and motivation. While this consistently good set of scores may be accurate, it may be a product of the halo effect. The most likely cause of the halo effect is the rater being over impressed by a single characteristic. This impression 'spills' over to judgements of other characteristics and produces a 'halo' through which it is difficult to make accurate judgements of the other traits. The halo effect can work in the opposite direction where an unfavourable characteristic reduces discrimination on other traits.

Leniency is the tendency to give ratings which are skewed in one direction – usually in a favourable direction. An analysis of many appraisal forms will show a substantial proportion of employees in the 'very good' category, a very large proportion of employees in the 'good' category, a few employees in the 'average' and 'poor' categories and practically no one in the 'very poor' category. Explanations for the leniency effect are not hard to envisage. Few managers will admit that they tolerate subordinates who are below average because they feel that it will be taken to reflect on their own abilities as a manager. In addition, many organisations have a policy of showing subordinates the ratings which their bosses have given them. Under these circumstances superiors are very reluctant indeed to give average or poor ratings. First, there is a high probability that poor ratings will be contested and involve a lengthy appeals procedure. Secondly, there may be a wish to avoid demoralising a poor worker.

The *error of central tendency* occurs because raters have a tendency to 'bunch' ratings together and not give extreme judgements. Consequently, most employees receive ratings that are within one point of the median rating and the discrimination of the judgements is usually poor.

The *contrast effects* may compound the situation still further. Judgements do not take place in a vacuum, they take place in a certain order and in a certain context. This sequence and the context can distort the ratings that are made. For example, a superior who has just correctly rated three subordinates as very superior will be rather less willing to give a fourth person the same rating.

The halo effect, leniency, central tendency and contrast effects may make ratings very suspect. In order to improve these judgements attention has been turned to more systematic methods of obtaining judgemental data for use as criteria (see Table 4.3).

TABLE 4.3   *Some ways of collecting judgemental data*

Basic technique	· rating scales
Scales with anchors	· behaviourally-anchored rating scales
	· summated rating scales
Employee comparison	· employee ranking
methods	· paired comparisons

Attempts to Improve Judgemental Data

The most usual attempt to improve judgemental data is to develop some type of *rating scale*. The first stage is to carefully define the number of scales which are to be constructed. It is generally pointless to produce more than about nine different scales.

The simplest type of scale consists of a *trait title* plus some kind of *continuum* anchored at both ends. For example:

Leadership   Good:–:–:–:–:–:Bad

The rater simply puts an X in the appropriate position.

This simple rating scale has two related weaknesses. First, the trait to be rated is ambiguously defined. To some people leadership involves having an iron will, a god-like judgement and the ability to dominate others. To others, leadership means paying acute attention to the wishes and preferences of a group and maintaining a happy, country-club-like atmosphere. Still other people attribute yet more meanings to the trait of leadership. If these simple scales are used, there is usually no reliable way of knowing which meaning is being used. The second weakness of simple rating scales is the ambiguity of the scale positions. For example, what does the cross in the extreme right hand box mean? Leadership on a cosmic scale or leadership that is just clearly discernable? Different raters will have different ideas and this divergence of opinion will contaminate the usefulness of the ratings as criteria.

In an attempt to improve judgemental data it is possible to be more specific when describing the trait and when defining the scale intervals. Examples are given in Tables 4.4 and 4.5.

TABLE 4.4 *Improved rating scales*

Improvement of trait description
CREDIT CONTROL

Knowledge of company guidelines and local area policy: setting and enforcing credit limits to assistant managers. Systematic checks on applications for credit.

GOOD   :____:____:____:____:____: BAD

Improvement descriptions of scale intervals
CREDIT CONTROL

	outstanding in top 1%	very good in top 20%	average	unsatisfactory in bottom 20%	very poor in bottom 1%	
GOOD	:	:	:	:	:	BAD

Improvement of both trait descriptions and scale intervals
CREDIT CONTROL

Knowledge of company guidelines and local area policy: setting and enforcing credit limits to assistant managers. Systematic checks on applications for credit.

	outstanding in top 1%	very good in top 30%	average	unsatisfactory in bottom 30%	very poor in bottom 1%	
GOOD	:	:	:	:	:	BAD

These examples demonstrate some extra points concerning the design of rating scales. The number of scale positions, i.e. five, raises the issue of how many points should be used. There is some evidence that people can reliably discriminate

TABLE 4.5   *A practical example of a behaviourally-anchored rating scale*

Security

Security is an important aspect of a branch manager's job. It includes taking normal care of premises and equipment, maintaining security of documents and maintaining proper security checks against fraud.

He is very security conscious and continually strives to improve the security situation. He regularly reviews areas with likely security weaknesses and ensures that a valid testing programme is implemented. Banking procedures are followed and forms and applicaitons are kept secure. Security of the premises is always maintained.

9

8

He is security conscious and ensures that a valid testing programme (twice per year, 15% sample) is implemented for checking agent's books against customer cards. Banking procedures are followed. Forms, applications and premises are maintained secure.

7

6

Security is generally good and there are only a few lapses in minor matters. Money and application forms are always accounted for and the premises are locked and checked each night.

5

4

He could be expected, at times to be a little lax about security matters and leave forms and documents lying around. Occasionally, money would not be banked sufficiently quickly, and a valid testing programme would be skimped.

3

2

He is a clear security risk. He makes no checks and locks nothing away. He cannot be relied upon to take even minimal precautions.

1

among seven positions on most continua: in favourable situations we are able to discriminate among nine positions and in unfavourable situations we are able to discriminate among only five positions. The number of scale positions chosen should generally lie within this range, with a preference for having more points at the upper end of the distribution. The rationale for this preference is quite straightforward. In most industrial situations raters are very reluctant to use the bottom two categories and when this is taken into account, a nine point scale becomes, to all intents and purposes, a seven point scale.

Some industrial psychologists prefer to use rating scales which have an even number of categories. This stratagem has the advantage of denying the rater the easy option of classifying people as average. He is forced to decide whether they are above or below average. However, the stratagem violates a simple fact of life, that on most human characteristics, the largest single group of people are those who are close to the average for the population.

The last example in Table 4.5 demonstrates one final issue. The description of the scale position (technically called the anchors) are only given for alternate scale positions. This often produces a clearer and less cluttered layout and it caters for the eventuality where a rater finds it hard to decide which of two scale descriptions apply to a particular individual.

The refinement of rating scales has been carried furthest by Smith and Kendall (1963), who developed *Behaviourally-Anchored Rating Scales* – BARS. Smith and Kendall reasoned that much of the unreliability of ratings arise from the fact that neither traits nor standards of judgement are sufficiently defined in most rating scales. Consequently must is left to the rater's imagination. If it is possible to construct rating scales which ask for specific judgements that are explicitly based upon behaviours which can be observed, then the agreement between raters should be much higher. Thus an ideal scale for collecting judgements would consist of two parts, (1) a clear definition of the trait to be rated, (2) a scale with descriptions of specific behaviours which would be observed at different levels. An example of a BAR is given in Table 4.5.

The construction of BARS usually proceeds in six steps. *Step One* involves the identification and definition of key aspects of job performance. Often this information can be directly obtained from the job description. *Step Two* concerns the production of the behavioural anchors. A sample of superiors, experts or job holders are asked to give specific examples of behaviours shown by people who are good, average and poor on that aspect of performance. Usually, their examples are written out on file cards. In *Step Three* the cards for the different traits are randomised and given to an independent group, who attempt to re-sort the behaviours into their

TABLE 4.6 *Abbreviated example of a completed summated rating scale*

C.B.R.I.

Name of person doing rating _____

Name of person being rated _____

EXPLANATION

Read each of the following statements. Then decide how often the person you are rating behaves in the way described. Show your decision by circling the appropriate letters under the statement by using the following code:

> A – Always
> F – Frequently
> S – Sometimes
> O – Occasionally
> N – Never

1 This person talks in a stimulating way
   A   F   S   O   N

2 This person frequently gives misleading and incorrect information
   A   F   S   O   N

3 This person is quick to grasp ideas
   A   F   S   O   N

4 This person belittles other people
   A   F   S   O   N

5 This person earns the highest respect from others
   A   F   S   O   N

6 This person refers important matters to the wrong people
   A   F   S   O   N

---

original categories. The anchors which are misclassified are rejected on the grounds that they are ambiguous. The *Fourth Step* involves placing a scale value upon the surviving anchors and the procedure is tantamount to the production of a Thurstone scale (see Edwards, 1957). A group of experts sort each anchor into one of, say, nine piles, according to whether it shows a high or low level of the trait involved. *Fifthly*, those anchors which produce a wide range of judgements are discarded. Finally, average scores of the remaining anchors are calculated and on the basis of these averages a selection is made so that the complete range from good to bad is sampled. Whilst it is possible to calculate the scale values of the anchors to several decimal points, in most practical situations it will be necessary to round them to the nearest integer.

The advocates of behaviourally-anchored rating scales point to two additional advantages: the process forces the organisation to give careful consideration to precisely what it means by success and failure and, because the scales focus on actual relevant behaviours, it is relatively easy to gain acceptance for them. Early research (for example, Taylor, 1968) suggested that BARS were better than 'ordinary' scales and that their accuracy approached a level which was equal to administering an ordinary scale to 'four' raters and taking the average rating. However, subsequent reviews (for example, Bernadin, Albares and Cranny, 1976 and Schwab, Heneman and DeCottis, 1975) are less enthusiastic.

Behaviourally-anchored rating scales is not the only attempt to reduce the errors involved in judgemental ratings. Summated ratings, forced choice questionnaires and methods of employee comparisons have also been used.

In some ways the *method of summated ratings* is similar to the BARS technique, except that the dimensions being rated are not made explicit and the behavioural anchors from several dimensions are juxtaposed with each anchor being presented in a standard Likert-type format. Raters are asked to say how often the individual exhibits that piece of behaviour. The rater answers every item and a score is obtained by marking each answer on, usually, a 1–5 scale. In the example given in Table 4.6 the score would be 21 (2 + 5 + 3 + 5 + 4 + 2 – alternate items being reverse scored).

It is claimed that the method of summated ratings give criteria in which the halo effect is noticeably reduced. However, a considerable leniency effect may remain. Bass (1957) produced a scoring procedure designed to overcome this problem.

Another way of using a questionnaire to obtain judgemental data which can be used as a criterion is the method of forced choice technique. It is effective in overcoming the problem of leniency error. Leniency error arises when raters want to be nice to the people they are rating and therefore tend to give ratings which put other people in a sociably desirable light.

A strategy to overcome this problem is to present two statements which are equally socially desirable but only one of which is a part of the criterion we want to measure. For example, both being happy and being efficient are socially desirable. A rater could be asked which of these traits is most typical of a worker. If the rater chooses efficiency then the worker has 1 added to his score, since efficiency is a part of the criterion. On the other hand, if the rater chooses happy, nothing is added. A scale is constructed of ten or more pairs of this kind and the criterion score is the total number of appropriate choices. Most forced choice questionnaires involve a variety of pairs and include pairs of favourable items and pairs of unfavourable items. Other formats are also possible. For example, it is possible to construct a tetrad involving a favourable pair and an unfavourable pair.

The disadvantages of forced choice ratings are relatively few. Sometimes, raters dislike making decisions of this kind. They may feel that both items of a pair apply equally to an employee or, in the case of unfavourable pairs, that neither of the pair apply. In practice the construction of forced choice questionnaires is time consuming. The items must be devised and then their social desirability must be established using an acceptable sample of 30 or more 'judges'. Uhbrock (1961) attempted to avoid some of this preparation by publishing the scale values of 2000 statements. Unfortunately the sizes of his samples of judges was small and ideas of social desirability have probably changed in the years since Uhbrock published his paper.

Employee comparisons are probably one of the least-frequently-used methods of obtaining criteria from judgements. There are two main approaches: rank order and paired comparisons. The *rank order* method is simplicity itself: the superior simply ranks his subordinates according to their perception of the subordinate's merit. Despite its simplicity, the rank order method has two related disadvantages. It often forces a discrimination where there is little difference between people and raters can find the task very difficult. To illustrate the problem of forced discrimination, suppose a supervisor in the pharmaceutical industry has four subordinates involved in running trials of an anti-arthritic drug. These subordinates can run 70, 60, 45 and 44 trials per month respectively and they are rightly ranked 1, 2, 3 and 4 by their superiors. However, this ranking implies that the difference between the first and second technicians is equal to that between the third and fourth technicians. The ranking also implies that there is a substantive difference between the third and fourth technicians where, in fact, the difference is quite tiny.

The second method of employee comparison, *paired comparison* technique, minimises some difficulties. The technique is also uncomplicated. Every possible pair of employees are compared in turn and the best employee in each pair is identified. An advantage of the paired comparison technique is that by using a number of psychometric procedures (see Edwards, 1957), measures can be obtained which are very discriminating and which have many of the properties of true interval measures. Unfortunately, the paired comparison method has a major disadvantage. It can only be used with fairly small groups of people. If it is used with large groups it becomes unwieldy because the number of combinations increases exponentially with the number of subordinates involved. A supervisor with six subordinates will need to make 15 decisions and a supervisor with nine subordinates will need to make 36 decisions. In practice this disadvantage limits the use of the paired comparison method to situations where no one has more than about 12 subordinates.

Both methods of employee comprison have an additional, and usually fatal, limitation. They are quite effective for producing criterion information about subordinates who come within the span of control of one person. But whenever more than one superior is involved it is difficult, and often impossible, to equate the standards used by the different superiors. In effect this limits the sample size to about 12 and for most purposes a sample of 12 is too small.

This description of the main types of criteria has established one fact very clearly. *No criteria are perfect.* This simple fact must be borne continuously in mind because the imperfections in the criteria will tend to reduce the apparent effectiveness of our methods of selection. The greater the criterion's inadequacies, the greater the selection system's handicap in predicting effective performers.

THEORETICAL REQUIREMENTS OF CRITERIA

The problems surrounding the use of criteria have led us to examine in detail the characteristics which criteria should possess. Landy and Trumbo (1980) present an impressive list of 14 separate requirements which can be reduced to three main issues: reliability, validity, and practicality.

Reliability of Criteria

To be of any use, a criteria must be reliable. A full consideration of the concept of reliability is given in chapter 6, and for our present purposes, it is sufficient to note that reliability is, in essence, concerned with consistency. Thus criteria should be consistent. If two sets of criteria data for the same individuals are collected at different periods of time, they should yield very similar results. The level of reliability will vary according to the criteria chosen. Ghiselli (1966) suggests that training data can be very reliable. On the other hand many authors suggest that sales figures are often too unreliable to use.

Reliability of criteria can be boiled down into three main issues: the inherent unreliability of criteria; the time interval between sets of data and the foibles of human judgement.

A clear example of *the inherent unreliability* of some types of criteria is given by a Dutch diamond broker who chose to evaluate its agents by using their sales figures as a criterion. Accordingly, they collected sales returns for the third week in September but, before making decisions on the basis of this information, they had the wisdom to check the reliability of weekly sales returns. They collected the same data for their agents in the second week of October, correlated the two sets of data and obtained a correlation of −0.2! This is not an isolated example of the inherent unreliability of criteria. Jenkins (1946) summarised the situation at that time:

> Various predictive efforts in World War II have failed because the very performance that was to be predicted has proved inherently unstable. Number of hits scored by an aircraft gunner on a towed sleeve is a criterion possessing a delightful degree of objectivity. All studies of this criterion, however, find the individual scores so low in reliability as to be without value.

Often the reliability of criteria can be improved by basing them on a longer time interval. In theory, the appropriate time interval should be determined empirically. For example, the diamond brokers could have collected two sets of monthly sales figures, two sets of quarterly sales figures, two sets of half-yearly sales figures, etc. They could then produce correlations for the different time periods and plot them on a graph to produce Figure 4.1.

On the basis of this graph, it could be concluded that half-yearly sales figures would be the optimum choice since the additional reliability of the yearly and two-yearly figures would not justify the additional delay. Although 'reliabilities' tend to increase with very long time intervals, in practice, however, the imperatives of a business environment prohibit studies of this kind: few organisations can afford the luxury of a four-year study (two years for the first data set and two years for the second) to determine whether to use half-yearly or two-year figures.

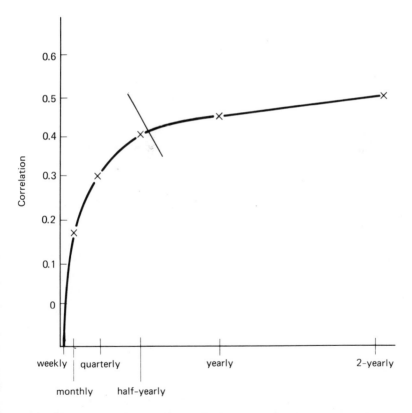

FIGURE 4.1 *Hypothetical reliabilities of sales figures based upon different time periods*

A slightly different issue concerns the *time interval between obtaining the two sets of criterion ratings*. Here the situation gives no surprise. The shorter the time interval between collecting the two sets of data, the higher the reliability. For example, Bass (1962) obtained a correlation of 0.6 when there were six-month intervals between collecting the two sets of data. When the time interval was 42 months the correlation fell to 0.3. This kind of relationship bodes well where the whole process of selection, from job analysis to final evaluation, takes place within a very short period of time, but it also implies that longer-term studies have to contend with an additional source of error since the same long-term forces which produce low long-term reliabilities may intrude between, say, the selection of a metallurgist and an evaluation, two years later, of his ability to develop new kinds of abrasives for polishing aluminium products.

The third issue concerning the reliability of criteria involves the *'foibles' of human judgement*. Jenkins (1946) provides another delightful scenario. Navy instructors were required to fill out a detailed form giving critical comments on various phases of each flight completed by each student. In actual fact certain instructors gave only a general grade, leaving detailed grading to a clerk who had not seen the flight. The clerk then dutifully supplied the detailed grades in a fashion which gave an over-all distribution of conventional form. In another example instructors saved all their forms to fill in at a weekend. Further doubts on the reliability of clerically-recorded data can be obtained from most examinations of medical records which almost invariably record body temperature of 98.6°F – in spite of known monthly cycles and well established differences arising from the way that the temperature is taken.

Thus, the research on the reliability of criteria makes quite depressing reading. According to orthodox procedure, the output of a selection system is compared with criterion data and if there is no relationship the selection system is abandoned. It is clear that many systems have been unfairly rejected. In many situations, it may have been better to keep the system but change the criteria.

Validity

Validity in the context of criteria can be taken to mean 'Do the criteria we use accurately reflect 'true' performance at work?' Whilst in theory it is an easy question to pose, in practice it is very difficult to answer. We have no direct telephone line to a deity in the sky who can tell us *for certain* the true answer. In the absence of a communication from an all-knowing deity, we must proceed one step at a time making logical deductions. The issues involved in the validity of criteria boil down to four main points: comprehensive coverage; contamination; dynamic nature of criteria; interrelationships among criteria.

Comprehensive coverage is important, as Ghiselli (1956) noted, because most jobs are complex and require the incumbent to achieve many objectives. For example, an operative in a nuclear reprocessing plant may be required to process fuel rods (1) quickly, (2) safely, (3) at minimal expense, whilst (4) maintaining good social relationships with his colleagues and superiors. Ghiselli also notes that each of these objectives can be achieved in different ways. As a trite example, one worker may achieve his objectives by means of brute strength, another may use craft and guile, whilst another may achieve the same results by charming his colleagues to do his work for him. Furthermore, each of these methods could be evaluated in several different ways, for example, by examining personnel records, by examining output figures or by questioning a worker's superior. This example is clearly a simplification but it implies that there are 36 different criteria which could be used with the job of a nuclear fuel-processing operative. In theory we can only be totally conclusive if we use all 36. In practice it would perhaps be adequate to use a sample of six or seven criteria. This sample should be carefully drawn so that most salient features are represented. *It is quite clear that, except in very unusual circumstances, a single criterion is not adequate.* Smith (1976) gives a list of 11 authors who have made the plea for the use of multiple criteria.

Probably the most famous exhortation to use multiple criteria is Dunnette's (1963a) call to junk *the* criterion. He says:

Much selection and validation research has gone astray because of an overzealous worshipping of *the* criterion with an accompanying will-ò-the-wisp searching for the best single measure of job success. The result has been an oversimplification of the complexities involved in test validation and the prediction of employee success. Investigators have been unwilling to consider the many facets of success and the further investigation of the prediction of many success measures and instead persist in an unfruitful effort to predict *the* criterion. Thus, I say: junk *the* criterion.

Notwithstanding these theoretical exhortations, it is clear that, in practice, most studies only use one criterion. Lent, Aurback and Levin (1971a) found that 85 per cent of studies used only *one* criterion.

Contamination of criteria is also concerned with the content of criteria but it focuses upon things which should *not* be present. Unfortunately criteria are particularly susceptible to insidious forms of bias which may remain undetected, and even when they are detected they are often difficult to quantify and remove. The number of potential contaminators is almost endless, but two categories are particularly important: job contaminators and illusory successes.

Some criteria are contaminated by job influences since workers rarely run the same race. There may be differences of equipment, design of product or the length of product run. A clear example of contamination by job influences is when crude sales figures are used as criteria for salesmen: some salesmen sell popular lines and some salesmen have very favourable territories. In other situations, departmental power and prestige can be important contaminants. This departmental power and prestige can help even mediocre employees to corner a lion's share of the resources and to land the plum assignments, while more talented employees in other departments are left to be content with the crumbs. This phenomena can be seen in the Civil Services of many countries in the world: a first posting in the Treasury is often an almost automatic passport to a high-flying career.

Illusory success was highlighted by Wallace (1974), who noted that it is difficult for us to predict success itself but we are more successful in predicting who people *say* are successful. In some organisations at least, the road to the top is paved with mimicry. The implications can be startling –

> If we are, indeed, embarked upon a venture which will lead us to pick people who can get good ratings, especially from the big shots, what are the implications for progress in business and societal endeavour? How to succeed in business by satisfying the guardians of the *status quo*.

A slightly different perspective arises out of the phenomenon of 'policy capturing', where criteria are used which reflect the point of view of the organisation's decision-makers. In other words, the criteria attempts to 'anticipate or predict how (and on what bases) operating managers will make their decisions' (Klimoski and Stickland, 1977). Policy capturing does not necessarily contaminate criteria. In some situations the explicit objective is, rightly or wrongly, to forecast future decisions.

The *dynamic nature of criteria* is often overlooked but it needs to be considered because the nature of criteria change over a period of time. For example, in the early days of computing economy of computer time and computer memory were important criteria which could be used to judge the success of programmers. However, in the last few years the costs of computer memory and computer time have fallen dramatically. User friendliness and ease of interfacing with other systems are now more important aspects of a programmer's work. Clearly, in today's situation it would be silly to continue evaluating the selection system on its ability to select programmers who economise upon computer memory. This is possibly an extreme example but, in other contexts, a gradual accumulation of obsolescence can affect criteria and this may produce an apparent lowering of the effectiveness of a selection system. Bass (1962), for example, investigated the effectiveness of three tests and 'peer' ratings over a 48-month period by seeing how well they predicted supervisors' opinions of salesmen. He found that all methods of selection became less effective as time progressed and after that a three-year period, meritorious performance is less contingent upon ability in comparison to esteem and popularity.

Practicality of Criteria

In an attempt to meet the objections in the two preceding sections there is a temptation to produce more complex and comprehensive criteria. Often there is a tendency to produce an exhaustive list of criteria which is too long, too time-consuming and too expensive for use. The practicality of criteria must be borne in mind. The main considerations are:

1. Cost
2. Acceptability to the organisation
3. Time taken to collect data
4. Time at which data is available
5. Acceptability to collector
6. Ease of analysis
7. Volume of information available

If these considerations are violated it is much more difficult to persuade organisations of the need to produce criteria against which the selection system can be evaluated.

In the haste to get a selection system 'off the ground' there is a compelling temptation to avoid the intricacies and difficulties of obtaining satisfactory criteria. It is alluring to proceed directly to the production of personnel specifications and the testing or interviewing of candidates. The lure should be resisted, for as Krug (1961) notes, a 'program of personnel selection can be no better than the criteria which define it'.

5 Attracting a Field of Candidates, Application Forms, and Handling the Response

The previous chapters on job descriptions, criteria and personnel specifications have dealt with the preparation which is undertaken before a vacancy arises. The more thoroughly this preparation is undertaken, the easier it is to deal with events when the vacancy actually arises – when an employee hands in their resignation or an expansion plan is agreed and extra employees need to be recruited. There is very little 'theory' involved at this point. Practical administrative experience is the greatest requirement.

ATTRACTING A FIELD OF CANDIDATES

A later chapter will demonstrate the statistical importance of attracting a large number of suitably qualified candidates, but for present purposes a commonsense rationale is sufficient: the greater the number of applicants, the greater the probability that one of them will provide a precise fit with the personnel specification. However, two particular points should be noted with care. First, there is an emphasis upon *suitably qualified* candidates. A large number of applications from non-runners who are patently unsuitable is a handicap rather than advantage. Secondly, the generalisation 'the more applicants the better' is only true up to a certain point. It takes time and effort to process applications. A very large number of applications can overwhelm the capacity of the recruiters and, under these circumstances, the care and consideration given to each application is degraded. In the light of the costs involved in dealing with large numbers of applicants and the deterioration which it may entail in the decision process, it is sometimes said that in ideal situations there should only be one applicant: the one who is eventually hired. In practice, however, it would be dangerous to adopt this approach. As a general rule of thumb the recruitment process should aim to produce a field of about ten well-qualified applicants, and probably in addition there may be a collection of applications from less suitable people. Success in attracting a good field of qualified applicants will largely depend upon where and how the job is advertised.

RECRUITMENT MEDIA

Internal advertising is usually the cheapest and quickest way of advertising a vacancy. At its simplest it involves an announcement of the vacancy at a meeting, a memo on notice boards or an insert into the company newsletter. Internal transfers of this type have a number of advantages:

1. The process can be completed quickly.
2. More will be known about the applicant.
3. There will be fewer formalities and legal implications.
4. Training requirements are reduced because the employee will already know much about the organisation.
5. Advertising costs are reduced.
6. General morale can be improved if it is felt that the company looks after its present employees and gives them 'first refusal' of any openings which arise.

However, internal recruitment also has a number of important disadvantages. The most important is the long-term consequences for the organisation. A policy of internal recruitment denies the company access to new ideas and approaches. Without even being aware of the situation, the organisation can become smug, complacent and out of touch. Another disadvantage arises from the tricky diplomatic situations which arise when an internal application is refused: a high proportion of rebuffed employees resign within a very short period. One of the disadvantages of internal recruitment is that it often does not solve the problem: it merely transfers it elsewhere.

Internal advertising can work in a way which avoids merely transferring the recruitment problem elsewhere. Existing *employees*

may pass on the information to someone who is looking for a job.
Often this is a suitable approach because:

1. The applicant can find out a lot about the job from existing employees and they are therefore likely to make a better decision.
2. The home circumstances of the applicant are likely to be appropriate, for example, he/she is likely to be a local person.
3. The applicant, if appointed, will try hard not to let down the person who recommended them.

   In addition, the employee who makes the recommendation has a vested interest in making sure that the person he recommends comes up to scratch. Generally they act as a source of guidance and advice which may make both induction and training easier tasks. To have a recommendation of this kind accepted by management may motivate existing employees. The main disadvantages of seeking recommendations from existing employees is the diplomatic situation which can arise if a recommendation is refused. Furthermore in some situations, especially in small organisations and units, it may not be in the organisation's interests to be dependent upon a small cohesive group of friends. Strauss and Sayles (1980) maintain that two-thirds of newly-hired employees learn about their job through informal recruitment of this kind.

   The decisions about whether to recruit internally needs to be taken in the light of specific situations and circumstances. The most usual pattern is to rely exclusively upon internal recruitment at senior management levels. Ironically, perhaps, this is the level at which it is most important to ensure an inflow of new ideas and expertise into the organisation.

   Vacancies boards are perhaps the second easiest recruitment media. Often a smart, up-to-date notice board outside the entrance of the organisation is a good way of advertising a vacancy. They tend to attract local recruits as they travel to work. Traditionally vacancies boards have been used as a recruitment media for skilled and semi-skilled jobs, but there is no intrinsic reason why they cannot be used for secretarial, professional and managerial jobs. Vacancies boards have two main disadvantages. First, if the organisation has a chronic labour turnover problem, the situation is clear for all to see. Secondly, the trivial task of keeping the board up to date, especially the removing of past vacancies, seems to defeat even the best managed organisations.

Future vacancies files contain information from two main sources, the documents of unsuccessful applicants for other vacancies and the details of speculative applications of people who have contacted the company on the chance that a suitable vacancy may exist. Future vacancies files can be cheap and very effective. People are often delighted to think that a company has not simply discarded their past applications. However, future vacancies files need to be managed carefully. An effective system of classification and cross indexing is necessary and there must be regular procedures to weed out files which are too old or where several job offers have been refused.

Government employment agencies can be found in most towns and their services are free. They can offer nationwide services and in many situations government agencies also undertake the preliminary sifting of applicants. Unfortunately these agencies have two problems. First, the service may have a poor image and some employers may believe that good applicants will use other methods. Consequently, some employers only use the government system as a medium of last resort. The second problem arises from the link between the state service and the payment of unemployment benefits. Employers often complain that they become involved in a bureaucratic game. They claim that their time is wasted because many applicants from this source are not interested in the actual vacancy and merely want a certificate to say that they have attended the interview so that their unemployment benefit will continue. Much will depend upon the relationship with the government agency. Time-wasting can be reduced by giving a clear and specific job description and by making it clear that the organisation does not wish to interview grossly unsuitable candidates. Some organisations have a policy of informing the government agency if they think that an applicant was not a serious candidate.

Private recruitment agencies charge fees and tend to specialise in particular occupations, such as clerical, technical or managerial groups. The exact methods of operation can vary from merely acting as a clearing house for applications to managing the whole recruitment process. The fee will depend, in part, upon the services used. Many agencies maintain a register of suitably qualified personnel and often a preliminary interviewing service. The advantage of using private agencies are that they have an 'up market' image and a company can avail itself of expertise as and when it is needed rather than having to bear the cost of employing specialists on a full-time basis. They have a further advantage because some applicants prefer to make their initial approach to an intermediary rather than to a specific company. The main disadvantage of private agencies are the fees and the fear that agencies will take a short-term view and will recommend unsuitable applicants in order to claim their fee. In practice, these disadvantages do not necessarily occur. Private agencies can be a cost-effective method of recruitment and only a small proportion of the agencies engage in short-term unethical activities.

Headhunters are a particular type of private recruitment agency and they are almost exclusively used for top jobs. The rationale for the use of headhunters is that the ideal candidate is probably not looking for another employer and is too busy in competently discharging his duties to read job advertisements. Therefore, if the post is an important one, a company or organisation should act proactively, and seek out the best person for the job. Headhunters perform this service, usually by using an extensive network of contacts, monitoring trade media or by identifying the employees of competitors and suppliers. Once they have identified a 'prospect' headhunters will research their performance in the current job and the previous career. If the results are positive, contact will be made and the vacancy discussed in general terms at a neutral venue. The company's name is only revealed to the prospect and the prospect's name is only revealed to the company when all checks have been made and where preliminary negotiations have been successful. Discretion is one of the main advantages of the process. The main disadvantage is the cost. There are also ethical considerations not least of which is the propriety of the present employer 'hoarding' talent which could be better used elsewhere. Headhunting executives, to obtain specific technical and commercial knowledge from competitors, involves serious legal dangers.

Unions and professional organisations can often be an excellent source of recruits – especially when there is a strong tradition of employing only union members. In some professional bodies, including the British Psychological Society and the American Psychological Association, the system is highly organised and the methods include appointments memoranda and offering facilities at conferences and conventions. Unions and professional organisations can be useful recruitment media even when systems of this kind have not been highly developed. An informal telephone call to the branch secretary can often produce a useful field of candidates.

Probably the majority of jobs are advertised in a *newspaper*, and a number of decisions have to be made. First, it is important to decide upon the category of newspaper to be used: should it be national, regional or local. Secondly, specific newspapers must be chosen. To a large extent certain newspapers specialise in certain types of job adverts. They may even specialise further by carrying specific types of job advertisements on certain days, for example, Monday, Civil Service; Tuesday, creative and media; Wednesday, academic and teaching; Thursday, sales; Friday production.

Even when a publication, or combination of publications, have been chosen, a further choice of the type of advertisement is necessary.

Lineage advertisements are the cheapest type and are used for small advertisements where you pay for the number of lines used. The advertiser has no control over the appearance of the advertisement but the finished product may look cramped, hard to read, and will appear along with scores of similar advertisements.

Semi-display advertisements allow the use of differing typefaces and give headings and more space. The advertiser still has little control over the final appearance but the result is easier to read and is more distinctive. The main disadvantage is its increased cost. Some guidelines for producing lineage and semi-display advertisements are given in Table 5.1.

Classified display advertisements are the most expensive and are usually spread over several columns. The advertiser has almost total control over the final appearance, and pictures, diagrams and logos can be included. Fordham (1975) draws attention to the need for creative talents in copy-writing and visualising in order to obtain maximum benefit. He suggests that a display advert should achieve four objectives. They are:

1. Attract reader's attention. It must catch the reader's eye and clearly identify the audience to which it is directed.
2. Arouse interest in the company and the job.
3. Explain the remuneration in terms of salary, benefits and prospects.
4. Incite the reader to action (that is, make an application).

The same considerations apply to job advertisements in the technical press except that the readership is usually much more

TABLE 5.1 *Guidelines for producing newspaper advertisements*

1 Get a copy of the paper you intend to use.

2 Be careful over *timing*. Avoid Bank Holidays, Budget Days, days when there is a lot of news. Fridays are said to be good days to advertise a job.

3 The first few words are crucial, start with the title of the job to be filled, or the type of work. If possible, start your advertisement with a word that begins with A, B or C – it will then get to the top of the column.

4 The first line or headline must catch the reader's eye and arouse interest. So start with the most interesting information and work down to less interesting information.

5 Use short words and short sentences. One sentence should contain one thought. Use plenty of paragraphs.

6 Generally, it is best to avoid box numbers. They lower the response, and should only be used in special circumstances.

7 Salary or salary range should be quoted whenever possible. References to 'attractive salary' are meaningless and a waste of space. Benefits should be included. Prospects for promotion can also be included.

8 Inclusion of telephone numbers increase response rate – but be sure to brief the people who may answer the telephone.

9 In some cases give information about the company, its size, location and product.

10 Tell people how to respond – for example, call at the office, write or telephone. Is an application form available?

specific and since trade journals appear less frequently, timing is a crucial element in success.

Liaison with educational institutions may be an important way of recruiting young employees. The liaison can operate at three levels. At its simplest level an employer simply writes to a school or appropriate college and sends details of vacancies as they arise. At a more organised level personnel officers will establish an informal relationship with the school's career teacher. At its most systematic level the college or university will offer facilities for advertising and interviewing applicants.

The *electronic media* are a relatively untapped method of recruitment. Local *radio* and *television* are a potentially powerful media but the cost is high and only a very short, general, advertisement can be transmitted. Consequently the use of these media can produce too many ill-suited applications. *Electronic and moving 'billboards'* suffer the same disadvantages, in perhaps a more acute form. The advent of *teletext* and the use of *cable TV* offer a way around this limitation and allow the presentation of a simplified job description so that potential applicants can make an informed decision.

Whatever recruitment media is chosen to attract a field of candidates, it should be remembered that an important secondary function of the advertising will be to *enhance the image which the public has of the organisation*: job advertisements will be noticed by a substantial proportion of suppliers, competitors and customers and it will play a part in forming their image of your organisation. Similarly, a job advertisement will receive a great deal of attention and speculation from present employees. It can fill them with pride and it can also fill them with shame.

The media chosen to attract applicants has also three *implications for equality of opportunity*, and the wrong choices can lead to secondary discrimination. First, media should be chosen so that all suitable applicants, regardless of sex, race or creed have a roughly equal chance of seeing the advertisements. Secondly, under the vast majority of circumstances the text of any advertisement should not state or imply that any one sex, or racial group is more suitable or will be given favourable treatment. Thirdly, while it is unlikely to evoke legal action, it is bad practice to produce advertisements and recruitment literature which presents the sexes and racial groups in stereotyped roles.

Before the advert appears it is vital to make two administrative checks: Is any additional information promised in the advertisement available? Have arrangements been made to handle the replies (for example, have the office staff and telephonist been briefed)?

METHODS OF APPLICATION

The job advertisements should clearly state how the applicant should apply. The most common methods are:

1. Personal visit 'on spec' to the personnel department.
2. Telephone
3. Written response

THE APPLICATION PACK

The usual result of a telephone or written contact is to send the potential applicant an application pack which will consist of four items:

1. A short letter thanking the applicant for their interest stating the closing date, and drawing attention to the enclosures
2. An application form
3. A description of the job
4. A reply envelope

APPLICATION FORMS

In the vast majority of cases a well-constructed application form is an essential part of the selection process and it can serve *five functions*. First, the most important function of an application form is to select a shortlist of applicants who will be invited to an interview. Secondly, a good application form should be an aid to the interview itself. It should be easy to read, provide a framework for the interview and provide convenient spaces for the interviewer to make short notes. The third funciton is to build up a future vacancies file: the applicant may not be suitable for the present job but they may be suitable for one that arises in the near future. Fourthly, an application form can help to analyse the labour market and identify the recruitment media which brings the best kind of response. Using this information, recruitment advertising can be targeted with pin-point accuracy and wastage can be reduced. The fifth function of an application form is often overlooked but is of great importance. The application form fulfils a public relations function. The form will be distributed to, perhaps, 100 people and even if they decide not to apply, they will give the form close attention. A well-produced form will help to project an image of an efficient, fair and well-run organisation. A scruffy, badly-typed form, run off on antique quarto size, poor quality paper, will also convey its own image.

Most firms will need three separate application forms in order to cater for different categories of staff. They are:

1. A form for school leavers
2. A form for professionally-qualified staff and management
3. A form for other employees

Basic examples of these forms are given at the end of this chapter (Tables 5.7, 5.8 and 5.9) and permission is hereby granted for them to be reproduced provided the source is acknowledged. In circumstances where they are not professionally printed, it is suggested that they are photocopied onto company letterheaded paper. In some situations a bespoke form will be needed. Tables 5.2 and 5.3 give guidelines on the construction of application forms and their contents. For more precise guidance it will be necessary to refer to standard texts such as Edwards (1975) and Tavernier (1973).

TABLE 5.2   *Checklist for constructing an application form*

1 It should be marked CONFIDENTIAL and *treated* as such. Completed application forms should not be circulated – if the successful applicant finds out that you have circulated his form, he may not trust your word again.

2 In general, arrange items in a chronological sequence.

3 The layout should give enough room for the answers.

4 If the form is to be used as an interview guide, allow room for interviewer's comments.

5 Use clear and concise words – that is, short words and short sentences.

6 Standardise form sizes – use A4 paper.

7 Avoid underlinings – use different sizes of type instead.

8 Choose good quality paper.

9 Instruct applicant to complete the form in BLACK ink so that it will photocopy.

10 It *must* contain the name and address to which it should be returned.

11 It *must* contain the closing date for the return of the completed form.

12 It should contain a warning not to send testimonials or the originals of other documents (these can be requested at a later stage).

TABLE 5.3 *Checklist for contents of application forms*

Application forms should start with the type of job sought and the date of any previous applications. They should also cover some *of the following items:*

1 *Personal details*

    (a)   name and address and telephone number
    (b)   date and place of birth
    (c)   sex, marital status, dependants
    (d)   height, weight, state of health

2 *Family background*

    (a)   relations employed in company
    (b)   occupations of other members of family

This section needs handling with care. Young people in particular may be sensitive about the status of their parents' jobs. However, this information is often useful.

3 *Educational background*

In general, do not ask for details of education before the age of 11. Possible items are:

    (a)   schools attended (name and type – with dates)
    (b)   examinations taken, and grades obtained
    (c)   school offices, scholarships, or prizes
    (d)   college or university; nature of courses; grades obtained; dates; offices held; extra curricular activities

4 *Vocational training*

    (a)   type of training, for example, apprenticeship/articles
    (b)   nature and place of training
    (c)   professional qualifications; date of qualification; present grade of membership
    (d)   fluency in languages: written, oral

5 *Employment history*

Complete chronological record of all jobs with

    (a)   dates
    (b)   nature and scale of duties and to whom responsible
    (c)   name and address of employer
    (d)   reasons for leaving
    (e)   starting and finishing salaries

TABLE 5.3 *cont'd*

Allow plenty of space for details of last employment and ask when they would be free to start work.

6 *Leisure interests*

(a)   hobbies
(b)   membership of societies and offices held

The exact range, depth and intensity of these interests can be ascertained at interview.

7 *Self-assessment*

Towards the end of the form ask the applicant about

(a)   his likes and dislikes
(b)   special job interests
(c)   future aims and ambitions

CURRICULA VITAE

At senior managerial and professional level and jobs where written communication is important, it is generally better to ask applicants to send copies of their curriculum vitae (CV) since the way that an applicant lays out their CV and communicates information about themselves may be a valid indicator of how good they will be at the job. However, the use of CVs may give rise to two problems. First, information from different applicants is likely to be given in a different order and in different formats. Inevitably this makes the initial sifting procedure more difficult and tedious. At its worst it can mean that some good applicants omit important information. In order to avoid this difficulty, requests for a CV should specify essential information which must be included. The second problem arises because an executive may not have produced the CV himself, but may have ued the services of professional agencies who prepare CVs for a fee. In these circumstances it is clearly inappropriate to use these CVs as a guide to the applicant's ability to communicate in writing.

PRODUCING A SHORT LIST

Very occasionally it is possible to make a decision solely on the basis of the information given in a written application. More often written applications are used as a first sieve to decide which applicants are to be invited to take part in the next, more extensive stage of selection. The most common sieving procedure is to sort each application into one of three piles:

1. *Possibles*: applicants who seem to have a good chance of succeeding at the job
2. *Doubtfuls*: applicants who are at the margin of suitability
3. *Rejected*: applicants who are clearly unsuitable

The objective is to end up with about six applicants in the 'possibles' pile. If there are fewer than this number, reconsider the candidates in the doubtful pile to see if any can be reclassified, perhaps using slightly less stringent criteria. If the first sieve results in more than six 'possibles', it is they who are subject to further scrutiny.

After a decent interval of about a week, applicants who are doubtful and rejected are informed of the decision.

THEORETICAL ISSUES IN ATTRACTING A FIELD OF APPLICANTS

There is remarkably little published evidence about the issues underlying attracting applicants. At best there are a few descriptive surveys giving a few basic facts. For example, a British Institute of Management and Institute of Personnel Management (1980) report surveyed the way in which 335 companies recruited managers. It found that 77 per cent of companies recruit managers internally and that the most common sources of external recruitment were the local press and the national press. But as Table 5.4 indicates, the pattern varies according to both the managerial function and the managerial level involved.

The same survey also examined the company's perceptions of the different recruitment methods and the results are shown in Table 5.5.

In general terms it appears that most companies are satisfied with the supply of suitable applicants and least satisfied with the public relations aspects of the recruitment media. As a generalisation, satisfaction is highest with internal recruitment and the local press, whilst satisfaction is lowest with professional registers.

Pollock and Lake (1983) give the results of a survey of 50 employers' and 50 recruitment consultants' views of the requirements

TABLE 5.4 *Use and satisfaction with recruitment media*

Recruitment media	% of companies using media for									Satisfaction with method (1–5 rating)
	Senior managers	Middle managers	Junior managers	Engineers	Sales/marketing	Personnel	Computer	Accountants	Technical	
National press	65	45	20	48	66	35	29	40	39	3.5
Local press	28	56	71	59	44	49	55	53	50	3.7
Trade journals	38	45	36	49	40	48	51	45	57	3.2
Private agencies	11	21	28	18	16	13	27	26	18	2.7
Selection consultants	35	15	6	14	18	14	11	18	12	2.8
Headhunters	15	3	1	4	5	6	0	6	5	2.5
Government agencies	12	25	28	27	17	19	19	19	26	2.2
Professional registers	6	8	6	9	7	4	6	10	10	1.9
Personal recommendations	26	24	21	27	27	20	21	16	25	–
Direct application	10	18	20	19	15	13	16	11	20	–
Internal recruitment		77		–	–	–	–	–	–	4.1

SOURCE British Institute of Management and Institute of Personnel Management (1980).

TABLE 5.5 *Perceived advantages and disadvantages of recruitment media*

Recruitment media	Over-all effectiveness	Cost effectiveness	Speed	Suitability of applicants	No. of Applicants	Public Relations	Confidentiality
National press	+	–		+	+	–	–
Local press	+	+	++	+	+	–	–
Trade press	–	––	–	++	–	–	–
Private agencies		––	+	+		––	
Selection consultants		––	–	++	–	––	++
Headhunters		–	–	++	–	––	++
Government agencies	–	+	–	+	–	––	–
Professional registers	––	–	–	++	+	–	–

KEY –– very poor
     – poor
     + good
     ++ very good
     +++ excellent

SOURCE British Institute of Management and Institute of Personnel Management (1980).

of CVs. The majority preferred a clear working document with no photograph. Most preferred to have details of the last job first and information about the duties, responsibilities and achievements under each job rather than a table of appointments followed by a description. Details of educational background, salaries and benefits (including whether a car had been provided in the last job), nationality, a clear statement of career aims were considered to be especially important information.

The applicant's view of recruitment media is an important issue but there has been even less research into this aspect. The results of one survey by the Consumers' Association (1983) are given in Table 5.6.

TABLE 5.6 *Applicant's use and success with recruitment media*

Recruitment media	% Use	% Success
National press	47	11
Local press	56	22
Trade press	30	15
Agencies	22	11
Specialist agencies	27	28
Job centres	56	11
Professional and executive register	39	7
Speculative applications	42	23
Personal contacts	50	51

SOURCE Consumers' Assocation (1983).

Some Unanswered Questions

Clearly research in this area is in its infancy. The data which exists is sparse, at descriptive level and focuses largely on the perception of custom and practice. We know very little about which advertisements and recruitment media are successful in terms of attracting applicants who will make good employees. We know little about the processes which lead potential applicants, especially those applicants who are contented in their present job, to attend to the recruitment media. We know little about the processes by which employers use the information in CVs and application forms to select a short list of candidates. We know little about the way that recruitment methods affect a company's public relations. These uncertainties mean that attracting a candidate and handling the response is, at present, more an art than a science.

TABLE 5.7   *School leaver application form*

School Leaver

APPLICATION FORM

Please return this form to:

No later than:

_____

1.   POSITION APPLIED FOR:

_____

2.   PERSONAL DETAILS:

Surname: _____   Forenames: _____

Address: _____   Telephone No: _____

_____   Date of Birth: _____ Age __ yrs

_____   Place of Birth: _____

_____

Name and address of next of kin:

_____

_____

_____

_____

_____

Occupation of next of kin _____

Names of any friends or relatives already working with this company

_____

_____

_____

3. SCHOOL HISTORY
   (since age 11)

   Names of schools attended   Dates

   _____ to _____

   _____ to _____

   _____ to _____

   What school subjects did you *like* most

   _____

   _____

   What school subjects did you *dislike* most

   _____

   _____

   Please list all the examinations you have taken (if you are taking exams in the next few months, list them here but leave the results column blank)

subject	exam (e.g. CSE)	result

   May we approach the headmaster of your last school for a reference? YES/NO

   _____

   _____

4. HOBBIES AND PASTIMES

    What are your hobbies & pastimes?

    Have you ever won any awards or prizes for your pastime?

    Please give details of any spare-time job you have had:

from	to
from	to
from	to

    _____

    _____

5. FUTURE PLANS

    What sort of work interests you most?

    What job would you like to be doing in 5 year's time?

    _____

    _____

6. GENERAL

    When could you start work with this company?

    How did you hear of us? (Give name of newspaper etc.)

    _____

Signed _____ Date _____

THANK YOU FOR YOUR INTEREST IN THIS COMPANY

TABLE 5.8 *Senior management application form*

Senior Management

APPLICATION FORM

Please return this form to:

Not later than:

---

1. POSITION APPLIED FOR

---

2. PERSONAL DETAILS

Surname: Forenames:
Address: Telephone Number:
                                  Date of Birth:
                                  Marital Status:
                                  Ages of children (if any):

Name and address of next of kin:

Do any of your friends or relatives work for this company (give name)?

---

3. WORK HISTORY

Name & address of your present (or last) employer:

Title of Job:
Details of duties and type of work:

Current salary:
Date and job title when you started work with this employer:

If you have already left your last job, give date of leaving:

Reason for leaving or wanting to change employers:

Name and address of your *last-but-one* employer:

Title of Job:

Details of duties and type of work:

Date and Job Title when you started work with this employer

Date of leaving and reason for leaving this employer

Names and addresses of other previous employers	Job Title	Dates	Reasons for Leaving

---

4. EDUCATION & TRAINING

(from age 11)

Please list the names and types of school and colleges you have attended   dates

Please list all the exams you have taken   results

Please list any training you have received. Include night school, day release, apprenticeship, in-company courses and correspondence courses

dates

---

5. MEDICAL HISTORY

Please list any serious illness you have had in the last 5 years. If you are a registered disabled person, give your certificate number.

Would you be willing to have a medical examination? Yes/No
Name and address of doctor

---

6. GENERAL

Please list any hobbies or pastimes you have and give details of any prizes or awards you have won. Also list any spare-time jobs.

When could you start work for this company?

How did you hear of us? (give name of newspaper etc.)

___

7. REFERENCES

Please give the names and addresses of THREE people who know your work. One should be your present (last) company – we will not approach your present employer without your permission. Do not give the names of relatives.

___

Signed   Date

TABLE 5.9   *Application form*

APPLICATION FORM

Please return this form to:

Not later than:

___

1. POSITION APPLIED FOR

___

2. PERSONAL DETAILS

Surname: _____ Forenames: _____

Address: _____ Telephone Number: _____

_____ Date of Birth: _____

_____ Marital Status: _____

_____ Ages of children (if any):

_____ ___ yrs ___ yrs ___ yrs
___ yrs ___ yrs ___ yrs

Name and Address of next of kin:

_____

_____ Telephone: _____

Names of friends or relatives in this company   Position

_____   _____

_____   _____

_____   _____

_____

_____

3. WORK HISTORY

Name and address of your present (or last) employer:

_____

_____

Date and job title on starting: _____

Title of present job: _____

Brief indication of type of work:

_____

Reason for leaving:

_____

_____

Salary of present (or last) job: _____

If you have already left your last job, give the date of leaving:

_____

Names and addresses of other previous employers	Job Title	Dates	Reasons for Leaving
_____	_____	_____	_____
_____			_____
_____			_____
_____			_____
_____	_____	_____	_____
_____			_____
_____			_____
_____	_____	_____	_____
_____			_____
_____			_____

4. EDUCATION AND TRAINING
(from age 11)

Names and type of school and colleges you have attended   dates

_____   _____

_____   _____

_____   _____

_____   _____

_____   _____

Please list all the examinations you have taken   results

Please list any training you have received. Include night school, day release, apprenticeship, in-company courses and correspondence courses.

         duration

_____   ____ to ____

_____   ____ to ____

5. MEDICAL HISTORY

Have you ever suffered from:

– Backtrouble	Yes/No	When?
– Nervous troubles	Yes/No	When?
– Dermatitis	Yes/No	When?
– Alcoholism	Yes/No	When?
– Epilepsy	Yes/No	When?

Would you be willing to have a medical examination? Yes/No
Name and address of doctor

If you are a registered disabled person, give your certificate No.

6. GENERAL

What are your hobbies and pastimes?

Have you every won any prizes or awards for your hobbies?

Please give details of any spare-time jobs you have had:

When could you start work with this company?

How did you hear of us? (give name of newspaper etc.)

_____

_____

7. REFERENCES

Please give the names and addresses of TWO people who know your work. One should be your present (last) company, but we will not approach your present employer without your permission. Do not give the names of any relatives.

_____   _____

_____   _____

_____   _____

_____   _____

_____   _____

_____

Please feel free to add any extra relevant information on a separate sheet

I certify that the information I have provided is correct

Signed _____ Date _____

THANK YOU FOR YOUR INTEREST IN THIS COMPANY

6 Requirements of Measures – Psychometrics

Once the short-listed candidates have been identified, the next stage is to subject them to a procedure which measures the personal qualities listed in the personnel specification. As subsequent chapters will show, there are many different measures to choose from. Eventually a decision between the different methods will need to be made. The most logical way is to set out, in advance, the requirements which good selection methods should meet.

In practice, there are four main requirements. In order of pre-eminence they are practicality, sensitivity, reliability and validity.

PRACTICALITY OF MEASURES

Except in the most unusual situations, practicality is the most important requirement. Even if a measure has all other virtues, if it is impractical its use will not be sustained.

Acceptability to those Involved

The employment of any selection device depends upon whether people perceive it to be useful. This perception does not have to be unanimous but there must be a consensus at the appropriate level and place within the organisation. Probably most important are the perceptions of *Senior Management* since, in the last analysis, they decide the employment of the organisation's resources. The perceptions of *selection specialists* are also important. Their experience and technical knowledge adds weight to their views. The technical aspects and practicality are probably the most important considerations to selection specialists, although tradition will play a significant part.

A selection method must also obtain the approval of the *candidates*. At the very least, the results will be distorted if candidates disapprove and they fail to take the proceedings seriously. Cronbach (1970) gives a delightful example of the importance of the candidates' perceptions: an Italian bus company discovered that applicants would travel 100 miles further than necessary to be tested in Rome because candidates believed that the more elaborate testing facilities in the capital gave them a fairer chance.

Finally, the method of selection may attract the attention of *political and pressure groups*. Again Cronbach provides an example, 'The British military selection programme had to satisfy a Labour cabinet insistent that poor boys have a fair chance to become officers'. More recently, some companies have abandoned certain selection methods in favour of less efficient ones because they are unwilling to attract the attention of minority groups and become involved in protracted litigation which would prove costly even if they sustained their case.

Operational Aspects

At a practical level, operational aspects of measures are also important considerations. The main operational aspects are: cost-benefit, time considerations, manpower and facilities. The basic point is that a selection system must produce more benefits than its cost. The difficulty lies in establishing whether this is true. With care it is fairly easy to establish the costs of a selection system, but establishing the benefits is much more difficult and can in itself be an expensive activity (see chapter 11). The main costs are set out in Table 6.1. In a large organisation with a clearly defined selection department, the costs will be easy to identify since most accounting systems will treat the department as a cost centre.

The second operational aspect concerns *timing*. Flexibility and lead time ARE PARTICULARLY IMPORTANT. Generally, a selection system which can be quickly adapted to changing circumstances is more practical than a system which requires rigid adherence to predetermined procedures. Similarly, methods which can be completed within a short time span of two or three weeks are usually more practical than multistage procedures which drag on for several months.

TABLE 6.1   *Main costs in a selection system*

---

1   *Labour costs* of personnel involved in selection and associated clerical
    work

    – salary
    – pension contributions
    – holiday entitlements
    – employment taxes

2   *Set-up costs*

    – costs of training staff in selection methods
    – costs of engaging consultants
    – costs of maintaining records
    – costs of obtaining criterion measures

3   *Equipment and accommodation costs*

    – rent or apportionment of accommodation costs
    – heating, lighting, cleaning
    – rates and taxes
    – cost of materials, for example, tests
    – stationery, postage, telephone

4   *Applicant costs* paid to applicants

    – travelling expenses
    – accommodation expenses

5   *Advertisement costs*

The different selection methods vary in the demands they make
upon able and qualified *manpower*. Unfortunately the situation is
complicated by the fact that the need for qualified personnel is clearer
for some methods than others.

The final aspect concerning the practicality of a measure concerns
the *facilities* it requires. Graphology and reference checks require
negligible facilities. Tests require booklets and answer sheets: they
also require small pieces of equipment. Some work sample tests, such
as test of ability as an airline pilot, can require expensive simulators.

On its own, practicality of a selection method is not enough:
selection at random with a pin is very practical but few organisations
knowingly use methods of this kind! Practicality must be supplemented by sensitivity, reliability and validity.

SENSITIVITY OF MEASURES AND SCORING SYSTEMS

Sensitivity and Discriminability

Other things being equal, the more a measure discriminates among applicants, the more useful the measure will be. Some selection methods are less discriminating than others. For example, one of the authors was involved in a selection situation which used eight different measures on the same group of people!

1. *Prework* consisted of a report, prepared by participants in advance.
2. *Tests* consisted of the results of a battery of pencil and paper tests.
3. The *work questionnaire* attempted to assess participant attitudes.
4. The *inbasket exercise* was typical of those described later in chapter 9.
5. The *group discussion exercise* produced ratings by observers.
6. The *group problem solving* exercise also produced ratings by observers.
7. *Presentations* on a topic of the participant's choice.
8. The results of an *interview* by senior managers.

For some of the participants, reports from their managers were also available. To ensure comparability between the methods, the participants were placed in one of five categories A to E (E being the most favourable) and the results can be seen in Figure 6.1.

In this example, interviews were the least discriminating method in which 125 ratings out of 170 (75 per cent) were placed in the middle category and no ratings were given in the top category. The reports from managers were also relatively indiscriminating with well over half of the ratings begin given in the middle category. The most discriminating measure was the tests, in which the middle category remained the most 'popular', but there was a reasonable number of ratings in each of the five categories and the distribution showed the characteristics of the normal curve.

Scoring Systems

The scoring system used to report the results of the measure is closely related to the degree to which a measure can discriminate. Crude

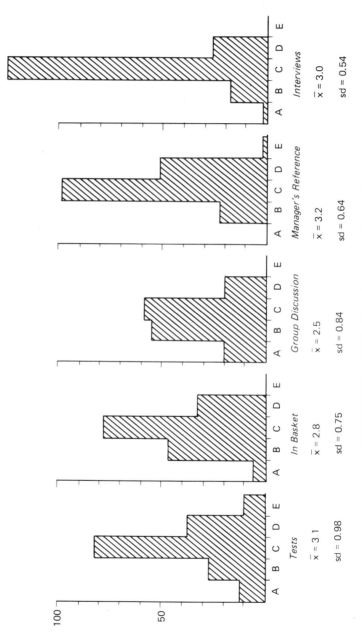

FIGURE 6.1 *Distribution of scores on five predictors*

measures can only validly adopt a crude scoring system and complex scoring systems should be used only with measures with good discrimination.

The initial score given by a measure is the *raw score* and at their simplest they consist of the number of right answers. However, on their own, raw scores have very little use and can be quite misleading as the cautionary tale of John Michael demonstrates. On arriving home one day he informed his mother that he had 'got 10 for arithmetic today'. Mummy, being delighted that her offspring was at last showing some gumption, decided to encourage the simpleton by buying him a new bicycle. John Michael had faithfully reported his raw score of 10. What he had not reported was that the test was out of 200 and that the average mark of his classmates was 120! Adequate scoring systems aim to prevent misunderstandings of this kind. In essence, there are three main types of scoring systems: intuitive, positional and systems based upon the normal curve.

Intuitive Systems

The simplest system is based upon pure intuition in which someone experienced in selection has stored in their memory experience of past situations. These memories may or may not be accurate. Current information can be matched with a past situation and an evaluation made.

Positional Scoring Systems

Except in the crude sense that, on most measures, the higher the score the higher the potential, the raw score is not very useful. To make sense of a score, it is necessary to compare the score with those obtained by similar people. In other words, it needs to be compared with a set of NORMS – a table which shows how a representative sample of people would have fared on the measure. Great care should be taken in choosing appropriate norms. Usually it is better to use 'local' norms, but recent work by Hunter, Schmidt and Hunter (1979) suggests that they should not be based on small samples of less than, say, 400 people. As the name implies, positional systems refer to the position of individuals in respect to those in the normative sample and there are four main systems.

The simplest positional scoring system simply allots an *above average or below average category*. Although it is simple and quick, this method wastes so much information and is so crude that it should be used only when all else fails.

Ranking is only slightly more complex and gives better discriminations. By convention, the best candidate is given a rank of 1 and so on until the worst candidate receives the highest number. However, rankings are best avoided: they can magnify small differencees and they can shrink large differences. Furthermore, a rank in itself does not indicate a level of merit or competence; the top rank can mean that an individual is merely the best of a bad bunch; the bottom rank could mean that an individual is only slightly worse than a field of superb candidates. Ranking systems are also notoriously difficult to analyse.

A *five-category grading system*, as used in Figure 6.1, places an individual into one of five categories: A, B, C, D or E. It is slightly more sophisticated than a ranking system. It is easily understood and is sufficiently refined for many personnel decisions. The most ubiquitous version of this system is as follows:

A = Top 10% of candidates
B = Next 20% of candidates
C = Middle 40% of candidates
D = Next 20% of candidates
E = Bottom 10% of candidates

This scheme has the advantage of placing the maximum discrimination at the extremes of the spectrum and it prevents over-interpretation of scores.

Percentile scores are the most refined type of positional score. Percentile scores attempt to place a person in place in a representative queue of 99 other people who have been arranged in order of their scores. Thus someone with a percentile of 52 would be 52nd in the queue. Percentile systems are easily understood by the layman and they allow fine discriminations. Their main disadvantage is that they do not accurately portray the difference between two scores. For example, there will only be a small absolute difference between two people at the 55th and 60th percentile, while there will usually be a substantial difference between two people at the 90th and 95th percentile. It should be noted that a percentile score says nothing about the percentage of questions answered correctly. The *decile system* is similar to the percentile system but gives a cruder classification. It tries to place people in a representative queue of 10. The decile system is rarely used but it has the advantage of avoiding over-interpretation of scores and it does not require such large standardisation samples to obtain a set of norms.

Scoring Systems based on the Normal Curve

If a large sample of people are taken and one of their characteristics such as height is measured, the results can be cast into a frequency diagram, as shown in Figure 6.2. When the midpoints of each class interval of the frequency diagram are joined, it is highly likely that a normal curve is produced in which most people are near the centre and there are fewer and fewer people at the extremes. The normal curve has two main characteristics: the mean and the standard deviation. The mean shows the average score and the standard deviation is a measure of the spread (see Figure 6.3). It is possible to construct several scoring systems based upon the normal curve. There are five main ones.

Z scores are the simplest type of score based upon a normal curve, and they simply state how many standard deviations a person is above or below the mean. Someone whose Z score is exactly average would

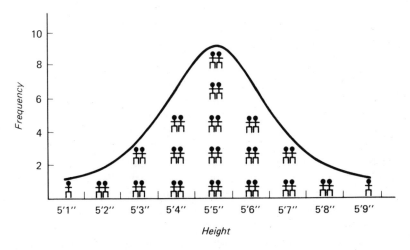

FIGURE 6.2 *Normal curve showing height of a sample of 36 women*

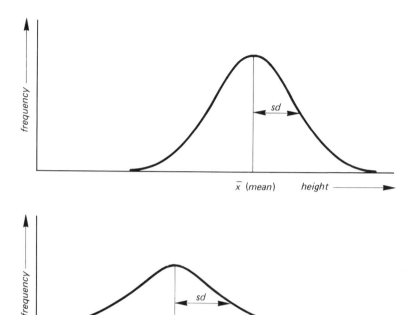

FIGURE 6.3   *Two examples of a normal curve showing how mean and standard deviation may vary*

have a score of 0: someone whose Z score is −2 would be two standard deviations below average. It is easy to obtain a Z score from a raw score: simply subtract the average from the raw score and then divide the result by the standard deviation. In most practical situations, Z scores are not used because they involve decimal points and plus or minus signs which are notoriously liable to be omitted when copying out results. Furthermore, Z scores appear to be crowded because most people lie in the −2.5 to +2.5 range. Although simple Z scores are rarely used, they are important because they form the basis for the other types of standard scores: quotients, T scores, stens and stannines. To obtain a standard score, the Z score is usually multiplied by a constant to expand the range. Then a further constant is added to remove any minus sign.

The *quotient system* is probably the best known standard score system. It is frequently used with intelligence tests and it is usually based on a mean of 100 and a standard deviation of 15. Thus someone with a Z score of +1.5 would obtain an IQ of 122.5 (ie 100 + 1½ × 15). Just to add some confusion, it should be noted that some tests use quotients based upon a mean of 100 and a standard deviation of 20. Unfortunately quotients offer too fine a discrimination for most measures and they invite over-interpretation of trivial differences.

T scores were named after Thorndike, and they adopt a mean of 50 and a standard deviation of 10. Although T scores are convenient and practically the whole population will have a score between 1 and 99, they are rarely used because they still invite over-interpretation.

Sten scores (standard scores to ten) are used by some of the most popular psychological tests. The system adopts a mean of 5.5 and a standard deviation of 2. Ninety-nine per cent of the population have scores between one and ten. Stens have the disadvantage of involving half points and analysts need to allow two digits in their computations to cater for those who score the maximum.

Stannines (standard scores to nine) are similar to stens except a mean of 5.0 is adopted. Consequently, decimal points are needed less often and the huge majority of people have scores between one and nine. It is possible to convert between percentiles, quotients, stens, etc., but to avoid confusion it is better, within an organisation, to adopt only one system.

RELIABILITY

The Standard Error

Even if a measure is both practical and sensitive, it will be inadequate if it is not also reliable. Reliability is often defined as the extent to which scores on a measure are free from random error. Reliability is usually, but not always, synonymous with consistency. The best way of establishing the reliability of a measure is to use it repeatedly on the same object. For example, 100 specimens of one person's handwriting could be obtained and each specimen independently rated on a trait such as extroversion. The 100 ratings of this one person could be collated and a histogram produced. Like most distributions, the histogram would have a mean and a standard deviation. The mean could be taken to be the 'true' position and the standard deviation could be taken as an index of how much random factors influence measurements. Usually, this is called the *standard error* of a measure. In approximately two out of three situations the random factors will be less than one standard error and consequently in two out of three situations we can be sure that the true score lies within one standard error of the score we observe. Thus, the standard error of measurement is particularly important in interpreting a score, as it tells us the confidence we can have in our observations. Providing the scoring system is held constant, measures with smaller standard errors are to be preferred. In essence, this analysis follows the classical analysis explained in more detail by Campbell (1976, p. 189ff) which views a score as two separate components: the true score and random error. Lumsden (1976) provides a witty, provocative and disturbing critique of this view.

Correlation Coefficients and Reliability

Estimating reliability by measuring the same thing a large number of times is usually possible in the physical sciences. In industrial psychology, however, this method is usually impractical. Few volunteers are prepared to submit to 100 interviews or be content to complete a questionnaire *ad nauseum*. A different method of establishing reliability is needed. Instead of obtaining 100 scores from one individual, it is usually easier to obtain, say, two scores on 100 people. The two scores can then be correlated with each other and the correlation can be used as an index of reliability since, if a measure is reliable it should produce two very similar scores for each person and therefore produce a high correlation. Furthermore, given a few statistical assumptions, it is possible to calculate a standard error from a correlation using the formula:

$$\text{standard error} = \text{standard deviation} \times \sqrt{1 - \text{correlation}}$$

Often it is more convenient to express reliability in terms of a correlation because the computing procedure for a correlation automatically reduces scores to a common scale. Thus under most circumstances the correlation coefficients can be interpreted as shown in Table 6.2. Thus it can be seen that a correlation of 0.9 implies random variance of only 19 per cent, whereas a correlation of 0.3 implies that 91 per cent of the scores are made up of random factors. Under most circumstances selectors are reluctant to use measures with reliability coefficients less than 0.7, because at this level about half of the score is determined by random factors.

TABLE 6.2   *Interpretation of correlation coefficients for reliability*

Correlation	0.9	0.8	0.7	0.6	0.5	0.4	0.3
Verbal label	excellent	good	acceptable	poor		abysmal	
% Random variance	19%	36%	51%	64%	75%	84%	91%
% Systematic variance	81%	64%	49%	36%	25%	16%	9%
Signal/noise ratio	4.2	2.7	0.9	0.6	0.3	0.2	0.1

Attenuation of Range

The use of correlation coefficients to estimate reliability is complicated by the way in which the sample is obtained. The sample must reflect the population on which the selection method is to be used. In particular, the sample must cover the whole range of the population because if the range is attentuated, it will produce a lower coefficient of reliability and make the proportion of error variance seem much larger.

In a selection situation it is often possible to obtain only samples of successful candidates or job holders and this usually involves an *attenuation of range* which reduces the reliability coefficients obtained. Fortunately, provided the standard deviation of the sample and the standard deviation of the unselected group are available, it is possible to correct for the effect of attenuation using formula 3.1 (Appendix I).

Methods of Obtaining Reliability Coefficients

To obtain a correlation coefficient it is necessary to have two scores for each candidate. The different ways of obtaining these pairs of scores give rise to the three main methods of estimating reliability.

Parallel form reliability is used when there are two equivalent versions of a measure. Sometimes this type of reliability is termed the coefficient of *equivalence*.

Parallel form reliability has a number of disadvantages. First, and obviously, it is necessary to produce a parallel form of the measure. This increases costs and can involve extra delay. Consequently, parallel form reliability is only used when different versions of the measure exist for other reasons. A second difficulty is the problem of ensuring that both versions are equally satisfactory. If one of the versions is less satisfactory than the other, the correlation between them will reflect the reliability of the least satisfactory version. The consecutive administration of the two measures produces a third set of difficulties. For example, in responding to the first version a candidate may be more alert, give greater thought to the answers and be less sure about the purposes of the procedure. In responding to the second version, the candidate may have become bored or so sophisticated that he can perceive the purpose of the procedure and adjust his responses in order to fool the selector. These influences arise from procedures to estimate reliability and not from the measure itself. This will tend to produce an underestimate of reliability. A fourth probelm with parallel form reliability is the influence of temporary and irrelevant states in the candidates. For example, if both versions of a measure are administered on a day when a candidate is feeling on top of the world, then the score on both versions may be a little higher. Another candidate may be operating in the face of what feels like a terminal hangover and both of these scores are depressed. Because these temporary influences operate on both versions they tend to inflate the observed level of parallel form of reliability.

Test-retest reliability, in spite of its name, is relevant to other selection measures. To establish test-retest reliability, the same measure is readministered to a sample after a short interval. Often this type of reliability is termed *stability* (see Cureton, 1971).

Test-retest reliability does not entail the problems arising from changes from one version to another, but additional issues arise. Some candidates will learn from their first experience and their scores will show subsequent improvement. Differential changes will tend to depress the level of the reliability coefficient obtained. The time interval used in a test-retest study may be of crucial importance. A very short interval such as one or two days increases learning effects. On the other hand, a long interval of a year could encompass genuine changes. These genuine changes are, wrongly, included as error and thus the reliability estimate is depressed. Most test-retest studies involve an interval of between one and three months.

Internal consistency is a type of reliability which has some similarities to parallel form reliability and at its simplest it consists of a *split-half reliability*. In essence the two scores used to compute the correlation are obtained by dividing the items of a measure into two equivalent halves. In principle this can be done with most measures, but in practice it is easiest with psychometric tests. For example, one half of a psychometric test might consist of the odd-numbered items and the other half might consist of the even-numbered items. A score is then obtained for each half and the two scores correlated. This initial correlation is an appreciable underestimate of the true reliability. It is known that short scales are less reliable than longer ones and the initial split-half correlation is based on scales that are only half the length of the actual scales. The initial estimates must therefore be corrected for length using the *Spearman-Brown formula* (see formula 3.2 in Appendix I).

Split-half correlations have one particular disadvantage. The way that the items are divided among the two halves is arbitrary. With very short measures which are not uni-dimensional this can unduly reduce the level of the reliability estimate. For example, supposing there is a short test of arithmetic ability covering the operations of add, subtract, divide and multiply. It is quite likely that the test designer used a spiral omnibus format in which the first and fifth questions are additions and the second and sixth questions are subtractions and so on. The unwary might then attempt an odd-even split-half reliability which would correlate additions and divisions against subtractions and multiplications. It is probable that the resulting coefficient would be smaller and one obtained from two halves, both of which contained all four types of arithmetic problems.

An alternative to the split-half method is the *item-whole* correlation, which also applies mainly, but not exclusively, to psychometric tests. Here the score on each item is correlated with the total score. There are as many correlations as there are items, and since it is mathematically wrong to take a simple average of a set of correlations, the median item-whole correlation is usually chosen. The item-whole correlation may be spuriously high because there is self-contamination: that is, the score of an item is included in the total score against which it is correlated. A correct analysis would make appropriate subtractions from the total score before it is correlated with an item.

Probably the best indices of a measure's internal consistency are *coefficient alpha* and *Kuder-Richardson's formula 20*. These indices, in effect, compute the mean values of all possible split-half reliabilities. The Kuder-Richardson (1937) formula is generally used where the items are scored in terms of pass and fail and Cronbach's (1951) alpha is used when items are marked on a continuum.

Inter-rater reliability is an issue where a measure involves some subjective evaluation by a judge, such as evaluating an interview or performance in a discussion group. In these situations a check should be made on the consistency of the raters. Usually, an unambiguous scoring system is devised and raters are trained in the use of the system. Next, two markers *independently* classify a small, but representative, sample of results. Differences between the two markers should be discussed and reconciled. The markers then independently score a full sample and the two sets of independent marks are then correlated. An inter-rater reliability less than 0.9 is not normally acceptable. Some authors, such as Cattell (1957) and Guion (1965), refer to inter-rater reliability as Conspect Reliability.

Length and Other Aspects of Reliability

Where a measure is obtained by adding up subscores, the number of subscores used can have a strong influence upon reliability. The classic situation of this kind is where a test score is obtained by adding the number of correct answers to a series of questions. The same principle applies to combining the scores given by several interviewers or by combining the references from several sources.

In general, the more subscores that are aggregated in this way, the more reliable the measure will be (see Gulliksen, 1950). Guilford (1965, p. 465) gives a formula for calculating the number of subscores needed in order to obtain a total score of a given reliability. The logic is quite simple. A score consists of two parts. The first part is a true reflection of a person's ability. The second part consists of random errors such as misunderstanding the wording of a question or a momentary surge in concentration and it distorts the true score. For each individual subscore, these distortions will be relatively large, but when subscores are aggregated the random errors tend to cancel out. The more subscores that are aggregated, the greater the probability that the cancelling out will be exact. However, there are two important qualifications to this generalisation. The additional scores must be as good as the scores to which they are added: simply adding rubbish will reduce reliability. Secondly, there comes a point of diminishing or even negative returns because candidates become bored or even annoyed by a long-winded procedure and they lose motivation.

VALIDITY

Definitions of Validity

Even if a measure is practical, sensitive and reliable, it is a poor measure unless it is also valid. For example, the circumference of the head might be suggested as a measure of a candidate's intelligence. This measure would be practical since it would only take a few seconds to obtain. It would be discriminating because the circumference of heads varies by up to 75 mm. It would be reliable because, with reasonable care, a second reading would give more or less the same answer. Yet head circumference is unlikely to be used because it is not valid as an index of intelligence: it has only a very slight relationship with intelligence itself.

Whilst everyone agrees that validity is a 'good thing', there is much less agreement upon its definition. A traditional definition is that validity answers the question, 'Does a measure gauge what it purports to measure?' Anastasi (1982) affirms that validity concerns *what* is measured and *how well* it is measured. It tells us what can be rightly inferred from a score. Gulliksen (1950) is more direct and says, 'Validity . . . is the correlation with a criterion'. Anastasi and Gulliksen's definitions are important because they focus attention on the fact that *the essence of validity is the correctness of inferences that may be made from it*. Thus, in a strict sense, measures do not have validities. It is the inferences made from them which have validities. A measure can be used for different purposes and it can therefore have different validities. The relativity of validity contrasts with the specifity of reliabilities – given a specific sample and method, reliability will remain static. Indeed, Cureton, Cook, Fischer, Laser, Rockwell and Simmons (1973) seem to imply that provided the length of a test is held static, the reliability will remain the same.

A more technical definition of validity is the systematic variance which is related to a criterion. The technical definition needs more explanation. In the previous discussion on reliability scores were divided into two parts, the random (error) variance which produces the unreliability of a score, and the systematic variance which produces the true score. This systematic variance can be further subdivided into those parts which are unrelated to a particular inference (for example, test familiarity, bias, seniority, length of service) and the part which is related to a particular criterion (for example, ability, personality). Validity is concerned with the size of the latter portion.

Types of Validity

Over the years many different ways of assessing validity have evolved but, despite the valiant efforts of professional organisations, there is no universally agreed method of classifying methods of establishing validity. The American Psychological Association (APA) (1954) initially distinguished four types of validity: content validity, concurrent validity, predictive validity and construct validity (Cronbach and Meehl, 1955). This view was subsequently revised (APA, 1966) and in 1974 a three-fold classification was made into content, criterion-related, and construct validity.

Content Validity

Content validity is often divided into two types: face validity and content validity proper. This distinction is essential because *face validity* is not, in the true sense of the earlier definitions, a type of validity at all. Face validity is concerned with people's perceptions of a test's validity: not with validity itself. This does not mean that face validity is unimportant. Indeed, in many situations it has greater practical importance because it can determine whether an organisation decides to adopt a measure and it determines the level of rapport with candidates.

The importance of face validity seems to increase with the age and seniority of the applicants. Fortunately, face validity can often be improved by using examples and wording that are appropriate to the group concerned. In 1950 Adams reviewed the literature on face validity and suggested a small correlation of 0.31 between true validity and face validity as assessed by students. Adams also quotes a study by O'Rourke who had judgements made on proposed tests for the postal service. He demonstrated that one test with great face validity possessed little or no true validity.

Content Validity boils down to a matter of sampling: does the measure adequately cover the operations which are relevant to success in a job? For example, if a job required general mathematical ability and an interviewer asked only questions concerning additions and division, the interview would not have content validity because subtraction and multiplication would have been overlooked.

An advantage of content validity is that it is usually easier to establish than other kinds of validity. The first stage is to define the domain to be measured by systematically examining job descriptions and consulting experts. On the basis of these enquiries a specification is built up. It is then easy to identify and rectify any omissions. Sometimes it may be necessary to employ judges to categorise behaviours. The judges should be carefully chosen and inter-judge agreement must be taken into account. Content validation of this kind is particularly pertinent to job samples since it is necessary to demonstrate that the sample is in fact representative of the job itself.

Unfortunately, content validity involves a number of practical and conceptual issues. In practice it is often difficult to define the domain of tasks to be sampled and experts may not be available. The conceptual difficulties are much greater. Guion (1977, 1978), Tenopyr (1977) and others have pointed out that content validity is evaluated by showing how well the content of the measure samples the class of situations about which conclusions are to be drawn. In other words, content validity is about *the construction of measures*. But this lies outside the earlier definition that validity is concerned with the *inferences made from scores*. Messick (1974) makes the point explicit, 'Content coverage is an important consideration in test construction and interpretation, to be sure, but in itself it does not provide validity. Call it "content relevance", if you would, or "content representativeness", but don't call it content validity'. Ebel (1975) underlines the same point, 'perhaps instead of content validity we should call it content reliability or job sample reliability. Perhaps we should, but I doubt that we will. Verbal habits are not easy to change. We are no doubt fated to live henceforth with somewhat imprecise terminology.'

Criterion-Related Validity

In a selection context criterion-related validity is usually the most important type of validity, and it is concerned with predicting an applicant's behaviour and effectiveness in certain situations. The word prediction in this definition must be taken in a broad statistical sense rather than in the sense of a sequence of time. Three main types of criteria-related validity can be distinguished: predictive validity, concurrent validity and synthetic validity.

Predictive validity is, from a scientific standpoint, the most desirable type of validity to establish. It refers to the extent to which a measure can predict the scores of applicants on some future assessment. For example, a company installing an optical fibre communication system might give applicants a test of finger dexterity. It does not use the scores on the test to select applicants. Instead it hires, trains and inducts all applicants. After a period of three months when the applicants have settled down in their jobs, the company collects information on how many circuits each applicant installs in a specified time. It establishes the predictive validity of the test by comparing the test scores with the production data, by plotting a scattergram with the test score along the bottom and the criteria score on the vertical axis as shown in Figure 6.4. The scattergram can then be inspected to see if there is a relationship between the measure and the criterion. Visual inspection can be arbitrary, so it is usually better to rely upon a correlation coefficient as a statistical index of the relationship between a measure and a criterion.

Although predictive validity has great theoretical appeal, in practice it is rarely used outside the armed forces and a few government organisations. The reasons are easy to determine. First, in its pure form, predictive validity requires an organisation to hire all applicants – even those who seem patently unsuitable. Few organisations

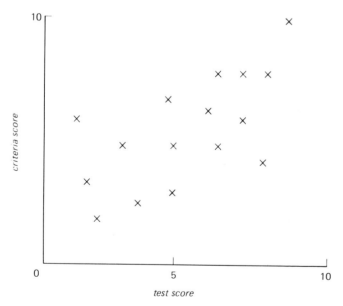

FIGURE 6.4 *Example of a scattergram between a predictor (in this case a test) and a criterion*

are prepared to sacrifice such large resources on the altar of scientific purity. Fortunately, in some circumstances it is possible to allow the worst candidates to be screened out and to then make a statistical correction to the results. There are two formulae. The first is used when the restriction occurs at an even earlier stage and where only some applicants are subjected to a measure, for example, only those who pass the interview are given tests. Thus when the restriction of range is in the predictor measure, formula 3.3 in Appendix I is used.

Restriction of range can also occur in the criterion data. Even the most affluent and tolerant organisation will fire or transfer the worst applicants who make a botch of everything they touch and who are a danger to themselves and colleagues. Furthermore, there is usually 'voluntary turnover' from poor performers who sense their failures and who decide to quit while they are ahead. Thus, even in the best planned predictive study, criterion scores tend to be higher for those for a perfect sample. To correct the restriction of range of this kind use formula 3.4 in Appendix I.

In addition to the necessity to hire all applicants, predictive validity has another practical disadvantage: it inevitably involves a time delay. This time delay can be very substantial. For example, to fully train a policeman takes more than two years. If it takes a year to amass data for a sufficient sample of recruits, then, allowing time for organisation and analysis of the study, predictive validity will take almost four years. In a commercial environment the organisation could become bankrupt while it awaits the results.

Concurrent validity avoids these practical problems, but is less pure from a scientific viewpoint. In essence, concurrent validity involves obtaining the measure and the criterion information at the same time. Usually, this means that a sample of existing employees are obtained and subjected to the selection measure in question. At about the same time criterion information is also collected. The criteria and the scores are then correlated in the normal way. The results of a study of concurrent validity are available within weeks or months and there is the further advantage that the method is relatively cheap. Unfortunately, concurrent validity also suffers from a number of disadvantages. Almost all concurrent studies suffer severe restriction of range: the worst employees will have been fired or transferred and the best employees may have been promoted to other work. This restriction of range will spuriously reduce the level of validity. A second problem arises from motivational factors: volunteer employees in a concurrent study may not be as motivated to produce their best performance whereas most applicants in a selection situation will try very hard. Motivational factors in concurrent validation will probably understate the actual validity. Cronbach (1970, p. 137) quotes an analysis of 70 studies in which concurrent validities were slightly smaller than predictive validities.

A special type of concurrent validity is the *nominated groups technique*, where two groups are assembled which are strongly believed to differ on a particular characteristic. The measure in question is applied to the groups. If the measure is valid, it should differentiate between the groups. For example, if a group of bank managers and a group of confidence tricksters were assembled and specimens of their handwriting given to a graphologist for evaluation, the bank managers should, presumably, achieve higher scores for honesty from the graphologist.

Synthetic validity is sometimes called job component validity, and was pioneered by Lawshe (1952) in an attempt to devise a method which is applicable to small firms. The first stage of obtaining synthetic validity is to analyse the jobs within an organisation in terms of the degree to which they require a certain characteristic. Next, the measure is applied to everyone in the organisation and the average score for each job is calculated. Finally, the average scores are correlated with the requirements. For example, a small company may be interested in evaluating a test of mental arithmetic. First it ranks each job on the level of mental arithmetic demanded, for example, accountant, estimator, general manager, supervisor ... janitor, tea lady. Secondly, everyone in the firm then completes the mental arithmetic test and the average score for each job is obtained. Jobs are ranked according to the average score of the occupants. Thirdly, the two sets of ranking are then correlated. Although synthetic validity was designed for use in small companies, it can be used in larger investigations. Probably the best example of this use is McCormick's 1959 study. Mossholder and Arvey (1984) provide a review of the current status of synthetic validity approaches.

Construct Validity

In essence, construct validity attempts to answer the questions 'What is the psychological meaning of the scores and how do the scores relate to other measures?' Cronbach and Meehl (1955) say that 'construct validation is involved whenever a test is to be interpreted as a measure of some attribute or quality which is not operationally defined.' The problem for the investigator is, 'What constructs account for variance in test performance'.

Although Cronbach and Meehl's comments specifically mention tests, the same considerations apply to other measures. Their definition, which has the broad support of most experts, seems to contain two related elements. First, construct validation is not particularly concerned with predicting behaviour which is operationally defined, for example, 'conducts an average of 40 blood group analyses per day'. Secondly, construct validation is concerned with the attribution of more general traits, which are usually derived from psychological theory, for example, 'is able to persist with highly boring, technical operations'. We can never open up anyone's brain and observe persistence of boredom. We can only infer these psychological constructs from behaviour. In this particular example it is easy to specify the behaviour which would indicate persistence and boredom. In many situations, the inferences are more complex, for example, what pieces of behaviour typify leadership or insight. Bechtoldt (1959), however, is not happy with the idea of construct validity. He feels that there is little essential difference between predictive validity and construct validity: they are both involved in the process of building scientific theories; in the case of construct validity the chain of inferences may be longer but the chain ultimately ends in some kind of observable behaviour. Bechtoldt rejects the idea of construct validity as merely a 'renaming of the process of building a theory of behaviour by the new term "construct validity"' and it, 'creates, at best, unnecessary confusion and, at the worst, a non-empirical, non-scientific approach to the study of behaviour.' A contrasting view is taken by Lumsden and Ross (1973) who say:

> it turns out that it is impossible to isolate validity questions from theoretical questions since an acceptable description must use the terms of a well developed theory and they identify two separate questions: (1) whether the construct ... is correctly formulated, (2) if so whether [it] reflects just the concept we suppose or others as well.

They suggest that construct validity confuses these two issues and suggest an alternative title of equivalence validation.

In practical terms construct validity is established in three main ways. First, there is correlation with a single alternative measure which is believed to be an accurate reflection of the construct involved. For example, suppose that a graphologist claims that the space between words in handwritten script is a reflection of intelligence. The construct validity of space between words could be established by correlating the size of spaces with scores on an established test of intelligence. To establish the full construct validity of a measure, many individual studies of this kind would be required. For example, we may need additional correlations with academic performance, and a rating by a superior. Unfortunately, the results of these studies may be contradictory – especially if the studies use small samples and alternative measures which are themselves questionable.

Factor analysis is a powerful tool in establishing the construct validity of a measure and is a way of simultaneously investigating several relationships. The use of factor analysis in this context is complex and best explained by an example. Suppose it was necessary to explore the construct validity of interview ratings: we wanted to know what psychological constructs are being measured. One way to do this would be to collect a series of scores on a substantial sample of individuals, for example, three tests of intelligence, two ratings of intelligence, a rating of verbal fluencey, tests of personality, sociometric ratings, and biographical information. Every combination of these scores could be correlated and a correlation matrix produced. In essence, factor analysis is a statistical technique for identifying the underlying trends in a matrix of correlations. A computer scans the matrix and when it locates a trend (a factor) it extracts its influence from the matrix. The computer then scans the remaining matrix for another trend – and so on until all the information is extracted. In extracting factors in this way, the computer combines together those scores which are measuring the same constructs and produces a more general composite which should overcome the drawbacks of its constituent scores. In this example there would be an intelligence factor, and probably factors concerning sociability and verbal fluency. It is then possible to correlate the interview scores with the factors to determine the factorial composition of interviews. This two-stage approach, involving first the extraction of the factors, and then a correlation of the measure in questions against the factors, is scientifically pure but cumbersome. In practice, the interview scores would probably be included in the analysis itself and the correlations between the interview scores and the factors would be produced in terms of loadings. The loadings could then be inspected to determine the factorial composition of the measure. By squaring the loadings and multiplying by 100 it is possible to calculate the percentage variance due to a factor. Table 6.3 shows how the loadings might emerge for our example.

The results from this hypothetical example suggest that the main component of interview scores is verbal fluency, which determines about 36 per cent of the differences between individuals. Among other things it suggests that intelligence plays a minor role and that 38 per cent of the differences between individuals are due to influences which are not included in the analysis.

TABLE 6.3   *Hypothetical factor loadings for interview scores*

Factor		*Loading on interview score*	*% of variance*
I	*Intelligence*	0.1	1
II	*Sociability*	0.4	16
III	*Verbal fluency*	0.6	36
IV	*Job experience*	0.3	9
		Variance accounted for	62
		Variance not accounted for	38
		Total variance	100

Thus factor analysis can be a powerful tool in establishing the composition of a measure. However, two very strong notes of caution are necessary. First, the sample sizes must be large – as a rule of thumb there should be four times as many applicants as there are scores for each applicant. Secondly, great care should be taken in determining which scores should be included in the factor analysis. The initial choice can artificially determine the factors which emerge. In the hypothetical example, the inclusion of several intelligence tests almost guaranteed the emergence of intelligence as the first and largest factor. However, the actual loadings with factors which do emerge should not be directly affected. In the hypothetical example also, intelligence emerged as the first and most important trend, but nevertheless it did not load (correlate) heavily upon the interview scores.

Factor analysis can help determine the construct validity of a measure in another way: it can help to determine the dimensionality of a measure. This arises most often when a total score is obtained by adding a series of subscores. For example, the total score on an arithmetic test is usually obtained by adding the scores from individual questions. In these cases the factorial composition of a measure can be explored by correlating the results of every question with the results on every other question. The resulting correlation matrix can then be factor analysed. The results of this analysis will show how many different qualities are being assessed by a measure. Some writers (for example, Lumsden and Ross, 1973) emphasise that measures should be unidimensional and theoretically this has an appeal analogous to discovering the basic elements in chemistry. However, it cannot be denied that, in practice, measures which are multidimensional can be useful in the same way that chemists find large organic compounds useful.

If a measure is multidimensional, the nature of the different dimensions can be assessed from the pattern of the loadings which emerge from the factor analysis. For example, a factor analysis of the questions in the arithmetic test might produce five factors. The first factors might have significant loadings on practically all questions and can be interpreted as a general numerical factor. Factor 2 might load mainly on questions involving additional problems and might be interpreted as an 'addition' factor. In this situation the results are fairly simple but generally the factor composition is more complex and less predictable.

Convergent-discriminant validity is usually associated with Campbell and Fiske's (1959) paper. In essence, convergent-discriminant validity is founded on the axiom that a measure *should* correlate with other measures purporting to gauge the same construct, and *should not* correlate with measures purporting to gauge different constructs. Thus, if ten measures are collected upon candidates for a post of accounting clerk, and three of these measures (test score, arithmetical questions at interview and reference from superior on candidate's arithmetic ability) concern arithmetical ability, then the intercorrelations should show a certain pattern. Table 6.4 shows that with valid measures, the three measures of arithmetic ability show high intercorrelations among themselves but do not show correlations with other variables such as temperament or biographical details. If the measures are invalid they show both some correlations among themselves and some correlations with irrelevant measures. The

TABLE 6.4   *Hypothetical correlation patterns for valid and invalid measures using convergent-divergent method of assessing validity*

	A1	A2	A3	0	0	0	0	0	0	0
A1		0.6	0.6	0.1	0.1	0.1	0.1	0.1	0.1	0.1
A2			0.6	0.1	0.1	0.1	0.1	0.1	0.1	0.1
A3				0.1	0.1	0.1	0.1	0.1	0.1	0.1
0					0.6	0.1	0.6	0.1	0.1	0.6
0						0.1	0.1	0.1	0.1	0.1
0							0.1	0.6	0.1	0.1
0								0.1	0.1	0.6
0									0.6	0.6
0										0.6
0										

Correlations for valid measures

	A1	A2	A3	0	0	0	0	0	0	0
A1		0.6	0.2	0.1	0.1	0.1	0.1	0.1		
A2			0.2	0.1	0.1	0.1	0.1	0.1		
A3				0.1	0.6	0.1	0.6	0.1		
0					0.6	0.1	0.6	0.1	0.1	0.1
0						0.1	0.1	0.1	0.1	0.1
0							0.1	0.6	0.6	0.1
0								0.1	0.1	0.6
0									0.1	0.1
0									0.1	0.1
0									0.1	0.6
									0.6	0.6
										0.6

Correlations for invalid measures

patterns shown in the lower half of Table 6.4 are quite clear cut and indicate that the third measure of arithmetical ability is invalid. In practice, however, the results are often less clear and subjective decisions become necessary. An excellent example of convergent-discriminant validity is given by Thomson (1970) who showed that the ratings given by managers and psychologists had higher convergent validity than ratings obtained from supervisors.

Evaluating Validity Coefficients

Whichever method is used to estimate validity, the time arrives when it is necessary to decide whether the validity is sufficient. Usually this decision boils down to evaluating whether a correlation coefficient is big enough. The issues raised in the other sections of this chapter show that this is a complex decision which needs to take account of many factors. However, Smith (1984) has suggested that the following benchmarks may be used as a rule of thumb guide:

over 0.5	excellent
0.40 – 0.49	good
0.30 – 0.39	acceptable
less than 0.3	poor

It must be emphasised that these are only general guidelines and that many factors must be taken into account.

Evidence on the actual validities of various measures will be discussed in subsequent chapters, but some indication of the general level is given by Ghiselli (1966), who collected together many validity coefficients for psychological tests. He concludes, 'Taking all jobs as a whole . . . it can be said that by and large the maximal power of tests to predict success at the job itself is in the order of 0.35'. Rundquist (1969) noted that validity coefficients rarely exceeded 0.5 and suggested the existence of a *prediction ceiling*. In 1974 Wallace provided statistical models to suggest that validities in the region of 0.5 are as much as can reasonably be expected. This ceiling may not necessarily reflect the true validities of the measures as much as the way in which we obtain our estimates. He gives a hypothetical example of a measure which has a true validity of 0.8 and a reliability of 0.9. He then goes on to ask 'what criterion reliability would be required under these assumptions to obtain an uncorrected validity coefficient of 0.5?' Wallace obtained the answer 0.7 and he goes on to point out that very few criteria even approach this level of reliability. The situation is further compounded by the fact that most validity studies involve some restriction of range which further reduces obtained validity coefficients. The logic of these arguments lead to the conclusion that many of the validities reported by Ghiselli and others are marked underestimates. The point is neatly demonstrated by Sparks (1970). He generated data whose characteristics were known precisely and he demonstrates that observed validity coefficients of 0.17 to 0.22 which were insignificant became significant correlations in the range 0.4 to 0.45 when a number of scores were combined and when some inadequacies in the criterion were taken into account.

Unfortunately the situation is still more complex. It is often found that if a validity study is repeated with a different sample, the second validity coefficient is lower than the initial estimate. This phenomenon is known as *shrinkage* and it can arise in two ways. First, there are changes which occur over time, in terms of social structure, education, physical fitness, which alter the relationship between a measure and a criterion. In theory there is no reason why these changes do not increase validity, but in practice, they nearly always decrease validity coefficients. A classic example of the shrinkage phenomena is given by Kirchner and Dunnette (1957). They used a measure based on biographical data to select office staff in 1954, 1955, 1956 and obtained validities of 0.74, 0.61, 0.38 and 0.07 respectively, even though the method remained identical. Secondly, shrinkage is particularly large when measures are combined using the statistical technique of multiple regression. For example, multiple regression analysis might show that for a sample of 100 engineers working on the installation of a Gandalf Switch the combination 0.4 × an interview rating (IR), plus 0.8 × score on a mechanical reasoning (MR) test, plus 0.2 × rating of a reference (R) produces a validity coefficient of 0.64. However, 0.64 is almost certainly an overestimate. The multiple regression technique tends to include some of the chance variation in the scores and the validity is inflated.

When the formula $(0.4 \times I + 0.8 \times MR + 0.2 \times R)$ is tried out on a second sample, there is a different set of chance variations which do not match the formula and are rightly excluded. The obtained validity falls to 0.37 and it generates the impression that the validity has diminished. To overcome this difficulty a process of *cross-validation* may be adopted. Generally, a sample of 100 would be split into two parts – about 68 candidates would comprise the *main sample* and 32 would comprise the *holdout* sample. The initial validation would be conducted on the main sample, but the results would then be checked out by applying the formula to the holdout sample and recomputing the validity.

Taking all these factors into account, there seems to be an upper limit of about 0.65 for validity coefficients and these levels are usually only achieved by selection procedures which combine many different methods and which extend over a period of several days. Using these extended methods, Bray and Grant (1966) and Anstey (1977) obtained very high validities of 0.66 or higher and Jones (1981) obtained reliabilities of 0.65 to 0.86.

In an effort to raise the level of validity coefficients beyond the ceiling which seems to exist at about 0.65, many people have turned their attention to identifying moderator variables. The logic behind moderator variables is very simple. It starts with the idea that some people are more predictable than others. Then it seeks to eliminate the least predictable people. Finally it applies measures only to those predictable people who remain. For example, a bank might have difficulty in accurately selecting investment analysts using an interest test. On subsequent analysis it discovers that the interest scores of applicants who are neurotic are almost useless – sometimes a high interest score produces a good performance, sometimes a high interest score produces a poor performance. On the other hand, the interest scores of stable individuals are good predictors of future performance. Thus the bank would be able to improve its selection of investment analysts by first giving a test of neuroticism to select those applicants whose scores can be predicted and then giving the interest test to provide the basis for the actual selection.

Using this kind of rationale, Ghiselli (1960) was able to use a measure for the selection of taxicab drivers whose initial validity was 0.22 but, by concentrating on the third of applicants whose success was most 'predictable', he obtained a validity coefficient of 0.64. In the same paper Ghiselli describes in details how, by constructing a predictability index and using it to screen out individuals whose scores were not predictable, he raised two validity coefficients from 0.22 to 0.86 and from 0.15 to 0.78. Similar results were obtained by Frederiksen and Melville (1954). They used The Accountant Scale on the Strong Interest Blank as a measure of compulsiveness and in eleven out of fifteen cases they found it easier to predict the subsequent success of people who were not compulsive. The findings were less clear cut when the study was replicated using a separate sample (Frederiksen and Gilbert, 1960). Clearly the use of moderators could raise the levels of validity coefficients in selection contexts. However, a word of warning is necessary. Abrahams and Alf (1972a and 1972b) contend that much of the improvement brought about by use of moderators is illusory and is merely the consequence of pratfalls and artifact. Dunnette (1972) and others are less convinced by Abrahams and Alf's reasoning.

The Bandwidth – Fidelity Dilemma

Cronbach and Glesser (1965) draw attention to a dilemma which faces many selectors: should their selection system concentrate upon accuracy or spread. Suppose a personnel manager in the aerospace industry wishes to select mechanical engineers to install and test rotor blades of jet engines. He knows from past experience that successful engineers need to be conscientious and have good numerical ability, spatial reasoning and mechanical comprehension. Furthermore, for reasons beyond the personnel manager's control, the selection process is restricted to a 45-minute interview. What should the personnel manager do? Should he spend the entire time obtaining a very precise measure of one aspect of the candidate such as conscientiousness or, should he share the time of the interview, obtaining less accurate estimates on all four requirements? This essentially is the bandwidth-fidelity dilemma. Cronbach and Glesser (1965, p. 99) write:

> This dilemma may be described in the language of the communications engineer as a choice between 'wideband' and 'narrowband' tests. In using a particular channel, such as a telegraph wire, one may either crowd many messages into a period of time, or give a single message slowly and repetitively. The former, more varied message, has greater 'bandwidth'. The wideband signal transmits more information, but the clarity or dependability of the information received is less than for the narrowband signal except under ideal communication conditions. Random errors can seriously confuse the wideband signal; this is spoken of as a lack of fidelity. The tester's situation is analogous. If he concentrates on facts relevant to a single decision, he gets a much more dependable answer than if he spreads his effort. But, by concentrating, he leaves all his other questions to be answered on the basis of chance alone.

Cronbach (1970) comes to the conclusion that:

> While no general rule can be given . . . it is clear that the greatest amount of time should be given to the most important questions. When several questions are of about equal importance, it is more

profitable to use a brief test giving a rough answer to each one than to use a precise test answering only one or two questions.

The Relationship between Reliability and Validity

One of the oldest canards of psychometric theory is that reliability sets a ceiling upon validity. Indeed, in statistical terms, validity cannot exceed the square of the reliability. Thus, if a measure has a reliability coefficient of 0.9, the validity cannot exceed 0.81. Using strict statistical definitions this generalisation is true; the variance associated with an inference can never exceed the systematic variance of a measure. In some circumstances, however, the observed reliability is unduly low and in these situations it is perfectly possible for validity to exceed reliability. This occurs most often when measuring characteristics which change very quickly. For example, a measure of hunger may have a high validity but a low test-retest reliability – because, in the interval between the test and the retest some people may have eaten a snack. A less extreme example concerns a projective test where applicants are presented with an ambiguous photograph and asked to tell a story about it. Assessing the true reliability of this test is very difficult because it has a kind of self-destruct quality and subsequent administrations are never quite the same because the first administration has already structured the mental field. Tomkins (1961) compares the situation to hearing a joke – it is just not the same a second time, but this is no reason to question the validity of the first laughter. Furthermore, in ambiguous situations applicants may deduce that the selector wishes them to give a different answer the second time around (Winter and Stewart, 1977). Many measures stress imagination, creativity and variability in their instructions, for example,

> This is a test of creative imagination ... obviously there are no right or wrong answers, so you may feel free to make up any kind of story about the picture that you choose. The more vivid and chromatic the better ... Remember this is a test of creative imagination ... be as imaginative as you are able to be.

Winter and Stewart found that when such implicit expectations to be different were removed from the instructions, the reliability of the scores rose to a level where validity no longer seems to exceed reliability.

Validity Generalisation

The generalisability of validity coefficients has great practical significance and involves the question, 'If a measure is valid in the selection for one job, would it also be a valid method of selection for jobs in the same category – or even for all jobs?' If the answer to this question is yes, then a great deal of effort can be saved since only the general validity of the measure must be established. If the answer is no, separate validities must be established for each job or even each situation.

Unfortunately the traditional answer to the question is the pessimistic one: general validity cannot be assumed. Consequently, text books of a decade ago recommended that validity should be established for each specific application. The logic seemed quite compelling. Authors such as Ghiselli (1966) who collected and catalogued validity studies, repeatedly found considerable variability from situation to situation – therefore validity is specific, not general. So powerful was this logic that the view is enshrined in authoritative documents such as the Equal Employment Opportunity Commission's 'Uniform Guidelines for Employee Selection Procedures' (1978).

A more recent and sophisticated view suggests that, quite the contrary, there is considerable generalisability of validity coefficients across jobs and situations. The more recent view states that validity coefficients usually contain several statistical artifacts which must be controlled *before* comparisons are made. The first two of the artifacts have been noted earlier in this chapter: the *restriction of range* and the *reliability* of the criteria. Some validity coefficients are based upon studies of the population as a whole, while other studies are based upon highly selected samples. A restriction of range is likely to reduce the size of a validity coefficient and consequently this statistical artifact alone will produce different correlations even when the 'true' validity is constant. Similarly, some studies have used criteria such as training records and other studies have used criteria such as superiors' ratings. Again, these differences alone will produce different correlations even when the true validity is constant. The third statistical artifact is probably more potent, and has been considered at length by Schmidt, Hunter and Urry (1976) and concerns the *sizes of samples* used in validation studies. They note that typical validity studies use small samples between 60 and 70, and frequently the sample size is as low as 30. This assertion is supported by other workers such as Lent, Aurbach and Levin (1971a, and b) and Jones (1950). More recently Monahan and Muchinsky (1983), in reviewing three decades of personnel selection research, concluded that the mean sample size of validity studies increased from 76 to 100 to 119 in the 1950s, 1960s and 1970s respectively.

Even allowing for the gradual improvement, Schmidt *et al.* (1976) suggest that sample sizes are too small to be sure of detecting a measure's validity. They show that when a measure's true validity is 0.5 and the criterion reliability is 0.6, and where the range has been reduced by 40 per cent, a sample of 172 subjects are needed to have a 90 per cent chance of detecting the measure's validity. Schmidt *et al.* (1976) go on to give tables showing the sizes of samples required under various conditions. To support their arguments they quote a study by Brogden. In a well-executed large sample series of studies, it was found that when army occupations were classified rationally into job families, tests showed essentially identical validities and regression weights for all jobs within a given family. Further, new jobs also fit this pattern. Finally, these validities have held constant since the end of the Second World War when they were determined. Brogden has concluded that when methodological artifacts are controlled and large samples are used ... the obtained validities are, in fact, quite stable and similar across time and situations for similar jobs.

Pressing the argument home one stage further, Schmidt, Hunter and Pearlman (1981) report two empirical studies. They first examined validity figures for five categories of clerical jobs and indicated that with the possible exception of one of the ten tests, tests valid for one job family are valid for all job families. Their second study was not limited by the fact that the jobs were drawn from the same type of occupation. The 35 jobs included: dental assistants, radar repairers, military police, clerks, welders and personnel specialists. Again the results indicated general validity. Schmidt *et al.* (1981) conclude, 'Contrary to widespread belief in personnel psychology, these results indicate that task differences between job families within an occupational area have little or no effect on test validities and differences in test validity among entirely different jobs are small.' The empirical foundations of these two studies are quite extraordinary. Study 1 is based on a total sample size of 368 877, study 2 is based on 21 022 individuals. The total sample base is almost 400 000.

The implications of these findings are quite profound. At a banal level they suggest that over the last 30 years some industrial psychologists have wasted a great deal of effort in pursuing small-scale validity studies. Yet in most situations practical constraints, such as cost or the limited number of people actually in an occupation, prohibit large-scale studies. It would follow that only the largest organisations or government departments are able to conduct satisfactory validity studies. Fortunately, the results also imply that once established, the validity coefficients can then be generalised to other situations.

Part II
Predictors

7   Interviews

Interviews are a very common method of selection. Industry must spend enormous amounts of money each year paying interviewers' expenses and providing accommodation. Yet there is little evidence that the money is well spent. Psychologists have known for more than half a century that many interviews have little value. For example, in 1929 Hollingsworth conducted a study in which 12 experienced sales managers arrived at independent personnel selection decisions. The results were appalling. One candidate was ranked first by one interviewer and last by another. A second candidate was ranked sixth and fifty-sixth.

It is difficult to be precise about the efficiency of interviews: they vary so much. At one extreme there is the ten-minute interview by an untrained chargehand on the factory floor, with all the distraction of industrial production, and at the other extreme a three- or four-hour depth interview, or series of interviews, by properly trained personnel.

The major purpose of any selection interview is, of course, to identify the most appropriate candidate for the job in question, but interviews can and do fulfil other important functions. These might include, providing the candidate with information about the organisation and promoting good public relations. The additional functions of interviews are mentioned later in this chapter. To begin with, however, discussion will focus on the selection function of interviews.

THE SELECTION FUNCTION OF INTERVIEWS

In essence, the selection function of interviews can be divided into two parts: obtaining reliable and valid data about applicants and using this information to arrive at a decision. In some organisations these two aspects are dealt with by different people. Personnel specialists, for example, may focus on collecting data and line managers concentrate on decision-making.

Like any other selection method, interviews need to be both reliable and valid. Interview reliability revolves around two main issues: first, the extent to which different interviewers agree in their evaluation of candidates (inter-judge reliability) and second, the extent to which an interviewer makes the same assessment of the same candidate on different occasions (intra-judge reliability).

Although there are some studies that demonstrate high inter-judge reliability (for example, Latham *et al.*, 1980), most of the evidence is consistent (for example, Ulrich and Trumbo, 1965) and suggests that in general, inter-judge reliability is not high. Intra-judge reliability is often reasonably good but there are obvious complicating factors such as the influence of memory and bias.

In general terms, studies of predictive validity suggest that selection interviews do not provide particularly useful methods for predicting future job performance. Although recent reviews of the relevant literature (Reilly and Chao, 1982; Arvey and Campion, 1982) present a slightly more optimistic view, the mean validity coefficient is still less than +0.2. Despite this rather gloomy background research, the interview is still used widely and, as later sections in this chapter will show, there are some approaches available that might help to improve interview reliability and validity.

Obtaining Data and Information about Applicants

To obtain accurate information, the following requirements are necessary:

(a) The interviewer must have a clear grasp of the characteristics the applicants need in order to be able to perform the job.

(b) The interviewer must be able to 'question' the applicants in a way that is likely to produce information. He or she should not miss any major areas.

(c) The interviewer must be prepared and able to give the information required. Most interviewees are not prepared to divulge unfavourable information and many interviewees are not able to put into words their experience and capabilities.

(d) All candidates should be given an equal opportunity.

Research results on the data collection phase of interviews are rather depressing. Interviewers can have very different views of the qualities required to do a job. For example, one officer interviewing police recruits may be looking for candidates with deductive powers of Maigret or Sherlock Holmes. A second, equally expert, officer may look for affability and physical fitness. Consequently, unstructured interviews, where the interviewer asks any question he or she likes, tend to have low reliability (about 0.36).

Many experienced interviewers make use of structured interview guides; either semi-structured, where certain broad subject areas are covered, or structured interviews, where the interviewer follows a prescribed list of questions. It seems likely that a structured guide may provide the interviewer with a better basis for meeting the conditions outlined above (a – d). Following a guide will help to ensure, for example, that interviewers do not omit to cover any major areas of information. It may provide an interviewer with a better opportunity to give relevant information and also reduce the likelihood of distortion or bias. In fact, although there is little evidence to support the superiority of one interview structure over any other, the available evidence does suggest that the use of structured formats is beneficial (Schmitt, 1976; Mayfield, Brown and Hamstra, 1980).

A demonstration of how the use of a guide can aid data collection is provided in the study of Carlson *et al.* (1971), which revealed that interviewers who did not use a guide were less accurate in their recall of factual data than interviewers who did use a guide. In general, the reliability of structured interviews tends to be better than that of unstructured interviews, although highly structured interviews relying on predetermined questions can seem very artificial (see Schwab and Heneman, 1969).

Even when interviewers make some attempt to follow a structure and question the candidate about specific job-related issues, they do not necessarily use the interview to *obtain* information – often they spend more time talking *at* the interviewee and *giving* information. Daniels and Otis (1950) found that interviewees talked for about 30 per cent of the time – the remainder was spent in stony silence!

Of course this imbalance does not necessarily mean that the interview is not worthwhile. A productive *exchange* of information with the interviewers providing information on the organisation and job, and interviewees giving relevant and useful information about themselves could be extremely profitable. Unfortunately this does not always turn out to be the case.

When interviewers are clear on the qualities needed for good job performance, follow a sensible structure *and* give the candidates chance to speak, the candidates may not be prepared to give accurate replies. Weiss and Dawis (1960) checked the replies of interviewees with their former employers and other factual sources. The accuracy depended on the subject area of the question, but even for those areas where accuracy was greatest (e.g. job title and pay), about a fifth of candidates gave misleading replies.

Not all of the discrepancies are due to distortion and lying on the part of the candidates: their memory may be faulty and some of the employers may not have been able to give accurate replies. Nevertheless, most candidates upgrade or inflate information about themselves. If all candidates upgraded themselves by the same extent, the effect would cancel out and would not influence the selection decision but some candidates may seriously distort the answers they give.

Using the Information to Arrive at a Decision

Even if an interviewer has faultlessly obtained all the relevant information about candidates there remain problems on how the information is used to arrive at a decision. There are two main approaches. The CLINICAL approach is where the interviewer judges all the facts and then relies on his experience and intuition to arrive at a judgement. The second approach involves STATISTICAL and ACTUARIAL prediction where, in essence, the interviewer makes a series of ratings. These ratings are then used in a formula to determine a result. The clinical v. actuarial debate has raged for over 20 years. Although the outcome is hard to generalise, the actuarial approach seems to offer the advantages of consistency and accuracy (see Meehl, 1954), although even this rather tentative conclusion can be challenged (see Lewis, 1980).

In practice, it is clear that many interviewers adopt the clinical, intuitive approach. Research results indicate a large number of problems:

First, it is very difficult for interviewers to remember all the information obtained in an interview. Research suggests that at the close of the interview, the interviewer has forgotten much of the information obtained, particularly when an unstructured approach is used.

Second, many interviewers make a decision before all the information has been obtained. Springbett (1958) suggests that interviewers make up their minds in the first four minutes and then spend the remainder of the time looking for information which supports their snap judgement.

Third, there is the problem of differing standards. Some interviewers are hard to please and others are very 'soft touches'.

Fourth, there is the problem of how interviewers weight and integrate the information available to them. Hakel, Dobmay and Dunnette (1970) suggest that where selectors had information concerning scholastic standing, business experience and interests and abilities, selectors gave most weight to scholastic standing. Keenan (1976) suggests that interviewers of undergraduate students organise information under four headings:

1. Motivation to succeed
2. Knowledge about the job
3. Quality of university references
4. Academic performance

Some research has suggested that interviewers tend to give too much weight to negative information although more recent work suggests that interviewers tend to emphasise any behaviour which is unexpected (Bolsher and Springbett, 1961). This latter result is consistent with research from attribution theory (see below).

A review of the literature by Schmitt (1976) draws together a significant amount of information concerning the effects of various factors such as how positive and negative information is used, and the type of information that is most influential in interviews.

Interviewing as a Social Process

An interview can be described as a conversation with a purpose. In other words, it is rather like many of the social interactions that we take part in but with some particular constraints and purposes of its own. Herriot (1981, p. 165) describes it as follows:

The selection interview is a rule-governed social interaction with clearly defined reciprocal roles allocated to both parties. For example, it is considered appropriate for the interviewer to take charge of the situation and to ask questions of the applicant. The applicant is expected to wait until invited to do so before asking questions.

Using the framework of attribution theory (for example, Kelley and Michela, 1980), Herriot goes on to argue that the frequently observed low validities of employment interviews can be in part explained by the fact that the interviewer and interviewee may not have a common understanding of their roles, and/or the interviewer may misinterpret the candidate's behaviour. In essence, attribution theory focuses on the way we make judgements of others and provides a number of principles to help understand how such judgements take place.

According to attribution theory, an important feature that determines the view that we develop of another person is their 'in-role' or 'out-of-role' behaviour. Someone behaving in-role is merely behaving in a way that is appropriate to the situation. Thus their behaviour can be attributed more to the circumstances (even impatient people stand in queues sometimes) than to any personal characteristics they may have. When someone behaves out-of-role however, it may be more appropriate to attribute their behaviour to *them* rather than the *situation*. Ross (1977) refers to an important and pervasive attribution error that people are prone to make. In essence it involves attributing too much of the cause of behaviour to personal factors and too little to the situation. Herriot (1981, p. 168) shows how this might apply to the selection interview:

> When we apply this bias to the selection interview it would result in the drawing of dispositional inferences from in-role behaviour. In other words the good interviewee [who obeys the rules of the interview as seen by the interviewer] becomes the good applicant.

> Furthermore, out of role behaviour may be taken to indicate a bad applicant, rather than treated as valuable data appropriate to dispositional attribution in general.

What Herriot (1981) and other writers (for example, Lewis, 1980) draw attention to is the important fact that an interview is an interactive social process and is potentially subject to all of the associated problems of faulty communication and judgement by both parties. As such it is a personnel selection technique that is different in many important ways from other techniques such as psychological tests.

Improving the Interview

Various suggestions have been put forward in attempts to improve the nature of personnel selection interviews. Herriot (1981), for example, suggests that interviewers might be trained to reduce attributional biases of the type described above and that they could also be trained and instructed to negotiate appropriate roles with applicants at the beginning of interviews. Lewis (1980, p. 115) argues in a similar vein that interviewing involves making use of basic communication skills:

> The first is the establishing of a contract ... this is an explicitly stated agreement between two persons to do something, and has to involve the mutual communication of what each party sees as the objective of the meeting from their points of view. In employment interviewing this is rarely explicit, with the result that the interviewer and interviewee rely upon their own assumptions about each others' objectives.

Lewis (1980, p. 115) goes on to argue that interviewers should seek to develop and utilise 'counselling' skills which focus on the fact that the constituent parts of interviews are 'people with needs, feelings and abilities ...'.

As far as the purpose of the interview is concerned, Ulrich and Trumbo (1965), in an influential article, suggest that interviews should focus on the assessment of qualities such as motivation, adjustment and similar factors, whereas skills, aptitudes, biographical details, etc. can be assessed by other techniques such as application forms or tests.

The idea that experience alone can produce good interviewers or that most people are 'naturally' good judges of others is not supported by research evidence (for example, Carlson, 1967).

Even 'commonsense' is sometimes not as helpful as it may seem as far as interviews are concerned. Dipboye, Fontelle and Garner (1984), for example, have shown that it is *not* always helpful to preview the information on a candidate before conducting an employment interview.

In an attempt to maximise the quality of selection interviews, many organisations attempt to ensure that their interviewers receive some form of systematic training. It is difficult to generalise about the benefits of all interview training, but in as much as it is possible to draw general conclusions, it seems that interview training that involves opportunities for practice, discussion and feedback can be effective in improving interview performance. Howard and colleagues (Howard and Dailey, 1979; Howard, Dailey and Gulanick, 1979) have examined the value of five-day interview training courses that involve a mixture of practice, discussion, demonstration and feedback and the evidence that they present suggests that these courses are effective. The most common format for interview training courses involves trainees in conducting role play interviews at various stages.

Frequently their performance is recorded on videotape and played back to them together with feedback from the trainer and other trainees. It is rare for trainees to be shown an example of an interview being conducted an a 'model' fashion. Recent research work seems to suggest that the format of role play followed by feedback may be less effective than a format involving the use of *model interviewers*.

In the context of interview training the value of modelling remains unproven. Maybe interview trainers lack the courage, commitment or skill (or all three) to produce and use the model videotapes! In other areas, particularly supervisory training, behavioural modelling has produced some extremely impressive results (for example, Goldstein and Sorcher, 1974; Latham and Saari, 1979; Decker, 1982; Russel *et al.*, 1984). One point that must be made in connection with the use of modelling in training is that trainees need help and guidance concerning the aspects of the models' behaviour that should be attended to. As Landy and Trumbo (1980) point out, 'Observation without a system is seldom systematic, is subject to biases, and is not likely to be an effective or efficient training method' (p. 290).

In an attempt to help interviewers do a better job a variety of 'how to interview' guides exist (for example, Smith, 1982) and many courses are based on the sort of advice given in these guides. Many of the 'how to interview' courses and books are useful and cover ground that seems to be important in the development of interviewing skills (for example, types of questions to use, encouraging candidates to talk, common judgemental errors and how to avoid them). Despite the likely value of such training it is worth noting Arvey and Campion's (1982, p. 317) stricture:

> There is a dearth of guidelines and suggestions concerning the improvement of interview effectiveness based on *research* findings. Instead many guidelines, suggestions, how to interview workshops and techniques are founded on intuition, beliefs and what seems more comfortable, rather than on research results.

Whilst accepting Arvey and Campion's point that the available guidance cannot be supported by specific research evidence, it is for the most part based on sound psychological principles and experience and can be shown to produce positive results (for example, Howard, Dailey and Gulanick, 1979).

Behaviour during the Interview

Some fairly systematic information exists concerning what takes place during real life employment interviews and what links exist between behaviour during the interview and the outcome (for example, accept/reject decisions). Hollandsworth *et al.* (1979) identify three different types of communication that are important in interviews. These are verbal behaviour (that is, what is said), non-verbal behaviour (for example gestures, eye movement) and articulative behaviour (for example, loudness of voice, fluency of speech). Several studies have shown that non-verbal and articulative behaviour seem to be important in interview settings although many of these studies have been conducted in simulated rather than real interviews (see Hollandsworth *et al.*, 1979).

A study by Forbes and Jackson (1980) looked at the links between the non-verbal behaviour of candidates and how it is related to selection decisions in real life interviews. They found that in interviews where the candidate was subsequently rejected there was more gaze avoidance and eye wandering on the part of the candidate; there was also less smiling and head movement compared with 'accept' interviews. Accept interviews were also characterised by higher levels of eye contact. This research is interesting and informative but one must be careful not to draw erroneous conclusions about the causes and effects involved. It is not clear, for instance, whether lack of eye contact *causes* subsequent rejection or whether an awareness of possible subsequent rejection on the part of the candidate, the interviewer, or both *leads* to a lack of eye contact.

Hollandsworth *et al.* (1979) investigated the relative importance of various aspects of verbal, non-verbal and articulative behaviour in some real life interviews. After interviews, interviewers were asked if they would select each candidate. Their responses could vary along a four-point scale (not a chance, probably not, probably, definitely). The most important variable, in terms of its links with post-interview decision, was 'appropriateness of content'; 'fluency of speech' followed by 'composure' came next and 'personal appearance' was also important but to a lesser extent. What this study demonstrates fairly clearly is that *what* the candidate says is of paramount importance.

Keenan and Wedderburn (1980) present some data on the content of discussions during real life (graduate selection) interviews. Somewhat surprisingly, their study revealed that data concerned with academic aspects of university life (for example, a knowledge of subjects studied) were not extensively discussed. These are issues that the interviewees probably expected to be dealt with in detail, and with which they might have felt more comfortable, but as Herriot and Rothwell (1981) have shown, there appear to be considerable differences between applicants' expectations of what will be covered in the interview and by whom, and their actual experience. Keenan and Wedderburn (1980) divided the topics discussed into six general categories:

(a)   Family and school background
(b)   University life – non-academic aspects
(c)   University – academic aspects
(d)   Knowledge of job and company
(e)   Extra-curricula activities
(f)   Personal circumstances and requirements

The area that was most popular for discussion was (d) – knowledge of job and company. As Keenan and Wedderburn suggest, it could well be that this is the area where *interviewers* feel most at ease; thus, rather than spreading the discussion across a range of potential topics the interviewers focus the discussion on the topic that is most comfortable for them. It is interesting to note that knowledge of the job and company are the topics that produce most anxiety on the part of candidates; furthermore on the evidence of the topics discussed in these interviews it seems likely that the interviewers concerned were not following the guidance of Ulrich and Trumbo (1965) and attempting to use the interview to assess personal characteristics such as motivation and adjustment.

Different Interview Formats

Standard One to One Interviews

Interviews can take a bewildering variety of formats and can vary considerably in terms of content and the personnel involved. For example a 30-minute interview might be divided into six parts:

1.	Opening	2 minutes
2.	Obtaining information	15 minutes
3.	Description of vacancy	3 minutes
4.	Candidate's questions	4 minutes
5.	Closing	1 minute
6.	Taking notes and making a decision	5 minutes

Some interviewers prefer to describe the vacancy before they question the candidates, but the description may then colour the replies the candidates give. In fact (see below), it may even be preferable to remove discussion of the job from the interview altogether.

In general, the higher the salary the longer the interview.

Sequence Interviews

Some organisations use a sequence of interviews. Typically, there is first a short screening interview at a local venue. Then, there are one or more extended interviews at a national or regional centre. If there is more than one extended interview they may be specialised: for example, one interview could be devoted to personal history, and personal characteristics, while the second could be devoted to technical competence and job knowledge.

Situational Interviews

An interesting and potentially useful form of interview is the
'situational' interview (Latham *et al.*, 1980). In essence, this involves
conducting a systematic analysis of the job in question and identifying
some critical incidents (Flanagan, 1954) associated with good and
poor work performance. The incidents are then used as the basis for
interview questions in which job applicants are asked how they would
behave in situations similar to those reported in the critical incidents.
Latham *et al.* developed various questions to form the basis of three
situational interviews with three grades of employee in an American
Timber Company. The interviews contained between 10 and 17
'situational' questions. Interviewees' answers were assessed with the
aid of specially developed rating scales. The result obtained demonstrated that the interviews produced fairly reliable and consistent
assessments and that the assessments also predicted work performance ratings made by the interviewees' supervisors. Latham *et al.*
(1980, p. 426) noted that 'The present findings are particularly
impressive in the light of the low reliability and validity of other
interview methods'.

They also point out that the validities obtained are comparable
with those reported for assessment centres (see chapter 13) and
suggest with some justification that the inclusion of situational
interviews in assessment centres or with other batteries of psychological tests could improve the validity of the selection process.

Panel Interviews

In many organisations selection interviews are conducted, not by one
or two people but by a panel. Like sequence interviews, panel
interviews have the advantage of involving more than one person in
collecting information and taking the decision. They are also more
acceptable in many organisations, partly because they are seen to be
fair, since the decision is not left to one individual only.

Disadvantages include the fact that they may be more stressful for
both interviewers and interviewees and they can be extremely time
consuming and difficult to organise.

Recent research evidence (see Arvey and Campion, 1982) suggests
that well-conducted panel interviews can produce reasonably valid
decisions. This is supported by Rothstein and Jackson (1980, p. 280),

who argue that group consensus decisions should provide a basis for minimising various judgemental biases:

> Interviewers who tend to use very narrow or very wide category widths in their judgements . . ., or who tend to make more extreme judgements on some other basis, would have their decisions averaged with a group of other interviewers or raters.

Indeed some studies (for example, Landy, 1976) have shown specifically that reasonable validities can be obtained by averaging the judgements of different interviewers.

ADDITIONAL FUNCTIONS OF INTERVIEWS

It is important to remember that there are *two* main parties to every interview – the interviewer(s) and the candidate. In many interviews the candidate will be gaining important information conerning the job and the organisation, and on the basis of this and other relevant information will decide whether to accept the appointment or not – if an offer is made. Not all post-interview job offers are accepted by candidates, and in many cases it seems likely that information gleaned by candidates at the interview is crucial in their decision-making.

The decisions to apply for a job and, if it is offered, to accept or reject it, involve some self-examination and an attempt to compare one's own abilities, experiences and preferences with the requirements and opportunities of the job on offer. Inevitably this matching is sometimes not as efficient as might be hoped, resulting in labour turnover and costs to the organisation and individual concerned. Interviews provide one opportunity to improve this match by giving candidates realistic information about the job and organisation in question.

Some investigators have studied the effects of more extensive attempts to provide realistic job previews (RJPs). The evidence (see Reilly *et al.*, 1981) suggests that RJPs have little impact on turnover.

Reilly *et al.* suggest that the main advantage of RJPs lies in communicating a favourable organisational image (see Popovich and Wanous, 1982). Tenopyr and Oeltjen (1982, p. 586) make the following comments:

It can be concluded that it would be unfair to expect too much from RJPs. Their primary objective should be to take much of the discussion of job content out of the employment interview, which is not the best place to inform applicants about the job anyway, since interviewers often are not a credible source of information.

Recent research by Dean and Wanous (1984) assessed the effects of three types of previews (realistically specific, realistically general and no preview). They found that over-all job survival rates were not related to type of preview but that the *rate* at which turnover occurred was significantly different.

On the basis of the current evidence it does seem advisable not to use the selection interview as the sole means of providing the candidate with information. Whenever possible a realistic job preview should be provided on a separate occasion (before the selection interview). Makin and Robertson (1983) argue that the most effective form of realistic job preview should be based on first-hand experience (for example, by taking a work-sample test) rather than a second-hand method such as a film or audio-visual presentation.

AN OVERVIEW

At this point it is sensible to review some of the main issues that have emerged in the preceding discussion of employment selection interviews. First and foremost it must be recognised that the overwhelming bulk of research evidence demonstrates that interviews do not provide a good basis for the prediction of subsequent work performance. We must not, however, infer from this that interviews cannot play a useful role in the employee selection process. Taken overall interviews have received a 'bad press', but blanket generalisations that employment interviews *per se* are worthless obscures the fact that at a more detailed level of analysis there are some areas for optimism, and the available research findings do provide some helpful guidance.

One point that needs emphasising is that employment interviews have important consequences. Bad selection decisions can have severe and damaging financial and psychological repercussions. It is therefore worthwhile to invest time and effort in making the interview as useful as possible. An ill-prepared, untrained interviewer who takes a cavalier approach to interviews is never likely to produce good results.

Interviewers need to obtain accurate and useful information and use this information to make valid judgements. Appropriate training, planning the interview and perhaps the use of an interview guide can all help with this. There is evidence to suggest that interviews should focus on certain issues (for example, the motivation and adjustment characteristics of candidates), that other items (for example, detailed biographical information) are best left out of the interview and yet other items (for example, giving information about the job and organisation) are of questionable relevance during interviews. Above all an interview is an interactive social process and interviewers, and most likely interviewees, will benefit from some training, practice and feedback on how to avoid some of the common communication problems that arise in such interactions. Different types of interviews (for example, screening, panel, situational) serve different purposes and have different aims and it seems most likely that all parties would benefit from some clarity about their expected roles and the purpose and nature of the interview in which they are engaged.

In any study that examines interviews it is difficult to separate the validity or reliability of the interview as a device from the validity or reliability of the interviewer. Differences in interviewer effectiveness are likely to be a function of many factors; individual difference factors such as intelligence, personality and previous experience; the procedures followed during the interview and the complex *interaction* between applicant and interviewer. Despite the obvious conceptual distinction that can be made between the interview and the interviewer, surprisingly little research has focused on the characteristics of interviewers themselves, although there are exceptions (for example, Valenzi and Andrews, 1973 and Leonard, 1976).

Zedeck, Tziner and Middlestat (1983) have demonstrated the advantages that can be obtained from research focusing on individual interviewers rather than examining aggregate results based on several interviewers. They argue that future research should focus on the individual differences that exist between interviewers rather than mask these differences as many previous studies do by utilising data combined from several interviewers in an attempt to study 'the interview'. Their argument suggests that instead of studying *interviews* we should concentrate on *interviewers* and try to establish the personal characteristics, and interview strategies and styles of effective interviewers. Maybe such an approach will add significantly to our existing store of knowledge on the employment interview which, despite its flaws, remains the mainstay of many selection procedures.

8   Psychological Tests

DEFINITION OF PSYCHOLOGICAL TESTS

Psychological tests may be defined as a carefully chosen, systematic and standardised procedure for evoking a sample of responses from a candidate, which can be used to assess one or more of their psychological characteristics by comparing the results with those of a representative sample of an appropriate population. This definition implies a wider range of procedures than the common stereotype of pencil and paper questionnaires – although it remains true that the vast majority of tests are in fact pencil and paper tests. The definition involves six main components.

First, tests are *systematic* and are constructed according to some logical framework which guides the questions which are included, and the order in which they are presented. For example, most tests attempt to cover all relevant aspects of a characteristic and generally tests start with easy items and progress to more difficult ones. Thus tests may be contrasted with references, where referees may report any information they wish in any order they prefer.

Secondly, tests are *standardised*, so that all candidates receive fair and equal treatment. As a slight over simplification standardisation can be taken to mean that all candidates are:

1. Faced with *identical tasks*
2. Given *identical instructions*
3. Required to perform in very *similar settings*
4. Have their responses *evaluated in an identical way*

This standardisation in tests may be compared with interviews where many aspects may be allowed to vary, willy-nilly and candidates may be treated quite differently.

Thirdly, questions are only a small *sample* of the questions it would be possible to ask. The adequacy of this sample will play a major part in determining the adequacy of the test. A typical test will ask

152

between 100 and 300 questions: this may be contrasted with the much smaller number asked at an interview.

Fourthly, tests aim to evoke *responses* which can be scored: that is, the candidates must do something. This contrasts to selection devices such as biographical data, references, palmistry and astrology in which the candidate is essentially passive.

Fifthly, assessments are made in terms of *general human characteristics*, which are usually some type of psychological construct such as intelligence, extroversion or outdoor interests. This aspect differentiates psychological tests from work samples which are tests which focus upon specific jobs. This distinction is very useful and works adequately in most cases but the distinction between psychological tests and work sample is not clear cut: for instance, there could be considerable overlap between a psychological test of mechanical reasoning and a work sample test for a motor mechanic job.

Sixthly, the candidates' scores can be compared and interpreted in the light of the *scores of a representative and relevant sample*. It is these comparisons which permit statements such as 'Evelyn is in the top 10 per cent of applicants'.

Some authorities (for example, the British Psychological Society, 1980b) suggest that to avoid misunderstanding by the user the name 'test' should be avoided when these requirements are not met. Where appropriate the word 'scale', 'inventory' or 'questionnaire' should be used rather than 'test'.

CATEGORIES OF PSYCHOLOGICAL TESTS

The definition of psychological test encompasses a very wide variety of instruments and many psychologists have sought to categorise them: unfortunately they may be classified in different ways. So many different classifications exist that the classifications themselves need classification into meta categories. The first of these meta categories is based upon *what* the tests aim to measure. The second meta category is based upon *how* the tests attempt their measurement. A third meta category is based on the qualifications needed by the *test user*.

CATEGORIES BASED ON WHAT TESTS MEASURE

There are six main inter-related categorisations of test based upon what they aim to measure.

The most obvious categorisation is based upon the *type of psychological characteristic* being gauged. One possible framework was discussed in detail in chapter 3 on personal specifications. In essence, tests can be classified into tests of (1) mental ability, (2) manual ability, (3) personality, (4) interests and motivation. This classification is implicit in the catalogues of most test publishers and will be followed later in this chapter when specific tests are examined.

A second categorisation divides tests into *analytic* v. *analogous tests*. Estimating a candidate's suitability can be approached in two ways. Underlying characteristics such as intelligence or emotional stability can be analysed and matched to the underlying characteristics required by the job. Tests which seek to do this are termed *analytic* tests and they are at least implicitly based on some theory of human behaviour. This approach requires insight and understanding of the dynamics of action at a basic level and it carries the enormous advantage that general tests can be constructed and applied in a wide range of circumstances. The disadvantages of the analytical approach are that the insight and understanding may be wrong and that as abstractions they are one step removed from concrete observation and they may lack face validity in the eyes of some managers and applicants. The alternative approach is to produce analogous tests, which do not seek to understand why people differ in their job competence, they merely seek to reflect the job and a person's competence in that job. Seen in this light, work samples, in-baskets, (which simulate how managers deal with items that arrive in their in trays) and many situational exercises can be viewed as analogous tests. The big advantage of analogous tests is the apparent clarity of what they are measuring and their high face validity. The big disadvantage is their specificity to a job or group of jobs and all that this entails in terms of developing and validating a multitude of specific tests.

A third classification divides tests into *tests of aptitude* v. *tests of attainment*. It is a useful oversimplification to think of tests of aptitude as attempting to measure a candidate's 'inherited potential' which could be used to predict their performance at a later date. Achievement tests on the other hand represent a snapshot of where the candidate is now as a result of both the inherited potential and environmental factors such as education or experience. Unfortunately this neat distinction is severely strained in practice. Inherited abilities have to be measured via acquired skills such as speech and writing and consequently there are no pure tests of aptitude. Furthermore, the present attainments of a candidate are highly relevant to their future performance and consequently attainment tests can be used as measures of potential. Because of these difficulties Anastasi (1982) writes 'A useful concept that is coming to replace the traditional categories of aptitude and achievement in psychometrics is that of developed abilities', and she proposes a continuum with course-oriented achievement tests covering narrowly-defined technical skills at one extreme and culture fair tests of general ability at the other. At this point it becomes clear that the analogous tests, described in the previous classification, map on to the specificity pole of Anastasi's continuum, while analytical tests map on to the generality pole.

A fourth classification of tests according to what they measure divides tests into *measures of typical performance* v. *measures of maximum performance*. This distinction is best seen by a comparison of two professors T and M. Professor T (who shall remain nameless to spare his blushes) is a nice even-tempered fellow who is always pleasantly courteous without becoming overwhelming. Professor M (who shall also remain nameless in order to protect the livelihood of one of the authors) is usually rude, irrascible and petulant, except when in the presence of research sponsors when he scales the very heights of consideration, tact and human concern. A test of civility where professor T has the highest score would be a test of typical performance while a test of civility where professor M was superior would be a test of maximal performance. Many authors such as Cronbach (1970, p. 39) seem to prefer measures of typical performance on the basis that measures of maximal performance are responses to extreme or unusual situations which are not typical in a day's work. However, there is some suggestion that, in fact, measures of maximal performance have slightly higher validities.

Another categorisation according to what tests measure concerns the *level of the test*, and it is mainly used in connection with tests of ability. Most tests used in selection are designed for use with the general population ranging from the quite dull to the quite brilliant. But when candidates are drawn from a special group, these tests may not give sufficient discrimination. In practice these considerations apply at the top end of the range where most candidates can be expected to be clever. In theory it also applies at the bottom end of the ability range. A classic example is provided by the AH series of intelligence tests.

A final categorisation based upon *what* tests measure is often called the *power-speed continuum* and is also mainly relevant to tests of ability. Some tests have questions which are very easy: an intelligent candidate can answer each question in one or two seconds and an unintelligent candidate can still answer them but will take three or four times longer. These tests usually have fairly short time limits and the final score is largely determined by the number of questions attempted. Tests of this kind measure speed of thinking. Power tests, on the otherhand, tend to have longer time limits and the questions are steeply graded: a few questions are easy, some are average difficulty and some are so hard that even quite bright candidates cannot produce the correct answer not matter how long they take.

CATEGORISATION BASED ON METHOD OF MEASUREMENT

Tests can also be categorised on the basis of the method used to obtain their measures and most of the categories are self explanatory.

Tests can be divided into *group tests or individual tests*. The vast majority of tests used for selection purposes are group tests and they can be administered simultaneously to several candidates, consequently reducing costs. Group tests are relatively simple to administer and they can also be used in an individual situation. Individual tests require one tester for each applicant and the administration of most individual tests is complex. In industry individual tests are only used in extreme situations.

Tests can be categorised into *pencil and paper tests* and *apparatus tests*. The majority of tests used in selection are the pencil and paper variety because they are relatively cheap and easy to score. The use of apparatus tests is largely confined to psychomotor abilities such as manual dexterity. In general, pencil and paper tests tend to be group tests, while apparatus tests tend to be individual tests.

The *directness of the method* used can be used to categorise tests. Some psychological tests of arithmetical ability or verbal fluency, for example, collect data which is *directly* relevant to the characteristic they attempt to measure. *Self-report tests* work in a more indirect way via the candidate's perceptions and what he is prepared to divulge and these additional factors increase the possibility of error. For example, the question 'Are you usually good at organising your work?' may provide a misleading answer in two ways. First, a candidate may not be best judge of his/her own abilities: an executive may be so disorganised that he cannot recognise the trail of havoc and chaos he leaves behind. Secondly, a candidate may not wish to reveal the truth: only a stupid candidate would be prepared to indict himself by answering no to the question. Very little can be done about a candidate's lack of self insight, but wilful distortion can often be detected by a lie scale embedded in a test. *Projective tests* work in a different way by presenting a candidate with a vague stimulus. The candidate has so little information that they must use their own ideas and thoughts in order to make any response, that is, they project their own characteristics and motives into the vague situation which confronts them. There are two main projective tests. The Rorschach Ink Blot Test is widely known but, nowadays, it is rarely used. The TAT (Thematic Apperception Test) is occasionally used for selection purposes, mainly in the measurement of motivation.

CATEGORISATIONS ACCORDING TO QUALIFICATIONS OF TEST USER

In order to maintain confidentiality of test material, and to avoid incompetence or misuse of tests, they are often divided into categories according to the qualifications needed by the test user. Most publishing companies will only supply test materials to users with appropriate qualifications. One scheme (British Psychological Society, 1980a) divides tests into four categories. First there are simple tests, such as interest tests. These are tests which are easy to administer, have objective scoring and require minimum technical knowledge. Tests in this category may be released to responsible users such as teachers or personnel officers. Often tests in this category are used in a guidance or a training context. Secondly, there are relatively straightforward tests of attainment which yield one or two scores which are simple to interpret and administer. Examples of this category are tests of arithmetic, typing ability and some of the simplest measures of intelligence. The qualifications needed to obtain these tests is completion of a short course of about one week which covers background theory to test, administration scoring and test interpretation. The third category consists of more complex tests which may yield a series of subscores that need careful integration and interpretation. The use of these tests requires thorough knowledge of the principles underlying testing, together with specific training and wide practical experience. Good examples of this category are Cattell's (1965) 16PF test of personality and Bennett, Seashore and Wesman's (1974) Differential Aptitude Test Battery

(DATB). Users who are qualified to obtain tests in this third category must have successfully completed a further course of about a week which is largely devoted to matters of interpretation or be a psychologist possessing an appropriate degree. Usually there is a short follow up of about six months after the initial training to ensure the maintenance of proper standards. The final category consists of very specialised tests requiring extended and specific training even for psychologists. Individual tests of mental ability require a high degree of professional skill and experience for their proper administration and interpretation (for example, the Wechsler Adult Intelligence Scale (WAIS) Wechsler 1955) and postgraduate or extended specialised training is usually needed. Some of the projective measures of personality and some tests used in clinical psychology fall into this category.

SPECIFIC PSYCHOLOGICAL TESTS

There are so many tests available that a description of each one is clearly impossible. Consequently this section will only mention those which are most significant from a theoretical viewpoint or those which are used most frequently in industrial selection.

Tests of Intellectual Ability

Measures of Global Ability

Although it is hardly used in industrial selection, the *WAIS* is theoretically important because it is one of the best intelligence scales in existence and it has been called the 'paragon of intelligence tests'. Consequently the WAIS is often used to 'calibrate' other tests. The WAIS consists of 11 subscales which can be used to produce estimates of:

1. General intelligence
2. Verbal intelligence
3. Performance intelligence

The WAIS is an individual test which requires one highly trained tester to each candidate. This has the advantage of permitting the inclusion of a range of non-pencil-and-paper tasks, and it permits some flexibility in administration. In addition to the wide sampling of skills the WAIS enjoys excellent standardisation studies which have been conducted in most major countries. Unfortunately the WAIS is expensive to use because as a complex individual test it requires about one hour of a highly-trained administrator for each candidate.

Raven's Progressive Matrices (RPM) (Raven, 1960) is also a very highly-regarded test of mental ability. They are non-verbal tests and are less influenced by culture and linguistic ability than many others. The matrices consist of nine figures case in a 3×3 square. The ninth figure is missing but its contents can be deduced from the sequence of the proceeding eight figures. The candidate is required to identify the correct alternative which should form the ninth figure. The questions become progressively harder. There are three versions of the Progressive Matrices Test: the Standard Matrices, the Advanced Matrices for superior adults and the Coloured Matrices for use with children. The RPM can be administered as either a group or an individual test and they are supported by a vast literature of 1000 research papers. It has been argued that RPM form one of the purest measures of Spearman's general intelligence 'g'. The standard matrices consist of 60 problems and takes 25 minutes to administer. In essence, the matrices are power tests. The main weakness of the RPM is the absence of modern norms – especially for United States' samples. The matrices are occasionally used for selection – especially at skilled operative level.

A survey by Sneath, Thakur and Medjuck (1976) showed that the most popular test of general intelligence in British industry is Heim's (1967, 1968) *AH4 test*. It is a short test which can be completed in 25 minutes and consists of two parts. Part one involves 65 traditional verbal and numerical items such as 'help is to hinder as permit is to .... (a) ticket (b) allow (c) prevent (d) forbid' and '10, 25, 37, which number comes next?' Part two also involves 65 perceptual and spatial problems. The two subscores can be combined to produce a global score. The AH4 is a broad spectrum test which can be used when little advance information about candidates is available. Its reliability is greater than 0.9 and it shows a correlation of 0.69 with Raven's Progressive Matrices. One of the present authors found that the AH4 produced a correlation for senior managers of 0.70 with the WAIS. Thurstone and Thurstone's (1952) *Test of Mental Alertness* has many similarities with the AH4 and can be used as a substitute in appropriate situations. Heim, Watts and Simmonds (1970) have revised the AH4 to produce parallel tests, the AH2 and AH3, which yield three subscores (verbal, numerical and perceptual) in addition to a global score for intelligence. Unfortunately general population norms for the AH2 and AH3 are not available. The AH range of tests of general intelligence is completed by the AH5, AII6 (Arts Graduates) and AH6 (Science, Mathematics, Engineering) which are intended for use with above-average applicants.

The *Wonderlic Personnel Tests* (Wonderlic, 1959) are very useful as a screening device where a quick estimate of mental ability is needed. The 50 items take only 12 minutes to complete. Test re-test reliabilities greater than 0.8 are generally achieved. Several parallel forms are available and there is a large amount of standardisation data.

Batteries of Specific Mental Abilities

Although several of the measures of global ability also provide subscores on numerical, verbal and possibly perceptual abilities, in many situations a more detailed analysis is required. In general, the most important group factors of this kind are spatial ability, mechanical ability as well as numerical and verbal abilities. Several batteries have been constructed which contain tests to measure these and other abilities. Either the complete battery or individual tests from the battery can be used.

Probably the best battery of this kind is the *Differential Aptitude Test Battery* (DATB) developed by Bennett, *et al.* (1974). In an enthusiastic review of the original battery, Carroll (1959) wrote 'The authors have done such a thorough and technically satisfactory job that the reviewer finds it hard to make himself appear sufficiently critical'. The DATB consists of eight independent tests:

1.	Verbal reasoning	5.	Mechanical reasoning
2.	Numerical ability	6.	Space relations
3.	Abstract reasoning	7.	Spelling
4.	Clerical speed and accuracy	8.	Language usage

Most of these tests last about 25 minutes, and the complete battery takes almost four hours. The length of time involved is one of the battery's disadvantages. The battery yields estimates of numerical and verbal reasoning after 60 minutes testing and comparable estimates can be obtained after 20 minutes using tests such as the Thurstone Test of Mental Alertness. Clerical speed and accuracy is the shortest test which takes six minutes, including the practise items, but this test has a very low reliability. The DATB enjoys the advantage of parallel forms and excellent norms (Hodgkiss, 1979).

A possible alternative to the DATB is Morrisby's (1955) Differential Test Battery which includes tests of:

Verbal ability	Shapes
Numerical ability	Mechanical ability
Perceptual ability	Speed

The Morrisby battery is more time-efficient than the DATB but is more complicated to adminster and there are no parallel forms. Standardisation data is also less extensive.

Most government employment services have developed test batteries for specific mental abilities. The United States Employment service has developed the *General Aptitude Test Battery* (GATB) which consists of 12 separately-timed tests. The British Department of Employment has developed the *Department of Employment Vocational Aptitude Tests* (DEVAT). Both GATB and DEVAT are designed for use with average or lower than average ability groups and are primarily intended for vocational guidance. Neither of the batteries is generally available.

The *Flanagan (1960) Industrial Tests* constitute a battery of eighteen very short tests which attempt to measure:

Inspection	Electronics
Mathematics	Ingenuity
Comprehension	Memory
Expression	Arithmetic
Precision	Patterns
Co-ordination	Components
Reading scales	Tables
Vocabulary	Mechanics
Planning	Assembly

Unfortunately the battery has been heavily criticised on account of the low test reliabilities and the inadequacies of the manual.

Individual Tests of Specific Abilities

There are a large number of tests measuring specific abilities which are not part of a larger battery. Probably the largest group consists of tests of *mechanical ability*. Unfortunately many of these tests seem to be attainment tests which merely reflect the contents of a physics school textbook rather than a more general mechanical aptitude. The main exceptions to this generalisation are Vincent's (1974) *Mechanical Diagrams Test* and *Cox's* (undated) *Mechanical Tests*. Both tests give a diagram of a mechanical contraption of levers, pivots, pulleys or gears and require the applicant to forecast the consequence of some movement, such as a lever being pushed or pulled.

There are also several tests of *spatial ability*. Probably the most popular test of spatial ability is the *Minnesota Form Board Test*. The 20-minute test consists of 64 problems in which the applicant must match a design with one of five other designs. In some of the more difficult problems parts of the design have been rotated or turned over. The test is widely respected and Guion (1965) notes 'the test has a broad record of usefulness in engineering, architecture, military tactics, drafting, machining and . . . spatial imagery'. An alternative measure of spatial ability is the *Minnesota Spatial Relations Test* which requires equipment, and is essentially an individual test. It consists of a board in which patterns are cut out to form holes. Pieces which fill the holes are placed in front of the applicant in standard positions and the applicant is required to place the pieces in the appropriate hole. Unfortunately, as a test of spatial ability, the Minnesota Spatial Relations Test is inevitably contaminated by factors such as clumsiness.

Tests for Specific Occupations

Some tests of ability have been developed for specific occupations. Probably the largest group concerns *clerical occupations*. Often batteries of clerical ability contain tests of numerical and verbal ability plus tests of number and name checking and they may include tests of spelling, comprehension and vocabulary. Typical clerical test batteries are the *General Clerical Test* (Psychological Corporation, 1944) and 'Typing and Office Skills Tests' (Science Research Association, 1980). An interesting development is a battery developed by Saville-Holdsworth for the selection of word processor operators.

TABLE 8.1 *Listing of some tests of ability*

SOME TESTS OF GENERAL ABILITY

Name of Test	No. of sub-scores	Numer-ical	Verbal	Levels
WAIS	10	√	√	LAS
Raven's Matrices	0	×	×	LAS
AH4	2	√		A
AH5	2		√	S
AH6 (Arts Graduates)	2	?	√	S
AH6 (Science, Maths, Engineering)	3	√	√	S
AH2/3	3	√	√	A
Thurstone Test of Mental Alertness	2	√	√	A
Wonderlic Test	0	×	×	A
Watson-Glazer test of Critical Thinking	5	×	×	S
Saville-Holdsworth Critical Reasoning	3	√	√	A
Saville-Holdsworth Advanced Battery	7	√	√	S
Saville-Holdsworth Personnel Battery	8	√	√	A
Saville-Holdsworth Technical Battery	4	√	√	AS
16PF B Scale	1	×	×	A

KEY TO LEVEL *L = Below average; A = Average; S = Superior*

SOME TESTS OF VERBAL ABILITY

National Institute of Industrial Psychology Test 90A/90B
Verbal Reasoning from DATB
Verbal Scale from Morrisby
Saville-Holdsworth VTS

SOME TESTS OF NUMERICAL ABILITY

NIIP EA4, GT66, EA2
Numerical Reasoning from DATB
Numerical Scale from Morrisby
Saville-Holdsworth NT2
Flanagan Mathematics and Reasoning
Flanagan Arithmetic

TABLE 8.1   *cont'd*

SOME TESTS OF MECHANICAL ABILITY

Vincent Mechanical Diagrams
Cox Mechanical Tests
Bennett Mechanical reasoning (similar to DATB test)
Macquarrie test for Mechanical Ability
Saville-Holdsworth MT4
Mechanical Ability Test from Morrisby Differential Aptitude Battery
Mechanical Reasoning Test from DATB

SOME TESTS OF SPATIAL ABILITY

Minnesota Form Board
Minnesota Spacial Relations Test
Guilford-Zimmerman Part V: Spatial Orientation
Spatial Reasoning from DATB
Shapes Test from Morrisby Battery
NIIP Tests
Saville-Holdsworth ST7
Embedded Figures Test

Specific occupational tests have also been produced for jobs in the computer industry. A typical example is the Computer Programmer Aptitude Battery (Palormo, 1973; Simpson and Saville, 1975).

TESTS OF PERSONALITY

Controversial Nature of Personality Tests

The use of personality tests is much more controversial than the use of tests of ability for several reasons. First, many people feel that there are ethical issues involved in personality testing, and so there are. But although the quantitative nature of personality tests brings the issues into much clearer focus, the ethical issues are not restricted to tests. They apply to all means of personality assessment including interviews, references and application forms. Consequently it makes sense to consider the ethical issues of personality assessment in a wider context.

A second objection concerns the approach (for example, Cattell, 1965; Eysenck, 1970) which underlies personality tests. The trait factor-analytic approach to personality underlies the most commonly used personality tests, such as Cattell's 16PF (see next section). This approach lays emphasis on personalities rather than situational factors as determinants of behaviour. (Despite this emphasis trait theorists such as Cattell do recognise that both personal make-up *and* situations determine behaviour.) Nevertheless, many other psychologists, for example, Mischel (1968, 1977) argue that trait theories do not place enough emphasis on the part that situations play in determining behaviour. Pervin (1980) provides a useful summary of the debate.

Since the publication of Mischel's book, and its development of this issue, considerable attention has been given to the internal-external (or person-situation) controversy. First there was the debate about whether persons or situations control behaviour, then about whether persons or situations are more important, and finally, acceptance of the view that both are important and interact with one another. Eysenck's views (quoted in Pervin, 1980) on the issue are also worth noting:

> Altogether I feel the debate is an unreal one. You cannot contrast persons and situations in any meaningful sense, or ask which is more important, because clearly you will always have person-in-situations, and the relative importance of personality and situational factors depends on the nature of the situation, the selection of people, and in particular the selection of traits measured. No physicist would put such a silly question as: Which is more important in melting a substance – the situation (heat of the flame) or the nature of the substance!

What are the implications of this debate as far as personnel selection is concerned? Its seems that although trait theories may over emphasise the role of person-factors in determining behaviour, the results of personality tests do, nevertheless, provide some indication of how a person is *likely* to behave. Trait-based personality tests provide a relatively quick well-researched and reliable means of summarising someone's personality.

The final objection to personality test is pragmatic and rests on the belief that tests are simply too inaccurate for use as selection devices. Meyer and Bertotti (1956), for example, suggest that the accuracy of measures of personality is less than the accuracy of measures of interests, abilities or physical characteristics. Whilst this view may be correct, it does not follow that personality tests are not useful for selection purposes. There are just too many examples where personality tests have been found useful.

Some Personality Tests

Without doubt, the personality test most frequently used in selection is the 16PF test (Cattell *et al.*, 1970). The 16PF test was developed from a statistical analysis which located 16 recurrent personality factors from a mass of judgements and measures of personality. Cattell then set out to produce a scale of 13 items for each of the factors. The 16 scales were then combined to produce the 16PF test which takes about 40 minutes to complete. Originally there were two parallel forms (A and B) but subsequently two shorter forms (C and D) were produced which take about 20 minutes to complete but which give less accurate measures. Finally, forms E and F were produced to cater for subjects of lower socio-educational attainment.

The scores from the 16 scales are not independent of each other and they can be correlated to produce scores for higher order factors. The main higher order factors are:

1. Introversion v. Extroversion
2. Adjustment v. Anxiety
3. Dependence of feelings v. Tough poise
4. Subduedness v. Independence

Table 8.2 (p. 168) shows a list of the 16 scales and the appropriate second order factors. The second order factors are not simply the sum of the scores on the scales indicated in Table 8.2 but they *must* be calculated using an appropriate equation given in Cattell *et al.* (1970). Most of the scales in the 16PF test (forms A and B) have adequate reliabilities except the scales which measure intelligence (B), shrewdness (N) and self control (Q3). However, the reliabilities of all the scales on form C and form D are low and generally appreciably lower than 0.5. Consequently the short forms of the 16PF should not be used for selection purposes.

The 16PF test enjoys an additional enormous advantage. Because it has been extensively used for over 20 years a great deal of supporting research is available. Data has been collected on samples of more than 100 occupations and typical profiles can be constructed and used for interpretation. Furthermore, equations have been established which use the 16PF scores to produce scores on other factors such as creativity, academic achievement and leadership.

The Eysenck Personality Questionnaire (EPQ)

The EPQ is a short test which takes about 10 minutes to complete. It yields scores on psychoticism, extroversion, neuroticism and a lie scale. Since the extroversion and neuroticism are similar to two of the second order factors on the 16PF the EPQ can be used as a cross check. The existence of the lie scale is a useful feature but, unfortunately, very conscientious candidates often obtain high scores (see chapter 13). The EPQ has adequate reliabilities and substantial validity information. A previous version was called the EPI and did not possess a scale to measure psychoticism.

TESTS OF INTERESTS AND MOTIVATION

An interest may be defined as a liking for doing something: the performance of an activity which produces its own intrinsic rewards and a feeling of happiness and satisfaction. It would follow that if we find our work interesting we will devote more effort to its performance and be prepared to maintain our effort over a longer period. Consequently, interests may form a basis for selection and we should aim to place individuals in jobs where the interests and the work are consonant.

Unfortunately there is little empirical evidence to support this simple logic. Ghiselli and Brown (1955) suggest that there is only a low relationship between interests and job performance. The main exception to this generalisation concerns sales work where average correlations of 0.32 and 0.34 were obtained. These figures must be interpreted with care because they do not necessarily imply a lack of relationship between interest and proficiency. Consequently interest tests are seldom used for selection purposes.

168

TABLE 8.2 *Higher order factors and their primaries on the 16PF Test*

HIGHER ORDER FACTOR: INTROVERSION *V.* EXTROVERSION
Main Primary Factors

reserved	– warmhearted	A
sober	– happy-go-lucky	F
shy	– venturesome	H
self-sufficient	– group-oriented	Q2

HIGHER ORDER FACTOR: ADJUSTED *V.* ANXIOUS
Main Primary Factors

affected by feelings	– emotionally stable	C
apprehensive	– confident	O
tense	– relaxed	Q4

HIGHER ORDER FACTOR: FEELING *V.* TOUGH POISE
Main Primary Factors

Warm-hearted	– reserved (repeat)	A
humble	– assertive	E
shy	– venturesome (repeat)	H
tenderminded	– tough-minded	I

HIGHER ORDER FACTOR: DEPENDENT – INDEPENDENT
Main Primary Factors

humble	– assertive (repeat)	E
practical	– imaginative	M
conservative	– experimenting	Q1

Other Primary Factors not associated with 4 main higher order factors

concrete	– intelligent	B
expedient	– conscientious	G
trusting	– suspicious	L
forthright	– shrewd	N
self-conflict	– controlled	Q3

Key to 16PF bipolar dimensions

Factor		Approximate Label	
A	Reserved	– Warmhearted
B	Concrete thinking	– Intelligent
C	Affected by feelings	– Emotionally Stable
E	Humble	– Assertive

F	Sober	– Happy-go-lucky
H	Expedient	– Conscientious
I	Tough-minded	– Tenderminded
L	Trusting	– Suspicious
M	Practical	– Imaginative
N	Forthright	– Shrewd
O	Self Assured	– Apprehensive
Q_1	Conservative	– Radical
Q_2	Group Dependent	– Self-Sufficient
Q_3	Undisciplined Self Conflict	– Controlled
Q_4	Relaxed	– Tense

TABLE 8.3 *Some tests of personality*

16PF
EPQ,EPI
Guilford-Zimmerman Temperament Survey
Thurstone Temperament Schedule
Edwards Personal Preference Schedule
Gordon Personal Inventory
Gough Adjective Check List

Some Interest Tests

The Strong Vocational Interest Blank is one of the two most frequently used interest tests and it operates in a fundamentally different way to most other interest tests. The latest version of the test is the Strong-Campbell Interest Inventory (SCII). The inventory consists of 325 items and takes almost an hour to complete. The responses are then matched to the responses of samples from differing occupations. For example, there are scoring keys for farmers, bankers, sales personnel and accountants. There are 67 scoring keys for male samples and 57 for female samples. While this procedure gives very specific information, scoring is excruciatingly time consuming, even when only a handful of scoring keys are involved. Any substantial use of the SCII requires computer scoring and involves additional costs and delays.

The occupational basis of the Strong inventories is both a strength and a weakness, and it differentiates the Strong inventories from most other measures of interests which focus upon themes. The Strong-Campbell Interest Inventory included a modification which also allows the inventory to be scored for six themes: realism, intellectual, artistic, social service, economic and clerical. The scores on the themes can then be related to specific occupations. A banker, for example, would be expected to have high scores on the clerical and the economic themes, whereas an advertising executive would be expected to have a high score on the artistic theme.

A particular feature of the Strong interest tests is the volume of relevant research. Reliabilities are generally high (0.85, 0.82 and 0.75 over 3, 10 and 22 years respectively; Strong, 1951; Campbell, 1977). Both Anastasi (1982) and Guion (1965) report evidence of validity in selection of engineers, bakery shop managers and insurance salesmen.

The Kuder Preference Record (Kuder, 1960) is the other major interest test and it produces scores in terms of ten interest categories or themes:

1.	Outdoor	6.	Artistic
2.	Mechanical	7.	Literary
3.	Computational	8.	Musical
4.	Scientific	9.	Social service
5.	Persuasive	10.	Clerical

The Kuder also contains a validity scale which can be used as a check against carelessness or wilful distortion. Test completion takes about 40 minutes and applicants find the test rather tedious. The Kuder is not often used in selection although Tiffin and Phelan (1953) found that it could be used to identify who would be likely to leave employment after a short time.

The *Rothwell-Miller Interest Blank* must represent the best value of all interest tests in terms of information produced per minute of candidates time. It consists of nine lists of twelve occupations, and subjects are required to rank the occupations according to preference. The Rothwell-Miller Interest Blank takes about 15 minutes to complete and yield scores on the same categories as the Kuder, plus scores for practical and medical interests. Class exercises by one of the authors with undergraduate students generally produce rank order correlations in the range 0.6 to 0.8 between the Kuder and the Rothwell-Miller scores.

With the possible exception of the Strong interest inventories, most interest tests have been designed with the 16- to 21-year-old age groups in view. This may reduce their face validity to older groups.

Three recent tests developed by Saville and Holdsworth (1984) are particularly useful in this context. *The General Occupational Interest Inventory* includes activities from semi-skilled to supervisory levels and is suitable for people whose educational level is around the average for the population. *The Advanced Occupational Interest Inventory* includes activities from skilled and supervisory levels to professional and managerial and is suitable for people whose educational level is above the general population average. The availability of the two tests should make scores more precise and relevant. A particularly nice feature of both tests is their basis on a systematic analysis of job interests. Job interests are arranged in a hierarchy which starts with three categories that are similar to Fine and Wiley's (1977) job analysis categories of People, Data and Things (see Figure 8.1).

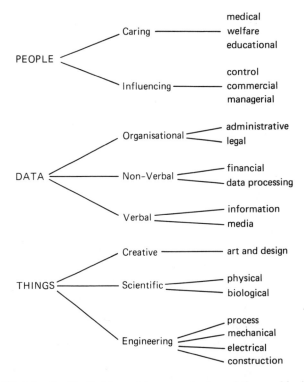

FIGURE 8.1 *Saville-Holdsworth's categorisation of the world of work*
SOURCE Saville and Holdsworth (1984).

Scoring is tedious, but it provides scores at all points of the hierarchy. As new tests, there is relatively little research data, but estimates of a reliability of 0.72 and above (generally 0.8 or more) have been obtained. Unfortunately validity data is sparse, and norms for the general population are not yet available.

Another innovation from Saville-Holdsworth (1983) is the test of the *Managerial Interest Inventory*. The inventory takes about 20 minutes to administer. Although the scoring is excruciatingly tedious, the test provides scores for interest in 12 management functions and 12 management skills. As an added bonus the test also gives an index of experience in both the managerial functions and managerial skills. However, the estimates are based on self-report by the subject, and might be virtually useless in a selection context (see Table 8.4).

TABLE 8.4   *Some interest tests*

Strong-Campbell Interest Inventory
Kuder Preference Record – vocational
Rothwell-Miller Interest Blank
Saville-Holdsworth General Occupational Interest Inventory
Saville-Holdsworth Advanced Occupational Interest Inventory
Saville-Holdsworth Managerial Interest Inventory
APU Occupational Interest Guide
Connolly Occupational Interest Questionnaire

Some Tests of Motivation

Tests of motivation are rarely used in selection and there are very few well recognised tests. Perhaps the most widely used are versions of the *Thematic Apperception Test* (TAT). Subjects are shown a series, usually four, of vague pictures and are asked to say what is happening in the picture, who the people are, what happened in the past and what will happen in the future. The resulting stories can then be analysed for the motives they contain. The main motives obtained from these tests are the achievement motive (n Ach), the affiliation motive and the power motive. Achievement motivation is probably the most extensively researched motive and detailed scoring systems are available (McClelland, 1963, 1976). Many authors (see McClelland and Bradburn, 1957; and Smith *et al.* 1982) have claimed a strong link between achievement motivation and entrepreneurial and managerial success.

Finally, *Rotter's External-Income Locus of Control* has been used, but it must be clear that it is not ideally suited for selection purposes.

CHOOSING AMONG TESTS

The first criteria governing the choice of a test should be its relevance to the items mentioned in the personnel specification and the psychometric properties – especially reliability and validity. Once these overriding criteria have been satisfied the following can be considered:

1. *Cost* of booklets, answer sheets, manual and scoring keys
2. *Delivery time*: several months may elapse between order and delivery
3. *Training needed for administrators*: its cost and availability
4. *Time required* for administration
5. *Time required for scoring* or *cost of scoring*
6. *Adequacy of manual*, which includes items such as:
   (a)   ease of understanding
   (b)   clear statement of purpose of test
   (c)   clear instructions for test administration and scoring
   (d)   clear instructions for scoring of test
   (e)   validity and reliability studies needed for correct interpretation of scores
   (f)   norms for relevant groups.

In addition it may be necessary to take into account the way the test was designed and constructed and the comments of reviewers.

OUTLINES OF TEST CONSTRUCTION

Test construction is a complex and technical undertaking which is best left to specialists in the field. As books by Adkins (1974), Gulliksen (1950), Cronbach and Glesser (1965) and Lord and Novick (1968) show, test construction can involve complex statistical models. Consequently, the following simplified description of test construction has two limited objectives: to give insight which will aid the evaluation and use of tests, and to help those who need to liase and converse with the psychometric mega-beings who actually construct tests.

The precise method of test construction varies according to the constraints of specific situations but the 'classic' method usually proceeds in seven major stages.

The first stage is to *define the domain* of a test. Probably the most important point is to define the aims of the test. This is a crucial decision upon which all else is built, and the way that the decision is reached is more an art than a science. Once the aims have been agreed, a specification of the test content can be produced. Generally the content can be divided into two parts: the subject matter and the mental operations. For example, the content of an arithmetic test can involve money, length, weight or time and each of these content categories can be subject to the mental operations of addition, subtraction, mutliplication and division, to produce 16 different types of problems. Clear thinking at this stage should help to ensure that the test adequately samples the domain.

Secondly, it is also necessary to *specify the type of question*. There are two major types of question: open-ended questions, and multiple-choice questions. Open-ended questions can vary from asking for several sentences on a topic (for example, what has been happening to the people in the picture), to the answer to an arithmetic problem (for example, $194+78=?$). Sometimes a subject is merely asked to fill in a missing word. Open-ended questions have the great advantage that the subject's responses are not limited by the viewpoint of the test constructor and the subject is required to produce the answer rather than just recog..ise it. Open-ended questions have the great disadvantage that, except in arithmetical problems, they are very difficult to analyse and score. Multiple-choice questions range from yes/no or true/false questions, to the most usual format consisting of a stem which poses the question, three or more plausible but wrong answers (distractors) and a correct answer. The construction of multiple-choice questions limits the replies a subject can give, and their preparation needs great care. They are, however, easy to score and analyse. The duration and length of the test also need to be specified in advance. Another consideration is the way that subjects will be asked to respond – should they make their marks on the test booklet or would it be appropriate to use separate answer sheets and so reduce costs?

The third stage is *to assemble items* according to the test specification. It must be anticipated that many of these items will not survive subsequent stages of test construction. Initially, about three times the number of final items is needed. Usually at this stage the questions are cast into an open-ended format and the directions for administering the test are drafted.

The fourth stage of test construction is to *try out the large initial pool of items* on a relatively representative population. If the test is to be timed, a time limit is not imposed at this stage. Instead, subjects are merely asked to mark where they are up to at various points.

The fifth stage consists of an *item analysis* of the responses obtained in the previous stage. At a very minimum this consists of calculating the percentage of the sample who pass each question. Unfortunately the decision of which items to retain and which items to reject is a dilemma. An item has maximum discrimination when it is passed by 50 per cent of subjects and it would follow that tests should be composed solely of items of average difficulty. However, in an extreme situation this would lead to half of the subjects receiving maximum marks, half receiving minimum marks with no-one in the centre of the distribution. In practice most test constructors avoid questions with very high and very low passes and then systematically sample the intermediate range. An adequate item analysis would investigate discrimination in addition to the difficulty of the item. Items which have high correlations with the total score are retained while those with low correlations are rejected. An excellent discussion item analysis is given by Guilford (1965, p. 493).

The sixth stage of constructing a psychological test is *selecting the items* to be included. Usually non-discriminating items are rejected first. Items of appropriate difficulty are then selected from those which remain. The items are usually arranged in an appropriate order, instructions added and the booklets printed. The most frequently used method of arranging questions is the spiral omnibus method which systematically works through all types of easy questions and progressively moving to harder questions. For example, an arithmetic test would start with very easy additions, subtractions, multiplications and divisions and then go on to average additions, subtractions, etc. before finishing on a very difficult division.

The seventh and final stage of constructing a test involves *researching the psychometric properties of the test* on a large representative sample and establishing norms, reliability and validity.

ADMINISTRATIVE ASPECTS OF TESTS

The first administrative decision is whether to use tests in preference to other selection devices. The main advantage of tests is their objectivity and, in most cases, their better predictive ability. However, the use of tests tends to involve a high set-up cost. But since many applicants can be tested simultaneously, the marginal cost of extra candidates may be quite low. In a later chapter on utility it will be shown that selection is important when:

1. There is a favourable selection ratio (that is, only a few applicants are accepted).
2. There is a wide range in ability to do a job (selection is a waste of time if everyone can competently perform the job).

These considerations apply to all selection devices including tests. In addition, however, tests are particularly suitable when the cost of making a mistake are high or when a large number of candidates are involved.

Test Security

Having decided to use tests, it is important to remember that most tests are supplied on a confidential basis. Tests would quickly lose their value if they became common knowledge and people could look up their answers in advance. In order to maintain test security they should be stored in a locked cabinet to which only registered testers have access. Tests should not be loaned to non-qualified testers and any requests for such a loan should be met with a tactful explanation that tests are provided on a confidential basis and that breach of this confidentiality could have important consequences for the person permitting the loan: registration by test publishers could be withdrawn and disciplinary action could be taken by a professional organisation. Test materials should not be photocopied and at the end of a testing session the number of test booklets should be counted to ensure that candidates do not take booklets away either intentionally or unintentionally. Breaches of test security should be reported to both the test publisher and the appropriate professional bodies.

Test Administration

Standardisation is a distinctive feature of tests and a part of this standardisation is to ensure that candidates have the same frame of mind when they are taking tests. Administration plays a key role in creating a uniform frame of mind and it merits careful and detailed attention.

Good test administration starts when the candidate is invited to take the tests. *The letter of invitation* should explain that test will be used and the part the results will play in the selection process. It is also worth reminding candidates who wear spectacles to bring them along. Good administration also involves *advance preparation*. Well in advance of the testing session, rooms of adequate size should be booked and supplies of test materials should be checked in case previous candidates have marked question booklets or in case stocks of answer sheets have been depleted. A day or two before the testing session test rooms should be checked for sources of noise and interruption and details of reception, marshalling and routing of candidates should be communicated to those concerned. Any introduction and explanations for candidates should be prepared. Several hours before the testing session the accommodation should be re-inspected to ensure that tables are properly spaced and that ventilation and heating are in order. An additional table should be available where the tester can lay out the materials in the order of administration. It is also helpful to have a table or other arrangements for bags, coats and umbrellas. There should also be an adequate supply of water and glasses, ashtrays, pencils, chalk or flip chart, and namebadges or nameplates. It is also essential that a DO NOT DISTURB sign is available for each entrance to the testing room and in some cases a QUITE PLEASE, EXAMINATION IN PROGRESS may be required for adjacent corridors. Half an hour before testing begins materials should be taken to the room, pencils and paper laid out on tables and stopwatches checked. Whenever possible, parallel forms of the tests should be taken to the testing room so that, if by chance a candidate has recently completed the test, or if the man with the hammer, pneumatic drill and siren strikes yet again, the test can be recommenced after dealing with the catastrophe.

Even with the best preparation, unanticipated events occur. The only course of action is to take these events into account when making an interpretation. This process will be infinitely easier if a contemporary account is available. Human memory is very fallible and much information is forgotten even after a short interval. Consequently, the use of a *test log* is essential. It should be prepared in advance and consist of the date, names of testers, list of tests used (in order), seating plan with candidates names. There should also be plenty of space to record occurrences which may have influenced the candidates. The candidates' behaviour such as acute anxiety, failure to settle down, attitude to testing, giving up before time, should also be recorded in the test log. Entries in the test log should be made in a discrete way in order not to raise the anxiety or distract the applicants. A useful ploy is to delay making an entry for one or two minutes after an occurrence.

A single administrator can usually cope with 8 to 10 candidates. Two administrators can usually cope with up to 25 candidates and three administrators can usually cope with 50 candidates. Where several administrators are involved, one administrator should be formally nominated to act as main administrator who is responsible for test materials, giving explanations, signals to start work, and keep the time. Assistant administrators should be responsible for distribution of materials, answering individual questions and marking tests. In general the administrators should arrive at the test room 20 minutes before the start of a testing session.

The main administrator should be responsible for introducing the session and his introduction should be worked out in advance. The introduction is crucially important and usually done badly. The experience of one of the authors suggests that postgraduate students need four or five practice attempts to introduce a session before it is accomplished competently. The postgraduate students were drawn from several universities and those possessing bachelor's degree in psychology required most practice, probably because of initial over-confidence.

The introduction must achieve two objectives: it must give the candidates the knowledge they need to complete the test, and it must put them in the right frame of mind. The introduction usually starts with the tester giving his name and job title and the name and job titles of his assistants. Then it is customary to welcome the candidates and check that they can hear the instructions absolutely clearly. This is followed by a fairly long explanation of the programme, arrangements for refreshments and estimated finishing time. The administrator should explicitly ask if candidates need spectacles for reading and check that they are available. Names of candidates without their spectacles should be recorded in the test log. The main investigator then invites general questions and when they have been dealt with a five-minute break is announced so that candidates can visit the cloakroom or collect spectacles.

When the group reassembles, the administrator needs to induce a frame of mind where the candidates lose any anxiety and develop a desire to do the tests as best as they can. To reduce anxiety the administrator suggests that candidates might like to take off their jackets to get comfortable and explain that the pencil-and-paper exercises are supplemented by other information such as references, interviews etc. and they are included in order to be fair to everyone and to try to get as much information as possible (note the avoidance of the words 'test' – especially the words 'intelligence test'). Next the candidate is reassured that full instructions will be given, and to ensure that everyone is dealt with fairly the instructions will be read from a card. Always explain that each part of the exercise will be preceded by practice items. Finally the candidates should be reassured that there are no trick questions and that their results will be strictly confidential. The candidates should now be ready for the instructions for specific tests being used and they should be read verbatim, either from the manual, or the instruction card for the test. Unfortunately some test instructions are inadequate, and they may need to be supplemented. The following wording can be suitably amended:

Before we go on to the first exercise, I would like to give you a few hints which will help you. First, remember to work quickly and accurately. Try to get as many right answers as possible. If you get stuck on any question leave it and go on to the next. It is unlikely that you will finish all the questions because tests are designed so that very few people can complete them. However, if you do reach the end, use any extra time to go back and check your answers. Generally, it is best to work backwards when you are checking your answers (then explain and demonstrate on the blackboard or flip-chart how to correct mistakes). If anyone would like to smoke they may do so but it may slow them down a little – and to avoid causing annoyance to others would smokers sit together on one side of the room ... Are there any more questions ... Good, the time allowed is ... The practice questions can be seen on ...

Marking Tests

The marking of tests should, in theory, be easy and accurate. All that is needed is a marking key which is placed over the answer sheet and the 'correct' answers counted. In practice there is no room for complacency. For example, the course records of one of the authors show that over half postgraduate students make at least one error when scoring the 16PF after an explanation and demonstration. One hundred per cent of a massive sample of two professors of psychology, blithely scored responses to form T of the Differential Aptitude Test, using scoring keys for form S! Mistakes in marking occur more often than we care to admit. They are unnecessary.

Indeed, it could be speculated that at least 5 per cent of the error variance in a typical validity study arises from poor marking procedures. Course records of one of the authors suggests that fewest mistakes are made on simple attainment tests such as the AH4 and the Thurstone Test of Mental Alertness, where it is only necessary to count the number of correct answers. More mistakes are made on scoring systems which involve subtracting the number of wrong answers or making a correction for guessing. Most mistakes are made with scoring keys which require differential weighting of replies (for example, some boxes have a score of 0, some 1 and some 2). In addition to these largely arithmetical sources of error there are two other major pitfalls. Careless markers frequently include duplicate answers where the candidate gives two replies to a question requiring only one reply. Careless markers may also wrongly include answers that have been cancelled by candidates. These errors are particularly prevalent on such tests as the 16PF where candidates are required to tick or blacken a box. Another source of error arises from carelessness of the candidates where they accidentally omit a line from the answer sheet so that their responses get 'out of sync'. Such errors are easy to locate on tests like the AH4 but are virtually impossible to identify on complex tests such as the 16PF or the SH Managerial Interest Scale. When a sudden change in the pattern of answers is encountered the marker should explore the possibility of this type of error and if appropriate it should be dealt with by repositioning the answer key and giving full credit for misplaced answers which are correct.

In general, markers should aim for a standard where there is no more than one error in marking a group of seven different answer sheets. The main requirement of good marking is to obey the instructions in the manual exactly. Aim to be as systematic as possible and establish a marking rhythm for each test. First examine the test for multiple answers, or answers which are ambiguous, and highlight them with a coloured pen. Do not give credit for ambiguous answers. Next score the test using the key, looking out for answers written in the wrong place. Always check that subscores have been added and transferred correctly. It is usually preferable to have all marking cross-checked by an independent marker. Finally it is always important to check that the appropriate norm tables are used in interpreting scores.

Test Profiles

Tests containing three or more subscores usually have a profile sheet. These aid interpretation but they should be filled in correctly. It is wrong to simply join the points of the profile as shown in the second diagram in Figure 8.2, as it implies that the scales are related to each other in some order of magnitude.

Instead, a histogram where bars protrude from the average can be used. An even better method is to mark the actual scores on a profile and indicate the standard errors surrounding the scores (see Warner and Thissen, 1981).

CODE OF PRACTICE IN USING TESTS

Tests can cause anxiety and mislead or put people at a disadvantage if they are wrongly used. Test use *must* be governed by a set of principles designed to preserve their confidentiality and usefulness to the community. The following items represent *some* of the ethical considerations:

1. Tests should only be sold to qualified users.
2. Test confidentiality should be maintained by secure storage and the prevention of 'leakage' by circulation or photocopying.
3. Testing should be carried out under standard conditions.
4. No one should be tested under false pretences: the testee should be informed of the uses to which the results will be put.
5. Test results are confidential and should not be divulged to those who have no right to them or who would not be able to interpret

them correctly. In general, tests should not be administered through the mail. The main exceptions to this rule are some simple tests of interest and some ability tests which have been developed for this purpose 'in house' and which are not used for selection by other organisations.

6. People should not be 'coached' for a test.
7. Never use a test which unfairly discriminates against a subgroup in society except, perhaps, as a temporary expedient, when the test is less discriminatory than alternative measures.
8. Tests should not be released without adequate research.
9. Tests should not make secret or harmful claims.

Additional aspects of good practice can be obtained from Anastasi (1982), 'Ethical Principles of Psychologists' (American Psychological Association, 1981), *Uniform Guidelines on Employee Selection* (USA Government, 1978), Division of Occupational Psychology (1983) and American Psychological Association (1974).

TAILORED TESTING

Tailored testing is probably the most significant development in psychological testing in the last two decades. As we shall see later, it holds the promise that an applicant can call at an employment office, be seated at a computer terminal and visual display unit (VDU), answer 40 to 50 questions within 10 to 15 minutes, and be classified as accurately as if he had completed a much longer test battery.

In essence, tailored testing is based on the notion that a test score is determined by very few items – those items in the difficulty band which lies above the 'floor' where all the answers are correct and below the ceiling where all the answers are incorrect. It is the difficulty band where some answers are correct and some are incorrect. In traditional tests where questions are ordered in level of difficulty a great deal of time is wasted getting up to the correct difficulty band and answering questions which are far too easy. Probably the best review of tailored testing is by Kilcross (1976) who describes a number of approaches to tailored testing.

Flexilevel tests probably form the simplest method which is based on conventional paper and pencil methods. Questions are arranged in two columns – the first column contains the easier questions and the second contains the harder questions. Across the top of the page is a

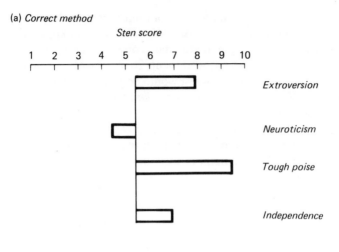

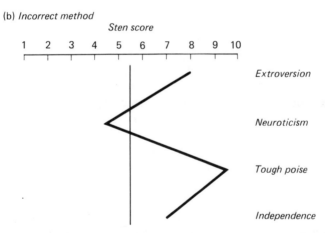

FIGURE 8.2 *Correct and incorrect methods of drawing psychometric profiles*

question of average difficulty and depending upon the answer to this question the candidate works down either the easy column or the hard column. Betz and Weiss (1975) compared this method with a conventional test and found marginally higher reliability (0.84 v. 0.80), and validity (0.91 v. 0.89), for the flexilevel test.

The next level of complication in tailored testing is to use *two-stage testing procedures*. For example, candidates are first given a routing test of say, 10 items. On the basis of their scores on this test, they are then given a subsequent test of, say, 20 items at an appropriate level of difficulty. Thus a candidate who scores 8, 9 or 10 on the routing test would be given the most difficult 20 items while a candidate who scored 4 or 5 on the routing test would be given the 20 items of middle difficulty. No candidate would be asked to complete all 100 items of the second test.

Flexilevel tests and two-stage testing represent the limit of what is feasible with conventional pencil-and-paper technology (see Lord, 1971). More complex methods have been attempted but they run the risk of involving complex instructions which baffle the candidate and produce invalid test results. In a selection context this might not matter since employers usually seek the most competent candidates and research suggests that it is the less able candidate who is most likely to produce an invalid test result. However, there are equal opportunity implications since minority groups with language difficulties may also produce an above average number of invalid results.

The practical use of tailored testing has been transformed over the last two years by changes in computer technology. It is now possible to buy a personal computer with high resolution graphics and memories of over 64k for less than the weekly labour costs of an average worker. Using this kind of technology, even a small company could obtain the benefits of the more advanced techniques of tailored testing. One of the more sophisticated designs are the *branching tests*. For example, a candidate sitting at a VDU may be asked a question at the 50 per cent level of difficulty. If he is correct the next question is the 75 per cent level while if he is incorrect he is asked a question at the 25 per cent level and so on.

Branching tests of this kind are very efficient, but there is the danger that on the basis of one question the candidate may be routed wrongly and there may be a tendency for the route to 'oscillate' widely as the program seeks appropriate items. To overcome these problems it has been suggested that there should be several questions at each node of the test.

The most sophisticated approach to tailored testing involves probability calculations and *item finding* in which each question is chosen almost independently of the other questions. On the basis of previous answers, the computer calculates a candidate's most likely level of ability, it then chooses the item in its memory which is most likely to add useful information to the calculation. This approach has many advantages. Urry (1977) points out that it is possible to decide in advance how precise the estimate of a candidate's ability must be and to continue testing until this level of precision has been obtained. The item selection approach also has profound implications for test construction. The unit of test construction becomes the item which can be linked to a difficulty level. Thus item banking becomes a real possibility in which a store of thousands of questions, whose difficulty level, reliability and discrimination indices is known, is set up (see Hambleton, Swaminathan, Cook, Eignore and Gifford, 1978). When a new test is required the test constructor chooses among the items and programs the appropriate questions into the computer. An interesting possibility is that tailored testing can be used recursively to improve the items it uses. If the item characteristics of a question are inadequate in some way such as being based on a small sample, the computer could 'slip' these items into a tailored test even though they were not required in order to estimate a candidate's ability. The results however could be used to refine the estimates of, for example, the item's level of difficulty and the revised information could be used for the next candidate.

Urry (1977) claims that tailored testing is very successful when applied to ability tests. It is economical and it requires only a third to a half of the testing time of conventional paper and pencil testing. Furthermore, the results may be slightly more valid: clever candidates are not given the chance to slip up on easy questions and poor candidates are not given the chance to guess difficult questions. As Urry (1977) indicates there are still more practical advantages:

1. Walk-in testing could be available in every personnel office.
2. Scores and reports of candidates' suitability for a range of jobs could be computed within seconds at the end of the test.
3. Administration of the test would be completely standardised by the computer thus reducing the training needed for personnel staff.
4. Increased confidentiality of tests since each candidate is only exposed to a few items.

As computer and information technology improves, the possibilities become almost endless and could revolutionise test publishing. Instead of maintaining stocks of tests and sometimes being short of *the* test which is required for a specific occasion, companies might simply telephone their local viewdata computer and download the tailored test they require. The results would be uploaded to the computer thus improving the background data on the items used and to enhance the reliability and validity of the results. In a really brave new world of tailored testing, test construction would be international. There would be no major obstacle to organisations in Wyoming, Winnipeg, Woomera and Whaley Bridge using and contributing to the same data bank!

9　Work Samples

The use of some form of test is a feature of many personnel selection procedures. Often these tests take the form of a pencil-and-paper psychological test (for example, general intelligence, numerical ability, aptitude or personality). To the designer of the personnel selection procedure the rationale for using the chosen tests will be perfectly clear. In a well-designed scheme job analysis and other preparatory work will have identified the psychological characteristics that are thought to be good predictors of successful job performance. Tests will then have been selected to identify the candidates who display the desired characteristics. From the point of view of the candidates, however, the justification for the chosen tests may well be less clear. This procedure of conducting a job analysis, inferring from this the desirable psychological characteristics and developing a set of predictors to identify these characteristics is probably the most common method for the initial design of selection schemes. The predictors produced in this way, whilst potentially valid, often require candidates to display behaviour that is rather *different* from the behaviour that they will eventually be expected to display at work. Thus an applicant for a job as a machine operator may be expected to take tests of general intelligence, numerical aptitude and mechanical aptitude. The potential machine operator may well *not* be asked to operate any machinery.

Wernimont and Campbell (1968) have commented on this traditional method of choosing predictors. They note that there seems to be an implicit or explicit insistence among applied psychologists that predictors should be somehow *different* from criteria. Furthermore, Wernimont and Campbell argue that for effective selection it would be more appropriate to make use of predictors that are not different from criteria. They argue in favour of using predictors that are realistic samples of behaviour and are actually as *similar to criteria as possible*. Asher and Sciarrino (1974) have made a very similar point arguing for what they describe as point-to-point correspondence between predictors and criteria. In other words, the behaviour that a predictor requires of the candidate and the conditions under which the candidate is expected to display this behaviour should be as similar as possible to the criterion (that is, actual work behaviour).

Over the past 25 years or so researchers have deliberately attempted to produce valid predictors that are as similar as possible to the desired criterion behaviours. Rather than using psychological tests or other 'signs' of behaviour this research has explored the extent to which realistic 'samples' of work behaviour can be used as predictors of subsequent job performance. This approach – 'work sampling' – involves identifying a task or set of tasks that are representative of the job in question and using these tasks for pre-employment testing. Figure 9.1 provides a comparison of the work-sampling and 'traditional' approaches.

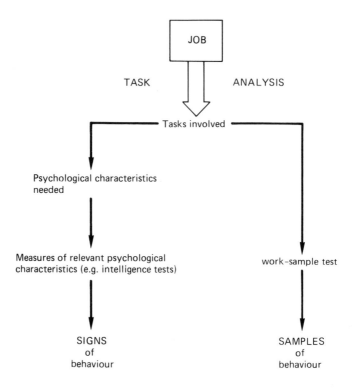

FIGURE 9.1 *A comparison of work-sampling and 'traditional' approaches*

TYPES OF WORK-SAMPLE TESTS

Work-sample tests have been developed and used for a wide range of different occupational areas. In the context of the current discussion it is interesting and informative to examine two issues: what types of work-sample tests have been developed and to what extent do work-sample tests provide valid predictors of future work performance?

In their review of work-sample tests, Asher and Sciarrino (1974) identify two main categories of tests – motor and verbal. A test was identified as 'motor' if 'the task was a physical manipulation of things, for example tracing electrical circuits, operating a sewing machine, making a tooth from plaster or repairing a gearbox', and was designated 'verbal' if 'there was a problem situation that was primarily language oriented or people oriented'. In a more recent review, Robertson and Kandola (1982) proposed a more comprehensive four category system – derived after examining many of the published studies concerned with work-sample tests:

(i) *Psychomotor.* This category is much the same as Asher and Sciarrino's (1974) 'motor' category and involves the manipulation of objects, for example, carving something out of chalk, typing, stitching a piece of cloth or using a sewing-machine.

(ii) *Job-related information.* Tests in this category examine the amount of information a person holds about a particular job. They are usually pencil-and-paper tests and although not work-sample tests in the simulation sense, they test applicant knowledge in areas thought to be directly relevant to work performance.

(iii) *Individual, situational decision-making.* Here the applicant is expected to take decisions similar to those taken in the job. This can be done more or less realistically by using in-tray exercises, for example, or more abstractly by presenting the applicant with a series of hypothetical situations and asking how he or she would respond.

(iv) *Group discussions/decision-making.* Tests of this sort involve two or more people being put together to discuss a particular topic and their performance in the discussion is evaluated. They are used widely for jobs where an individual's contribution within a group setting is an important determinant of job success.

As far as the validity of the different types of work-sample tests are concerned, Tables 9.1 and 9.2 give some information on the validity coefficients obtained from a total of over 60 different validation studies. Table 9.1 gives the median validity coefficients for each type of work sample test. Table 9.2 shows how the validity coefficients for each type of tests are distributed. The figures also show that psychomotor and job-related information tests have the highest validity coefficients. Situational decision-making is the weakest of the

TABLE 9.1　*Summary of validity coefficients for each type of work-sample test*

	Psychomotor	Job-related information	Situational decision-making	Group discussion
Median	0.39	0.40	0.28	0.34
No. of coefficients	78	27	53	27
Range	−0.07–0.80	0.03–0.72	−0.19–0.86	0.10–0.63

SOURCE　Robertson and Kandola (1982).

TABLE 9.2　*Distribution of validity coefficients for each type of work-sample test: proportions in each category*

	Psychomotor	Job-related information	Situational decision-making	Group discussion
Percentage of coefficients less than 0.30	26	30	52	26
0.30–0.39	24	19	15	13
0.40–0.49	23	19	13	13
0.50–0.59	9	19	10	10
Greater than 0.59	18	13	12	12

SOURCE　Robertson and Kandola (1982).

four categories and has the lowest median, the greatest proportion of coefficients below 0.30 and the smallest proportion above 0.50. At this point it is useful to look in some more detail at the nature of the tests involved in each of the four categories.

Work-sample Tests

(i) *Psychomotor tests*

In general, researchers and practitioners have devoted more attention to psychomotor work-sample tests than to the other three types of test. Psychomotor work sample tests also appear to have been the most successful form of work-sample test. As Table 9.1 reveals, psychomotor tests produce a smaller proportion of small validity coefficients (that is, 26 per cent below 0.30) and a larger proportion of large coefficients (that is, 18 per cent above 0.59).

For any type of work-sample test one of the most important stages in the development of the test is the identification of a suitable task (s) to form the basis of the work sample. The typical format for a work-sample test involves the following steps:

1. The candidate is briefed on the task(s) to be performed.
2. The candidate performs the tasks (unaided) and is observed by an assessor who is often an expert at the job in question.
3. The assessor's observations are used to produce judgements of the candidate's suitability for the job (often standardised checklists or rating scales are used).

Clearly, if the task(s) that form the basis for the work-sample are chosen badly the predictive value of the work-sample exercise will be severely diminished.

A good example of the development and use of a psychomotor work-sample test is provided by Campion (1972) who produced a test for maintenance mechanics. To develop the test Campion followed a procedure based on earlier work by Smith and Kendall (1963). Campion's procedure involved five stages:

Stage 1 Job experts produced a list of all tasks conducted by maintenance mechanics and indicated the frequency of performance and importance of each task.

Stage 2 Job experts with experience of screening applicants for maintenance mechanics' jobs, plus a personnel specialist, produced a second list of tasks related to the previous work experience that typical applicants would have had.

Stage 3. The experts identified the major dimensions of work behaviour (for example, use of tools, accuracy of work) that they felt discriminated between effective and ineffective performance on the job. Then each expert independently identified some critical behavioural incidents (Flanagan, 1954) to illustrate actual performance on each major dimension. At the end of stage 3 the experts pooled their information and discussed and reconciled differences of opinion.

Stage 4 In this stage the information produced in stages 1 to 3 was used to determine which tasks should be used as work samples. To ensure that the tasks chosen were representative of the normal job of a maintenance mechanic, *and* appropriate for applicants for the job, only those tasks that were common to stages 1 and 2 of the procedure were considered. The tasks chosen were also specifically relevant to the major dimensions of work behaviour identified during stage 3. Tasks finally selected included disassembling and repairing a motor and installing a pulley and belts.

Stage 5 In the final stage the tasks were analysed in detail to identify the various approaches that might be followed by an applicant, and scoring weights were assigned based on expert judgements.

The work-sample test resulting from this procedure was used in a concurrent validity study. The work-sample test results showed a much better relationship with a criterion measure of over-all mechanical ability than pencil-and-paper aptitude tests. The most popular example of a psychomotor work-sample test is probably the typing test (for example, West and Bolanovich, 1963; Ash, 1980) but many other investigators have developed and validated psychomotor work-sample tests for a wide range of jobs and a review of the work done can be found in Asher and Sciarrino (1974) and Robertson and Kandola (1982).

(ii) *Job-related information*

In the strict sense tests in this category are not work-sample tests since they examine the job-related knowledge that an applicant holds – but do not call for the performance of a work-sample. As Tables 9.1

and 9.2 show, job-related information tests compare reasonably well with psychomotor tests and such tests have been produced for various skills (for example, a farm knowledge test, Grigg, 1948; a naval knowledge test, Glickman, 1956; and a knowledge of sales-related information, Baier and Dugan, 1956).

Schmidt *et al.* (1977) have conducted a direct comparison of a job-related information test and a psychomotor work-sample test. Their study is interesting because it highlights the possibility that job-related information tests like other paper-and-pencil tests may be less appropriate for some ethnic minority groups. Schmidt *et al.* make the following point, 'It is well established that blacks and other disadvantaged groups average significantly below national (USA) means on most paper and pencil tests (for example, see Dreger and Miller, 1968, for a review of this research)' (pp. 187–8). They go on to demonstrate that, although well-designed and content-valid, the job-related information test that they used may be subject to similar problems. 'It can be seen that the written Machine Trades Achievement Test and each of its component subtests show large and significant minority-majority differences, while two of the three job sample subtests ... show no significant group differences' (pp. 193–4). The significance of ethnic differences is discussed in detail in chapter 12.

Schmidt *et al.* stress that the evidence that they present does not suggest that the job-related information test that they used is invalid as a predictor of performance. Indeed, the available evidence suggests that it may be quite a good predictor of job performance. What their research does support, however, is the view that paper-and-pencil tests (whether they are based on job-related information or not) may place some groups at a disadvantage. Schmidt *et al.* (p. 196) express it in the following way:

> Nothing in these findings implies that the written Machine Trades Achievement Test is invalid or fails to meet legal requirements ...
> The point is that, compared to the performance (work-sample) test, this test emphasises heavily those performance determining factors (and perhaps some non-valid factors) on which minority-majority differences are apparently large.

In short, then, whilst potentially valuable, job-related information tests need to be used with caution in situations where heterogeneous groups of applicants are involved.

(iii)   *Individual, situational decision-making*

Individual, situational decision-making tests involve placing applicants in circumstances that simulate, as closely as possible, the real
job. The simulations can take a variety of forms. They include
psychomotor simulators (for example, for pilots or air traffic controllers) and realistic in-tray exercises where candidates are given a
limited amount of time to deal with the contents of a typical in-tray
for the job in question. For managerial and administrative jobs the
most common form of situational decision-making test is probably
the in-tray exercise.

In the United States in-tray exercises have, for some time, been
used as one of the various exercises (for example, leaderless group
discussions, psychologial tests, interviews) that form the components
of managerial assessment centres (Bender, 1973) (see chapter 13 for
more information on assessment centres). In the United Kingdom the
personal experience of the writers suggests that in-trays are now used
widely; though as little as ten years ago they were apparently used
very little (Holdsworth, 1975).

A typical in-tray attempts to simulate the contents of an executive's
in-tray and includes letters, memoranda, hand-written notes, internal
company reports, telephone messages and so on. Usually a fixed time
is allowed for completion (often 1 to 1½ hours) and briefing notes are
provided describing the background to the job and company and
making it clear that no one is available for the candidate to consult. A
selection of the contents of an in-tray for department managers in a
large manufacturing company is given in Table 9.3 (Moss, 1984). In
common with most other work-sample tests the scoring of in-trays is
usually conducted by people with an expert knowledge of the job,
although the value of their assessments is likely to be improved by
training in the techniques of assessment (See Richards and Jaffee,
1972; Frank and Whipple, 1978). Following Fredriksen, Saunders
and Wand (1957), Gill (1979) outlines two steps involved in evaluating a candidate's performance: (i) an agreed prior classification of the
in-tray items is established (for example, irrelevant items, key items,
and so on) and (ii) evaluation of action first on key papers, and next
on the other ones. Gill (1979) notes that the available evidence
suggests that in-tray performance evaluations are usually related to
two major dimensions: supervision (a human-relations dimension)
and planning/administration (an intellectual dimension).

TABLE 9.3 *Selected contents from a departmental manager's in-tray exercise*

---

1. Memo from personnel manager concerning an outbreak of dermatitis caused by solvents.
2. Memo from sales manager to confirm a meeting.
3. Memo (handwritten) from a foreman concerning a disagreement with inspection over the quality of a product.
4. Letter from a customer concerning late delivery of an order.
5. Memo from a foreman pointing out a shortage of bolts needed for a current job.
6. Memo from the general manager placing restrictions on purchasing.
7. Memo from work study manager concerning erratic bonus earnings.

Note: Altogether the in-tray exercise contains 20 letters and memoranda.

SOURCE MOSS (1984).

As far as predicting future work performance is conerned, the in-tray appears to have a useful and unique contribution to make. Wollowick and McNamara (1969) found that in-tray exercises contributed a unique element to the prediction of managerial success. Gill (1979) reviews the available literature on in-tray exercises and arrives at the conclusion that there is some evidence for the predictive validity of in-trays although as Table 9.1 and 9.2 show, situational decision-making exercises such as in-trays appear to be less effective in general than other forms of work-sample tests. Gill also suggests that in-tray exercises appear to be particularly valuable for assessing a wide range of factors including: recall and insight, written communication, logical reasoning and problem-solving and the ability and willingness to make decisions, establish priorities and distinguish fact from opinion.

He also adds a note of caution 'We still need to know a good deal more about the relationships of overall in-tray performance to subsequent job performance and of the different dimensions of in-tray performance to the different dimensions of managerial effectiveness' (p. 195).

(iv) *Group discussions/decision-making*

Group discussion techniques seem to have been used almost entirely for the assessment of managerial potential within industry, commerce and the armed services. One of the most popular discussion exercises is the Leaderless Group Discussion (LGD). An example of an LGD is provided in Dulewicz and Fletcher (1982, pp. 199) who used the exercise as part of an assessment centre for Standard Telephones and Cables/ITT (UK).

Committee exercise: Six participants form an appointments committee set up to fill a vacancy within Geo-Systems Division. They are each given written details of a candidate to propose for the job; they, as a group are instructed to ensure that the best person is appointed to the job. However, each individual is told to try as hard as possible to get his own candidate selected. The candidates are allocated at random, and each has roughly the same number of strengths and weaknesses. The participants in turn present the case for their own candidate for up to four minutes. Then there is an unconstrained discussion for 40 minutes before (usually though not always) deciding on an appointee.

Unfortunately, although LGDs are used frequently it is not possible to draw unequivocal conclusions about the validity of LGDs. The main reason for this is that although LGDs are used often in assessment centres, it is rare to find studies that focus on the validity of specific components of assessment centres.

In an early influential paper, Bass (1954) suggests that LGDs may have some value in assessing leadership potential – but he also provides some important warnings. For example, he emphasises that LGDs must attempt as far as possible to approximate the real situation and that observers should assess the *behaviour* of candidates and not attempt to infer differences in personality traits amongst candidates (see Ungerson, 1974, for a summary).

As well as leaderless groups, it is also common to find group exercises where candidates (often in turn) are appointed specifically to take the lead in group problem-solving exercises (for example, Gardner and Williams, 1973) although it is probably more appropriate to classify problem-solving exercises such as these (frequently used by the armed services selection boards) as 'situational decision-making' rather than 'group discussion' exercises. Taken overall, group discussion techniques seem to display reasonable validity, although direct evidence is not extensive. Reliability is moderate (see Jones, 1981). They are nevertheless popular methods, particularly for managerial assessment.

ASSESSING TRAINABILITY

Much of the literature on work-sample testing focuses on people who are *already* trained and able to do the job and the function of the test is to identify the most suitable candidate. Often the problem is not to select from a pool of *ready-trained* candidates, but to choose candidates who are suitable for training. Various methods have been adopted to predict trainability, including the use of standard pencil-and-paper psychological tests (see Ghiselli, 1973). The progress of trainees during the early stages of training has also been investigated as a predictor of later training performance, with some success (for example, Gordon and Cohen, 1973). A practical problem with using early training performance as a predictor is that it is still necessary to select trainees in some way and the psychological and financial costs of training and then rejecting unsuitable candidates may be considerable.

Over the last 20 years or so various investigators have made use of work-sample tests to predict training success. Siegal and Bergman (1975, p. 326) have described the general format for work-sample-based predictors of trainability, 'The job seeker is *trained* [our italics] to perform a sample of tasks involved in the job for which he is an applicant and, immediately following the training, his ability to perform these tasks is measured.' In the UK the earliest work-sample trainability tests were developed by Downs (for example, Downs, 1968).

The essential difference between a normal work sample and a trainability test is that the trainability test incorporates a structured and controlled learning period. For this reason such tests have been described as taking a 'job learning' or 'miniaturised training' approach to performance prediction. In many cases trainability tests also involve the systematic observation of how things are done as well as what is done.

Downs (1968), for example, reports the development of carpentry and welding tests. The carpentry.test involved making a half lap T-joint and the welding test involved making several straight runs on mild steel. Since this early work a variety of work-sample trainability tests (mostly psychomotor) have been developed, both in the UK and the USA. Robertson and Downs (1979) provide a review of the UK work, and Siegal (1983) provides a brief review together with an example of how these techniques are developing in the USA. Tests used vary in length from 10 to 15 minutes to two hours or so.

(The candidate is asked to build the ushaded section of wall)

FIGURE 9.2   *Bricklaying trainability test*
SOURCE Robertson and Mindel (1980).

Work-sample trainability tests exist for many craft trades, for example, bricklaying (Figure 9.2), centre lathe-turning, capstan operating (see, for example, Robertson and Mindel, 1980), and for various other jobs such as dentistry (Deubert *et al.* 1975) and sewing-machining (Downs, 1973).

Guidance on the development and use of work-sample trainability tests is provided in Downs (1977). Most work-sample trainability tests developed so far have been concerned with psychomotor skills, but it seems likely that the approach could be of more general use. Robertson and Downs (1979) provide some advice on the factors that might need to be considered in any wider application.

As far as validity is concerned, the evidence for work-sample trainability tests is quite good as reviews by Robertson and Downs (1979), Robertson and Kandola (1982) and Siegal (1983) demonstrate. Table 9.4 provides a comparison of validity coefficients for work-sample tests using a trainability (job-learning) approach with other psychomotor work-sample tests.

BENEFITS AND LIMITATIONS OF WORK-SAMPLE TESTS

Applicants

From the applicant's point of view, realistic work-sample tests may have a number of advantages over traditional psychological tests. For

TABLE 9.4 *Comparison of validity coefficients for job-learning tests and other psychomotor tests using training criteria*

	Job learning	Other
Median	0.37	0.39
Number of coefficients	28	24
Range	−0.07–0.80	0.18–0.66
Percentage greater than		
0.29	64	75
0.39	36	50
0.49	25	16

Note: This table includes data from those tests where a job-learning approach was used (that is, involving a period of instruction on how to perform the work sample). The tests were not necessarily developed and designed using common procedures.

SOURCE Robertson and Kandola (1982).

a work-sample test the applicant is expected to perform some activities which very closely resemble the job that they have applied for; and which they presumably feel competent to carry out or be trained to carry out, that is, the tests have high face validity (see chapter 6). The high face validity of work-sample tests may have some beneficial influences.

One likely benefit of a work-sample test is that candidates themselves are provided with an opportunity to assess their *own* potential for the job. In other words, work-sample tests provide a basis for candidates to make *self-assessments*. Most recent reviews of the value of self-assessments in industrial and organisational contexts conclude that there is little to recommend their use. Major criticisms of self-assessments concern their excessive leniency (that is, people produce an inflated opinion of themselves) and their poor accuracy (see chapter 10). Despite these limitations there is some evidence to suggest that whilst some forms of self-assessment might not be particularly valuable, self-assessments based on *direct* job 'tasting' or experience are useful (see Makin and Robertson, 1983, for a review). Downs, Farr and Colbeck (1978) report the use of a trainability test with applicants for employment as sewing-machinists. Candidates were *not* selected on the basis of their test performance; all candidates were offered jobs. Ninety per cent of people graded A (the highest grade) started work whereas only slightly over twenty-three per cent of those graded E began work. Using Bem's (1972) theory of self-perception as a theoretical basis, Downs *et al.* (1978) argue that the individual makes a self-assessment (similar to that of the assessors) of their potential and that their future behaviour is determined by the nature of this assessment. It is not possible to be certain whether the reasons behind the rejection of the job by candidates who were poorly assessed was due to a change in their self-assessment, a change in their understanding of the nature of the job, a mixture of both or some other factor. What does seem clear from this research is that work-sample tests have the potential to help the applicant and the selectors to come to a decision. Work-sample tests may in fact represent the most effective way of providing candidates with a useful and realistic job review. They may also be used, and frequently are, in assessment centre settings, to provide candidates with feedback about various aspects of their job-related performance.

A second likely benefit of work-sample tests, in terms of applicant reaction, is that they may encourage positive attitudes on the part of the applicants. To a large extent this positive attitude may be a function of the high face validity of work-sample tests. Cascio and Phillips (1979) provide some evidence suggesting that the clear link between a typical work-sample test and the work itself is an important asset. In their study applicants were being assessed for both initial hiring and for promotion. When conventional tests were being used as part of these procedures, 5 to 10 per cent of job applicants, and 20 per cent of applicants for promotion, sent in complaints about the way that they had been tested. In their 17-month study of work-sample tests not one complaint was received. There is also further evidence to suggest that work-sample tests encourage positive attitudes in applicants (see Robertson and Kandola, 1982) and that they provide encouragement for highly-motivated candidates (Gordon and Kleiman, 1976).

In the United Kingdom legislation and the efforts of various groups have sought to ensure that personnel selection processes are fair and do not discriminate unfairly against any particular group (see chapter 12). In the USA similar legislation and moves have taken place. In practical terms 'fairness' in selection has proved to be a difficult concept to operationalise. Fairness is often considered in terms of the 'adverse impact' that a selection scheme has. In the USA adverse impact is operationally defined by the so-called '80 per cent' rule. According to this rule the *proportion* of minority group applicants hired should be no less than 80 per cent of the proportion of majority group applicants hired. In the UK, whilst there is no such firm rule concerning the degree of adverse impact, the general concept is used – 'adverse impact refers to the disproportionate rejection rate of one subgroup by comparisons with the rest of the individuals being assessed for selection' (Runnymede Trust, 1980, p. 45).

Cascio and Phillips have conducted a comprehensive study of the selection rates of different racial-ethnic groups, using work-sample tests. Working for an American city government they constructed 21 work-sample tests and examined their use over a 17-month period. Selection rates were 0.64 for whites, 0.60 for blacks and 0.57 for hispanics – clearly satisfying the 80 per cent rule.

As far as taking good selection decisions are concerned it is, of course, not sufficient merely to reduce adverse impact – such action provides no guarantee that appropriate candidates are being selected from any of the (minority or majority) groups involved. Indeed, the decision to hire in predetermined proportions, regardless of validity, is unlikely to produce fairer selection in more general terms.

A 'fair' selection system would use valid selection procedures – with validities that did not differ significantly between any of the groups involved. The available research suggests that in general, work-sample tests produce validities that are similar across majority and minority group applicants (see Robertson and Kandola, 1982 for a review). Indeed, in general, it seems that work-sample tests may have a beneficial effect on the fairness of selection procedures. There is evidence to suggest that they can tap factors that are important determinants of job success but only where racial differences are small (Schmidt *et al.*, 1977; Kesselman and Lopez, 1979).

Furthermore, when evaluators make judgements concerning applicants, based on work-sample test performance, it seems likely that these judgements may be less susceptible to race (or sex) linked bias (see Robertson and Kandola, 1982).

Organisations

From the organisation's point of view the benefits of a work-sample approach to personnel selection are clear and have been discussed earlier in this chapter.

When looked at from the perspective of the organisation these benefits need to be balanced against the limitations and difficulties associated with work-sample tests.

Work-sample tests are often more time consuming to administer than traditional psychological tests, and they are unquestionably more demanding in terms of resources. Since work-sample tests are designed to involve the core activities of jobs, they must of necessity incorporate into their format a requirement for some of the equipment and materials used in the job. In some cases this requirement may be neither difficult nor expensive to satisfy. An in-tray exercise designed to simulate parts of an executive job will, for example, usually need little more than a room, paper, writing equipment, a desk and perhaps a telephone. By contrast, where manual skills are involved, special equipment and premises may be needed. A work-sample test for a bricklayer, for example, requires bricks, mortar, tools and the space to build a small section of wall (see Figure 9.2). Tests for other craft trades (for example, capstan setting, centre lathe-operating, welding) require considerable, expensive equipment, machinery and premises. Not only can work-sample tests be costly in terms of machinery, materials, equipment and premises, they are also costly in terms of human resources. For most work-sample tests it seems sensible to have evaluators who are themselves skilled performers of the job in question. Although there is no conclusive research to support this, this has been the practice of many researchers and practitioners using such tests. Organisations will often find it costly or inconvenient to release skilled performers. The evaluator is required to observe and assess the quality of the candidate's performance. In many cases this means that the evaluator will need to observe the candidate as he or she carries out the work sample. Thus it is often difficult for one person to administer work-sample tests, simultaneously, to more than about three candidates. By contrast, with many traditional psychological tests, a qualified tester may be able to administer a group test to 10 or more candidates simultaneously.

Work-sample tests are related to specific jobs, and as such will need to be redesigned and validated as jobs change. Although this is true for all selection instruments, it may be more time consuming and expensive to redesign and validate a work-sample test than it is to redesign and validate a battery of pencil-and-paper psychological tests. Furthermore, there is a great variety of ready to use, standardised pencil-and-paper tests, but relatively few ready-made work-sample tests, and in any case it is fairly unlikely that a ready-made work-sample test will show sufficient similarity to the jobs conducted within an organisation.

Against the problems and limitations of work-sample tests, it should be borne in mind that such tests show good validities, appear to have the potential to reduce adverse impact and improve fairness, provide a realistic preview of the job, aid self-selection and are well received by applicants. The choice of when and where to use work-sample tests should be made on the basis of the likely balance of benefits and drawbacks as far as the specific situation is concerned.

In terms of predictive validity work-sample tests compare favourably with the more widely used pencil-and-paper psychological tests (see Table 9.5). In fact, work-sample tests produce better validities than any of the more conventional tests. Support for the idea that work-sample tests compare favourably with conventional tests is also provided by Gordon and Kleiman (1976). Their study involved a direct comparison of an intelligence test and a work-sample test for predicting success in a police training school. The work-sample tests produced consistently better validities than the inteligence test.

A very interesting, important, but currently unresolved question concerns the extent to which work-sample tests and pencil-and-paper tests predict overlapping or independent aspects of criterion perform-

TABLE 9.5 *Distribution of validity coefficients for work-sample tests and other predictors using job performance criteria*

	Percentage greater than		
	0.29	0.39	0.49
(a) *Work sample tests*			
Psychomotor	88	69	31
Job-related information	36	27	9
Situational decision-making	50	27	8
Group discussion	80	40	30
(b) *Other predictors*			
(from Asher and Sciarrino, 1974)			
Biographical data	97	74	55
Intelligence	60	51	28
Mechanical aptitude	73	48	17
Finger dexterity	39	24	13
Personality	42	22	12
Spatial relations	16	9	3

SOURCE Robertson and Kandola (1982).

ance. In essence, if work-sample tests and pencil-and-paper tests predict overlapping aspects of criterion space it is pointless to use both in a selection procedure. If, however, they predict independent aspects of criterion space, used together they could produce significant improvements in predictive validity. Future studies using both work-sample tests and pencil-and-paper tests on the same sample of people could examine the extent to which they predict independent aspects of criterion space. Such studies, if conducted over a period of years, might also throw light on two other important issues.

First, they might help to determine the extent to which the predictive value of work-sample tests deteriorates over time. The available evidence suggests that work-sample tests may predict early job-training performance well – but as time passes the job holder's performance may be increasingly at variance with expected performance, based on a work-sample test. The attenuation of predictive validity over time is common to all selection instruments. Work-sample tests, however, are very closely tied to the job, and may be more susceptible to attenuation over time. As working practices and the environment change, and as the job holder's skills grow, so the predictive power of the work-sample test might be reduced. Conventional pencil-and-paper tests attempt to measure more fundamental aspects of ability and temperament, and so on, and because of this, prediction based on them may be less susceptible to attenuation over time.

The second issue that future research might resolve concerns the relative value of work-sample tests and conventional pencil-and-paper tests. Although the results discussed earlier indicate that work-sample tests might produce higher predictive validities, the available results do not form a satisfactory basis for drawing general conclusions concerning the value of work-sample tests and conventional predictors (for example, tests of intelligence and personality). It is possible, for instance, that conventional tests are much more likely to be used in circumstances where they are entirely inappropriate and could not reasonably be expected to have any predictive power. Work-sample tests are less likely to have been used in this indiscriminate way because of their close link with their job and the lack of availability of ready-made tests.

10 Other Predictors

The principal method of personnel selection used in most organisations is the selection interview (see Robertson and Makin, in press). Psychological tests and work-sample tests are also mainstream methods of personnel selection that are used fairly frequently and seem to display reasonable predictive power (see chapters 6, 8, 9). There are, however, several other predictors that are worth considering, perhaps because they produce particularly good validities (for example, the use of biographical data), or because they are useful in special situations (for example, self-assessment), or because they are interesting and controversial (for example, handwriting analysis and astrology).

The purpose of this chapter is to provide a brief overview of some of these alternative methods, to examine their validity, and to assess their feasibility. The methods dealt with are:

Biographical data
Self-assessment
Peer-evaluation
References
Graphology (handwriting)
Astrology

BIOGRAPHICAL DATA

Many studies have demonstrated that various important aspects of work performance can be predicted accurately with the aid of biographical information (see Asher, 1972). In most selection situations there is a readily available source of biographical information about candidates, their application forms. Even the most rudimentary application forms provide some basic biographical data such as age, marital status, number of previous jobs and time spent in previous jobs. In its simplest form, using biographical data to assist in selection decisions is relatively straightforward. The basic procedure is to collect biographical data (using application forms, for example) and the links with successful job performance are examined, and used to make future selection decisions.

In some circumstances the use of biographical data in personnel selection may involve an approach to the problem of predicting a candidate's work performance that is rather different from the approach used when other selection methods are utilised. When using selection procedures such as interviews or psychological tests the specific areas to be examined in the interview or tests are normally derived from a systematic analysis of the job in question and there is a clear link between the nature of tasks involved in the job and the selection criteria used. When biographical data is used the link between the job and the criteria used for selection is much less clear. Specific types of biographical data are chosen, not because they have any clear relationship with the tasks involved in the job but because on a statistical basis they are good predictors of future performance.

(In chapter 11 a distinction is made between actuarial (or statistical) and clinical prediction.) The use of biographical data in personnel selection may seem to represent an extreme form of actuarial prediction, where selection decisions are influenced purely on the basis of statistical links between predictors and criteria.

Although biographical data can be used in this way, some work (for example, Owens, 1976) demonstrates that biographical data may represent much more than a collection of isolated items of information about a person's life. This work is discussed later in this chapter.

Using Biographical Data for Selection

In order to examine the use of biographical data in personnel selection it makes sense to identify the two main ways in which biographical data are collected viz. *application forms* and *biographical questionnaires*. The difference between these two data sources is largely a matter of quantity. A typical application form (or application blank as they are sometimes known) will request a fairly limited amount of information from candidates. A form such as those shown at the end of chapter 5 will cover items of personal information such as age, marital status, and education and employment history.

It is rare for an application form to ask for much more than rudimentary biographical information. A biographical questionnaire, by contrast, is specifically designed to provide detailed life-history information, often containing a large number of questions. Biographical questionnaires with over 100 items are not unusual (for example, Levine and Zachert, 1951; Baehr and Williams, 1967; Rawls and Rawls, 1968; Owens, 1971).

To some extent the distinction between application forms and biographical questionnaires is rather artificial and is further complicated by the fact that biographical data can be collected in a wide variety of ways including structured interviews.

As noted earlier, studies using biographical data to predict subsequent performance have been remarkably successful (Ghiselli, 1966, 1973; Asher, 1972; Owns 1976). Figure 10.1 compares the results obtained from biodata studies using other personnel selection methods.

As Figure 10.1 shows, biographical data produces consistently good predictions.

An illustrative study involving the use of an application form to collect data is that of McClelland and Rhodes (1969). They investigated the use of biograpical data to predict the job success of hospital

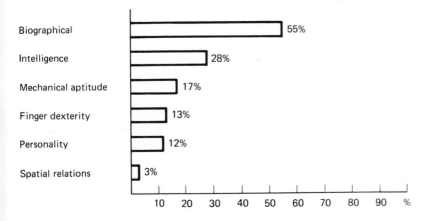

FIGURE 10.1 *A comparison of the validities obtained from biodata and other selection methods, showing validities of 0.5 or higher*

SOURCE Asher (1972).

aides and orderlies. The following biographical information was obtained from application forms:

1. Age
2. Marital status
3. Number of dependents
4. Education in years
5. Health impairment (that is, the absence or presence of any disability – other than spectacles)
6. Average tenure on past jobs
7. Related experience (that is, number of years in previous jobs in related fields)
8. Salary difference between present and last job
9. Restriction on hours available for duty
10. Number of months resident in local area

McClelland and Rhodes also used a well-established personality questionnaire – the Minnesota Multiphasic Personality Inventory (MMPI) – to attempt to predict job success. They found that both types of predictor (that is, the biographical questionnaire and the MMPI) helped to predict job performance. They note (pp. 53–4) that:

> In general the findings of this study are similar to many in which a sampling of biographical data, a personality measure or both, have been used to predict job performance criteria. . . . Biographical items were more important than MMPI scores for predicting composite job performance.

Despite the consistently good validities reported for biodata studies (see Schmitt *et al.* 1984) the method can be criticised in various ways. There are various criticisms and unresolved questions that may be asked concerning biodata, and Owens (1976) provides a thorough review of the relevant material. One of the more important issues concerns the accuracy of biodata. In other words, when people report on their life history and current circumstances, how do we know that the information is accurate? They may be lying and memory may be at fault. As Owens (1976) notes, there is not a great deal of evidence available concerning this question. Mosel and Cozan (1952) checked records of applications for employment and found high agreement between application claims and verifications by past employers on weekly wages, duration of employment and job duties. With one exception all correlations were 0.90 or over. Goldstein (1971) however, produced data suggesting that substantial falsification may occur (see chapter 13).

Another, in many ways more important, problem with the use of biodata has been succinctly summarised by Owens (1976, p. 625):

> Research involving biodata has been subject to more or less constant criticism on the basis that quite good prediction is achieved, but that it is accompanied by modest, if existent, gains in understanding. There has also appeared to be a not unreasonable feeling that research in this area has been somewhat insular, neither seeking nor defining its relationship to the larger body of psychology. Thus Guilford (1959) *has quite properly observed that biodata research has been characterized by an empirical shotgun approach to prediction, largely devoid of both theory and generality.* Similarly, Dunnette (1962) reviewed selected biodata applications to the problem of predicting managerial and executive success and stressed the need for moving beyond simple prediction to a greater emphasis on the finding of causal relationships.

More recent work on biodata, in particular that of Owens and his associates (Owens, 1976; Owens and Schoenfeld, 1979; Neiner and Owens, 1982), has focused on attempts to develop a much more coherent and theoretically sound basis for the use of biodata as a predictor of performance. Owens (1976) points out the intuitively appealing basis on which biodata rests. He argues that in essence biodata provides a measure or indicator of previous behaviour, that is, it provides 'A postmortem view of the development of the individual – an inverted pyramid of many recent and a few remote events the validity of which is limited chiefly by the insight of its author and by the memory and intention of the respondent' (p. 625). He then asserts, as many psychologists before him have asserted, that the best predictor of a person's future behaviour is what he or she has done in the past.

Thus Owens argues that biodata represents not merely a few isolated items of information about a person, but a much richer source of data which, if interpreted sensitively and insightfully, represents an alternative, factually-based, view of a person's life so far, which may be used to make predictions about the person's future life in a rational and coherent way. Current research is focusing on the methods used for collecting biographical data (for example, Eberhardt and Muchinsky, 1982) and on investigating Owen's proposal that biodata can provide a coherent view of individual development over time (for example, Neiner and Owens, 1982).

SELF-ASSESSMENT

Most decisions concerning initial selection are made by personnel specialists and other members of the organisation who are senior to the person assessed. This is clearly sensible in many respects but the person with most knowledge of the applicant – the candidate himself or herself is excluded from the decision-making process. Similarly, the insights of peers might be useful in making predictions but, again, traditionally they are excluded. The purpose of the following section in this chapter is to consider the contribution that self-assessment might make to personnel decisions.

Many reviews of the value of self-assessment in industrial and organisational settings (for example, Thornton, 1980; Reilly and Chao, 1982) conclude that there is little to recommend its use. The criticisms of self-assessments centre on three main issues (see Levine, Flory and Ash, 1977). First, it is expected that people will produce an inflated, that is, lenient picture of their own abilities. Secondly, that people are unable to make accurate or reliable self-assessments. Thirdly, that this leniency and low reliability will lead to poor validity.

Leniency

The evidence available supports the idea that self-assessments are lenient. Ash (1980) for example, found consistent overestimates of typing ability (51.4 words/minute) against a tested mean (39.6 words/minute). In fact, with the notable exception of Heneman (1974), all of the relevant research reviewed by Thornton (1980), Tenpoyr and Oeltjen (1982) and Reilly and Chao (1982) showed consistent overestimates in self-assessment. Despite the evidence confirming the leniency of self-ratings, it should be remembered that leniency effects can also occur in non-self-assessments. Makin and Robertson (1983) argue that the degree of leniency in judgements of self or others will be influenced by the purpose to which the assessments will be put. Despite some agreement concerning the detailed effects of disclosure and other factors, the existing evidence does provide the basis for some generalisations concerning leniency and self-appraisals. Makin and Robertson (1983, p. 22) summarise them as follows:

1. Leniency is common to all ratings, not just self-assessments.
2. Self-raters and other raters show individual differences in the extent to which they exhibit leniency.
3. The amount of leniency is affected by the perceived consequences to the rater whether it be self or another.

Accuracy and Validity

It is possible to assess the accuracy of self-assessments by, for example, comparing self-assessments with the assessments made by other people (see Thornton, 1980).

Such studies have produced mixed results, although most show some relationships between self- and other assessments. These comparisons are usually based on two sets of ratings (for example, a self-rating and a rating by a supervisor), and merely indicate the extent to which the views of two people correspond. The 'acid' test for accuracy of self-assessments involves comparing a self-assessment with some *objective* measure of performance rather than *subjective* ratings.

Some research directly compares self-appraisal with objective performance measures, (for example, De Nisi and Shaw, 1977; Levine, Flory and Ash, 1977; Ekpo-Ufot, 1979; Primoff, 1980). Ash (1980) compared self-assessments with objective measures for various forms of typing ability. The results showed that peoples' self-assessments corresponded more closely with objective assessments when the factor being assessed was straightforward and well understood (for example, simple copy-typing ability, a correlation coefficient of +0.59). For more complex skills (for example, typing tables) the self- and objective assessments corresponded less well (a correlation coefficient of +0.07). It seems clear from this, and some of the other studies mentioned above, that self-assessments may be more accurate for well-understood and familiar aspects of behaviour.

Relatively few studies have examined the value of self-assessments in selection situations. Reilly and Chao (1982) reviewed eight studies, four of which involved attempts to estimate the predictive validity of self-assessments. Reilly and Chao (1982, p. 32) make the following comments:

> Although several studies reported positive results, only three studies included validity coefficients with overall criteria. Based on these limited data (three independent coefficients, total N=545) an average weighted validity of .15 was calculated.

In summary, the value of self-assessment as a formal selection technique appears to be limited. Self-assessments does, however, have a more general role within the selection process. A decision to apply for a job, and a decision to accept a job offer, both involve self-assessment and a comparison of oneself with the requirements and characteristics of the job. One possible means of helping people to make a more accurate assessment of the match between their own characteristics and those of the job is to provide a realistic job preview (RJP). The argument here is that a realistic job preview should provide the basis on which suitable candidates will accept a job offer, while less suitable candidates will turn it down. Research into RJPs (for example, Wanous, 1977) has produced some promising findings, but most recent research (Reilly *et al.* 1981) seems to imply that RJPs are unlikely to be particulary useful as an aid to self-assessment, and in turn self-selection for jobs. However RJPs may have a role to play in transmitting a favourable 'image' of the organisation and as Tenopyr and Oeltjen (1982) suggest, taking discussion of job characteristics out of the employment interview (see chapter 7).

Most of the studies of RJPs make use of 'second-hand' means of transmitting information (for example, film-shows, books, talks or perhaps job visits). It seems likely (see Primoff, 1980) that to make an accurate self-assessment a good first-hand grasp of the nature of the job requirements is needed. One means of providing first-hand job experience involves actually doing the job – for example, a probationary period. This is expensive and time-consuming for both the individual and the organisation. A less expensive and less time-consuming method of previewing a job through experience may be gained with the aid of trainability or work-sample tests (see chapter 9). Indeed, there is some evidence to show that the sort of first-hand job experience provided by these instruments forms a good basis for self-assessment, and in turn self-selection (for example, Downs *et al.* 1978).

PEER-EVALUATION

As far as initial selection to an organisation is concerned peer-evaluation is likely to be of little value. It is clearly impossible for an employer to obtain peer assessments of a candidate who is coming from outside the organisation. For promotion decisions within organisatons peer-evaluations show reasonably high levels of validity (Lewin and Zwany, 1976; Reilly and Chao, 1982) though there are many problems concerning, for instance, the number of people and friendship patterns with the peer group. Kane and Lawler (1978) review some of the techniques that can be used for peer-evaluation. As Reilly and Chao point out, perhaps the crucial factor in the success of a peer-evaluation system is acceptance of the system by participants. Cederblom and Lounsbury (1980) found that 59 per cent of participants in such a system favoured discontinuation.

Taken overall, the potential of self- and peer-assessments as formal selection instruments for new entrants to organisations seems fairly small. Such assessments may have more potential for promotion nd other personnel development and placement decisions.

REFERENCES

In his review of the literature on reference reports in personnel selection, Muchinsky (1979) points out that 'Of all the more commonly used personnel selection devices, reference reports are the most underresearched' (p. 287). Muchinsky cites four studies examining the use of reference reports by organisations and concludes that over the 80 per cent of the respondents requested reference checks as part of their selection procedures. Whilst these studies show that references are frequently *requested* by organisations, they do not show whether they are *used* by organisations when making personnel selection decisions. References might be used to fulfil at least two different functions. First, they can be used to confirm information provided by the applicant. Secondly, they can be used to obtain views on the previous work performance or personal characteristics of the applicant. In the writers' experience some organisations take up references only *after* an employment offer has been made. References taken at this stage are used (probably) to confirm self-report information and as a last-minute check that the candidate is not grossly unsuitable. References taken up at this stage are clearly not being used to influence initial selection decisions. Muchinsky suggests that references should be used, if they are used at all, to identify a small proportion of people who should not be considered further. Many organisations do, of course, take up references early in the selection process. Reference checks are often elicited from previous employers but many other sources are used as referees and reference requests take a variety of forms, varying from a pre-prepared form (Table 10.1) to an open-ended invitation to provide information about the candidate.

TABLE 10.1   *A reference request form and letter*

Dear Sir,

The person named above has applied to this Company for employment and he has given his permission to ask you, as one of his previous employers, for a reference.

Since we provide many references ourselves, we know the time and trouble it takes to produce an accurate reference. However, we would greatly appreciate answers to the following questions. If at all possible we would like the form to be completed by the applicant's immediate superior.

We enclose a stamped addressed envelope and your answers will be treated in strict confidence

Yours sincerely,

Reference Form   Please return this form to

Not later than:

1. When did the applicant start employment with you?

2. What was the final Job Title?

3. What was the final salary?

4. Were there any breaks in employment?

5. What were the reasons for leaving?

_____

6. How satisfactory was the applicant in
   the following respects (please underline the appropriate answers)

– general conduct	excellent	good	average	poor	bad
– attendance	excellent	good	average	poor	bad
– timekeeping	excellent	good	average	poor	bad
– sobriety	excellent	good	average	poor	bad
– attitude to authority	excellent	good	average	poor	bad

_____

7. Was general health good?
   Is he/she registered disabled?

_____

8. Did you receive a reference for the
   applicant, if so who gave it?

_____

9. Would you employ the applicant again?   certainly   probably   possibly   no

_____

Any other remarks:

Date _____ Signature _____

Position _____

As far as the validity of references is concerned, the evidence is fairly consistent but not very exciting. Muchinsky (1979) concludes that 'Most of the available evidence on reference reports suggests that they are not particularly valuable as selection devices, although some notable exceptions have been reported' (p. 296). Reilly and Chao (1982) reviewed seven different studies examining the validity of references and show that validity coefficients greater than $+0.2$ are rare and they calculated that the average validity coefficient for the studies considered was $+0.14$.

In addition to fairly low validity coefficients there is a number of other drawbacks associated with the use of references for selection purposes. Like self-assessments, references appear to be prone to leniency errors. Browing (1968), for example, used a rating scale to obtain information and found that all of the mean ratings obtained were above 3 on a 4-point scale.

Obtaining references may also be a problem; Mosel and Goheen, for example, report a response rate of 56 per cent. Although Carroll and Nash (1972) eventually obtained a return rate of 85 per cent, a previous effort produced a return of only 35 per cent. Several practical questions concerning the collection and use of references are also important and, although some guidance can be found in the existing literature, it is clear that more research is needed before definitive answers are available. Mehrabian (1965) and Wiens *et al.* (1969) have suggested that there is a link between the referee's attitute to the candidate and the length of a reference. In a simulation study Wiens *et al.* found a difference in length of reference for 'liked' and 'disliked' candidates. Referees who 'liked' a candidate tended to write longer references. The differences in length were still apparent when specific instructions, 'You are to discuss his (her) character, intelligence, ability and perseverance at work' (p. 265) were given.

Other practical questions are: whether previous employers provide more valid references than other referees, the form in which references should be collected, and how the resulting data is scored or interpreted. Most research studies focus on references obtained from previous employers. Although it seems sensible to expect employers' references to be more soundly based, there is little evidence to support this expectation.

References can be obtained using an open-ended format, or as seems more common in research on references, a predetermined format is used such as, ratings on various dimensions (Browning, 1968), forced-choice questionnaire format (Carroll and Nash, 1972) or a checklist. It is also possible to use telephone rather than written reference checks. Again clear evidence on the superiority of one form of reference over another is not yet available.

After reviewing much of the literature Reilly and Chao conclude that 'The reference check has relatively low validity in employment settings. Even if validity were higher, the utility of reference checks would seem to be limited, because of low reliability, leniency error and poor response rates by previous employers.' (p. 38).

GRAPHOLOGY

Most of us feel that we are able to recognise our own handwriting and also the handwriting of close friends and relatives, suggesting that there is something individualistic and different about each person's handwriting. Perhaps, like finger prints, no two people's handwriting is the same. It is a relatively small step from this to suggest that it might be possible to draw inferences about someone's personal characteristics by examining his or her handwriting. Graphology, that is, handwriting analysis, is the examination of the features of handwriting in which the anlayst draw inferences about the writer. It has been estimated that 85 per cent of Continental European companies use graphology to help with personnel selection decisions (Sharma and Vardhan, 1975). Although usage in the United States and the UK is probably less, more than 3000 American films currently retain handwriting analysts as personnel consultants (reported in Klimoski and Rafaeli, 1983).

Despite its widespread popularity, the evidence for the predictive validity of handwriting analysis in personnel selection (and other) situations is not great.

A starting point in considering the value of handwriting in personnel selection is to examine the extent to which handwriting varies or remains stable. Several studies (see Harvey, 1934; Walner, 1975) have been conducted to assess the consistency of script features and by and large the evidence suggests that handwriting is stable over time; although there is also evidence to suggest that in certain circumstances handwriting does vary. Loewenthal (1975), for example, found that the handwriting of a group of students differed from normal when they were told to produce an example of their 'best' handwriting as if they were applying for a job. Downey (1919) observed variations in handwriting which seem to show some links with variations in mood and health. Predictably, perhaps, Wing and Baddely (1978) found reliable variations in handwriting after the consumption of alcohol! Loewenthal (1975) has demonstrated that handwriting can be faked. Students who were asked to fake the handwriting of methodical and original people produced samples that were reliably judged as such. In short then, although it may be possible to fake handwriting and some variations may be caused by situational and emotional factors, it seems that the important features of a person's handwriting are reasonably consistent over time. Loewenthal (1982, p. 91) presents an interesting view on this fundamental consistency:

> In spite of variations handwriting can usually be identified correctly as coming from a particular individual ... There are some people who, sadly, because of disablement, must use mouth or

feet to write with; and yet, regardless of the limb used to guide the pen, a given individual produces writing that is characteristically his. Handwriting is *not so much handwriting as brain-writing*.

Methods of Analysis

Like many others who attempt to assess human characteristics, graphologists do not adopt a single approach, although certain common features of handwriting are recognised as significant by most analysts. Klimoski and Rafaeli (1983) quote Patterson (1976), who identifies 12 features that are typically examined by graphologists including size, slant, width, regularity, pressure, form of connection.

Loewenthal (1982) outlines two major forms of handwriting analysis (graphoanalysis) – the *single feature approach* which involves the examination of specific features (for example, size, letter slant) of handwriting and single aspects of personality, and the *total approach* where several features are combined and related to personality, and an attempt is made to view handwriting as a whole rather than focus on individual features.

Klimoski and Rafaeli (1983) identify three approaches – the *trait approach* and the *Gestalt approach* which seem to correspond with Loewenthal's single feature and total approach respectively, and the *graphoanalysis approach*, founded by Bunker in 1929, which focuses on the study of individual features, but it also emphasises that people must be studied as a whole. Research to examine the validity of handwriting analysis is beset with problems including a lack of detail concerning the training and experience of the analysts involved, lack of information on the approach/method of analysis used, and a lack of control over the type of material used for analysis.

In a particularly well-controlled study, Rafaeli and Klimoski (1983) found that graphologists using the same method of analysis showed some agreement in their analyses of sample scripts and that the agreement was no worse when graphologists using different methods were compared. Klimoski and Rafaeli (1983, p. 195) conclude that 'Although different methods of handwriting analysis are unique, they do represent some unified framework of personality analysis'.

Some graphologists, for example, prefer to work from copied material, others like to use spontaneous script of an autobiographical nature – where the candidates' are asked to write something about themselves. Clearly the *content* of an autobiographical piece of writing may provide information over and above the cues provided in the nature of the handwriting itself. As a previous section in this chapter has shown, autobiographical data can provide a good basis for predicting future behaviour.

Rafaeli and Klimoski (1983) examined the effects that the *content* of the handwriting had on analysis. They asked handwriting experts to examine two types of scripts, 'neutral' descriptions of houses, and 'autobiographical' material written by the people being assessed. Contrary to their predictions, script content had little effect on the graphologists' assessments.

The Validity of Handwriting Analysis

The evidence is rather limited but it implies that handwriting analysis is a reasonably reliable method of assessment and is not influenced by script content or the procedure adopted. The evidence for *validity*, however, provides less encouragement for the graphology enthusiast. Studies reviewed by Klimoski and Rafaeli (1983) provide rather mixed findings – sometimes offering no support for the validity of graphology as a measure of personality (for example, Rosenthal and Lines 1972), and sometimes offering some support (for example, Lemke and Kirchner, 1971).

Studies looking at the validity of graphology in work situations are also ambiguous. Zdep and Weaver 1967 (life assurance agents) and Sonneman and Kerman 1962 (executives), provide some positive findings but Klimoski and Rafaeli (1983) criticise both investigations on methodological grounds.

Other studies (for example, Jansen, 1973) offer no support for handwriting analysis as a predictor of work-related criteria. In Rafaeli and Klimoski's (1983) study practising graphologists were paid to provide assessments of American real estate sales personnel. An objective index of performance and supervisor's ratings were used as criterion measures. The data offered no support for the validity of the graphologists' assessments. Taken overall, the evidence for the validity of handwriting assessment is not great, although it is fair to point out that the available evidence is not extensive.

ASTROLOGY

In March 1984 a national UK newspaper ran a series of articles
examining various aspects of astrology under headlines such as, 'Do
the stars shape our destinies after all?' (*Guardian* 19 March, 1984, p.
7). The articles represented a serious attempt by Professor Alan
Smithers to examine and interpret the statistical links between
astrological factors (for example, date of birth) and other factors such
as occupation, for a sample of one in ten of all 'economically active
persons' from the 1971 census. Correspondence and further articles
in the newspaper after these articles included the following

'In short I suggest that Professor Smither's data shows nothing more
than the random fluctuations of precisely the scale to be expected.'

'Professor Alan Smithers has shown that we will need to look at the
universe very differently from the approach now in vogue.'

Clearly both views cannot be correct!
     Most people have some knowledge of astrology and appreciate that
it involves attempts to relate human behaviour and characteristics to
the position and movements of the stars and planets. To some people
such a notion seems perfectly reasonable – to others it seems quite
ludicrous. Much of the evidence offering support for this fundamental notion is far from clear-cut. What is clear is that no one has
yet provided evidence enabling the notion to be conclusively rejected
or validated.
     Relatively little hard evidence exists on the extent to which
astrology is used for personnel selection (Robertson and Makin, in
press). Some sources provide advice on using astrological techniques
in vocational settings (Luntz, 1962) but little is known about the extent
to which it is used, nor is there much scientific evidence concerning the
extent to which astrological methods can produce valid predictions
relating to a person's work behaviour. Astrology is an ancient
discipline and although much modern astrology differs from traditional ideas many of the fundamental principles date back many centuries.
In essence astrology involves two separate but related acts. First the
astrologer constructs a horoscope (basically a map of the heavens at
the time of birth) and secondly the astrologer interprets the horoscope.
     Whilst individual astrologers might differ on some details, the
procedures for constructing the map appear to be fairly common. The

starting point for the construction of a horoscope is the place, date *and* time of birth of the person concerned. Most people are familiar with the 12 signs of the zodiac and many can also remember their own sign and that of some close friends and relatives.

Unlike the generalised astrological information provided in the popular press, 'serious' astrology involves producing a very specific horoscope for an individual person and taking into account much more than the relevant sign of the zodiac. Various textbooks provide outlines of how the procedure is conducted. Eysenck and Nias (1982) provide an overview and more information is given in Parker and Parker (1975).

Astrology, as a procedure for assessing people, draws on centuries of tradition. The *interpretation* of astrological data, as opposed to the *construction* of astrological charts, involves a subjective, holistic and intuitive act rather than straightforward and systematic inference. The following passages from a committed astrologer (Macleod, 1982) illustrate this:

> Each planet symbolizes a life-principle or energy. A way of gaining a greater understanding of these principles is to study myths, legends and fairy stories across many cultures. The circle containing a dot, which represents the Sun in a horoscope, symbolizes a source of life and vitality, a person's Will to Be, which will manifest itself according to the nature of the sign of the zodiac and the house position within the chart...The astrologer...has to move with the times and with an understanding of the cultural and social background of the individual whose horoscope is being interpreted. The drama of life and the archetypal roles remain the same, but the scenery and the costumes change. The astrological symbols that suggest that a man will become a great warrior, who will have many fearless encounters on the battlefield against opposing tribes, are equally valid symbols when they are found in the chart of a female political leader of this century.

As Macleod (1982, p. 107) also points out:

> The astrologer uses intuition. The chart has been studied and enters the subconscious, where it picks up the rules and structures of astrology acquired by time-consuming study of the tradition. The details are then synthesized by the brain in much the same way as they are synthesized by the computer. However, the

astrologer is now able to leave the mind free to sense the entirety of the chart, the pattern, and the potential within it. Feedback is now dependent upon the unique situation of the astrologer, the consciousness of the astrologer, and the astrologer's act of judgement which requires perception and active imagination. Intuition is used to interpret what cannot be measured by technique alone. Intuition refuses to be pinned down and placed under the microscope so that we can examine how it functions.

In other words she is arguing that astrology may be difficult to investigate with the methods of traditional scientific inquiry. The supporters of various other 'unscientific' pursuits make the same claims. Whilst there may be some validity in such a point of view it is equally fair to state that assertion alone is not enough to demonstrate the validity of a method or procedure. Astrology, like other methods of selection, must be investigated in a way that at least minimises the possible influence of chance factors, self-fulfilling prophesies and other artefacts. Otherwise such approaches will never be taken seriously by scientists.

When carefully-controlled studies of astrology are conducted the results do not provide unequivocal support for the proponents of astrology – on the other hand the evidence is such that many (though by no means all) scientists are prepared at least to suspend judgement for the time being. The most notable source of scientific evidence comes from the work of French psychologist Michel Gauquelin (for example, Gauquelin, 1978, 1980). Gauquelin has conducted extensive work examining the links between various factors (for example, occupation, character, sporting prowess) and astrological characteristics.

Some of Gauquelin's early work concentrated on the links between astrological factors and occupational groups. One early study, for example, used a sample of over 500 eminent French medical practitioners. The results showed that when compared with a control group drawn at random from the electoral register the eminent doctors were more likely to have been born when Mars or Saturn had just risen or just passed the midheaven. Several other positive results have emerged from Gauquelin's work linking ocupations with planetary positions, including, for instance, fairly large samples of successful artists (over 5000) and scientists (over 3500).

Gauquelin has also produced data showing links between personality characteristics and planetary positions. One study (Gauquelin,

Gauquelin and Eysenck, 1979) revealed links between extroversion–introversion and planetary positions at birth. Eysenck and Nias (1982) argue that results linking personality with planetary positions at birth shown that it is personality rather than occupation that is linked with planetary position. The link with successful members of occupational groups occurs because certain personality types tend to be successful in certain occupational areas.

By and large Gauquelin's research is carefully designed and fully documented. A recent review of the available work, including the Gauquelins' work, is provided in Eysenck and Nias (1982). On balance the evidence seems to suggest that there are some statistically significant patterns concerning the relationship between the positions of heavenly bodies and some aspects of human behaviour that are consistent with astrological thought, though many astrological ideas are *not* supported by data. Overall, the work seems to provide some evidence for what Eysenck and Nias (1982) describe as a 'connection between the affairs of man and the position of the planets at the time of birth' (p. 209).

It is also clear that despite the support provided for astrology by Gauquelin's work, most orthodox scientists remain sceptical. Eysenck and Nias (1982) provide a description and evaluation of the reaction of the scientific community to Gauquelin's work.

Despite the availability of some evidence to support astrology it must also be pointed out that even when evidence appears to be strong there may be alternative explanations of the results that do not invoke astrological ideas.

For example, one possible explanation of some of the apparently significant results involves using the idea of a self-fulfilling prophesy. Many people are aware of some of the various supposed links between astrological factors and occupational factors, some even get vocational guidance from astrologers. It is possible that knowledge of astrology (however slight) might influence peoples' occupational choices.

Indeed two studies referred to by Nias (1982) illustrates this point rather well. One study (Mayo, White and Eysenck, 1977) examined the link between the personality characteristic, extroversion – introversion, and signs of the zodiac. According to some astrological predictions people born under odd-numbered signs of the zodiac (for example, Aries, Gemini) should display extrovert characteristics and those born under even-numbered signs (for example, Taurus Cancer) should be more introverted. The results from the research did indeed produce the predicted pattern. Nias (1982), however, reports two other studies where, for people who were less familiar with astrology or did not believe in it, no such relationship was observed. In general, however, it seems unlikely that Gauquelin's research can be dismissed entirely – by this or any other currently available alternative explanation.

Within the specific context of personnel selection one final comment is in order. Even for research where evidence to support astrological ideas has been produced, the magnitude of the observed effect is often rather small and would not provide a basis for particularly powerful predictions of employment success – although the predictive value of astrological data may be quite unique and different from that obtained with other predictors. It is also, of course, true that, if planetary influences on human behaviour are eventually accepted, a significant new phase in our understanding of human behaviour will have been attained.

Part III
Evaluation and Other Aspects

11 Making a Decision and Estimating the Value of Selection

CLINICAL *V.* ACTUARIAL PREDICTION

Whatever methods are employed to obtain data from candidates (interviews, references, and so on), the information must then be used to choose the candidate who will be offered the job. There are many ways of making this choice but they can be divided into two main types – clinical *v.* actuarial.

As its name implies the *clinical method* follows the medical model in which an expert, or at least an experienced practitioner, reviews the available information, and on the basis of their experience and expertise the choice is made. The *actuarial method* follows the model of insurance assessment where various factors are quantified and then put in a formula which predicts the level of risk.

The main question is, which approach is the most accurate? This clinical *v.* actuarial debate has raged for over 20 years. Although the outcome is hard to generalise, the actuarial approach seems to offer the advantages of consistency and accuracy (see Meehl, 1954). Sawyer (1966) provides a more recent comparison of clinical *v.* actuarial prediction and concludes that although clinical prediction, in some studies, could equal the statistical method, there was no case where the clinical method was actually superior. Nevertheless, the clinical approach may be best in extreme situations, because the formulae used by the actuaries are based on samples which contain only a few extreme cases and therefore they produce a less solid base for decisions in special situations.

CLINICAL APPROACHES

Without doubt the clinical method is used far more frequently than the actuarial method, and the decision process often boils down to an intuitive 'gutfeeling' which is left at the end of an interview.

ACTUARIAL APPROACHES

In a very simple situation where there is only one score and only one vacancy, the choice of candidate is straightforward – the applicant with the highest score is offered the job. However, if there is more than one score they must be combined in some way. There are five major methods, the simple method, weighting scores, multiple regression, minimum cut-off points and profile-matching.

Simple Method

Slightly more rigorously, the selector goes through the personnel specification and eliminates those candidates who do not have all the essential characteristics. The surviving candidates are then reconsidered and awarded a grade on, say, a six-point scale for each of the points (essential and desirable) on the personnel specification. The grades are then summed and, other things being equal, the candidate with the highest score is offered the job. In essence the selector using this simple system is using on actuarial approach. Suppose the personnel specification calls for qualities of verbal-intelligence, assertiveness, conscientiousness and imagination – then the implicit formula is:

$$\begin{aligned}\text{predicted} \atop \text{suitability} = {(1 \times \text{verbal: intelligence}) + (1 \times \text{assertiveness}) \atop + (1 \times \text{conscientiousness}) + (1 \times \text{imagination})}\end{aligned}$$

Weighting Scores

The simple method has a number of disadvantages, one of which is the assumption that all items on the personnel specification are equally important. If this is not the case then it is necessary to multiply the important items by an appropriate weighting factor. For example, it might be decided that verbal intelligence and conscientiousness are three times as important as imagination, and assertiveness is twice as important. The formula would then be:

$$\text{predicted suitability} = \frac{(3 \times \text{verbal: intelligence}) + (3 \times \text{conscientiousness})}{+ (2 \times \text{assertiveness}) + (1 \times \text{imagination})}$$

Multiple Regression Approach

In most situations, using judgement, discussion and advice to determine these weights is the only practical course of action. However, under certain circumstances they can be obtained with much greater precision. If follow-up data is available for a sample of 70 or more applicants, it is possible to use the statistical procedure of multiple regression (see Guilford, 1965). In essence, multiple regression tries to establish the exact combination of selection measures which produces the best prediction of a candidate's suitability.

Guion (1965) quotes two studies which compared the efficiency of the multiple regression approach and more simple weighting approaches. Lawshe and Schucker (1959) used three separate samples and found that the average success in identifying hits for the weighting approach was 68 per cent and the average success for the multiple regression approach was 66 per cent. Similarly Trattner (1963), studying a series of 12 different jobs, found that the multiple regression produced slightly poorer estimates than a simple weighting approach. These results are surprising because, in theory, the multiple regression approach should produce optimum solutions. One possible explanation is that, in practice, imperfections in the test and minor violations of statistical assumptions mean that the power of the multiple regression approach is not used to the full. It must also be noted that simple weighting approaches require measures to be on the same scale (for example, sten scale) which has equal variance.

Use of Minimum Cut-off Points

The multiple regression approach is very powerful but it makes an important assumption: deficiencies in some characteristics can be compensated by strengths in other characteristics. For example, it might be that a slightly dull branch manager can make up for his relative stupidity by being extremely conscientious. Undoubtedly, compensation of this kind is possible – but perhaps only up to a point. Perhaps some minimum level of intelligence is needed below which a person cannot cope, no matter how conscientious they are. Companies often use these cut-off points and their use is implicit in the rejection of candidates who do not meet the 'essential' requirements in the personnel specification.

Profile Similarity Approaches

An alternative ploy to both weighting and regression is to look at the profile of scores on the different measures and compare the profile of a standard profile. The technique is particularly useful when hard criteria are not available. The first stage is to establish the standard profile: this is usually achieved by collecting data on a sample of competent present employees and working out the average scores. Each candidate's profile can be superimposed on to the standard profile and an estimate of the difference made. The candidate with the fewest differences is then offered the job. Instead of relying on subjective estimates of this kind it is better to calculate and sum the differences to provide an inverse index of similarity. Since large differences are usually more important than small differences, the customary practice is to square all differences before calculating the total. Figure 11.1 shows some of the complications which can arise with the profile similarity approach. The example is purely hypothetical and uses only four scores, but it shows that correlations should not be used in profile matching. Both Pearson Produce Moment Correlations and Rank Order Correlations are sensitive to shape rather than absolute differences. As the second example in Figure 11.1 shows, it is possible to obtain a high correlation even when massive absolute differences are present. On the other hand, distance measures are insenitive to the shape of a profile. Cattell's *et al.*'s (1970) pattern similarity coefficient produces an index which may be interpreted as an ordinary correlation but it is essentially a distance measure.

The use of data from present employees can produce difficulties. The sample of present employees will usually contain a mixture of good, bad and indifferent workers, thus the average profile may not provide a very good means of selecting out the worst employees. Similarly, the constitution of present workers reflects, in part, the job

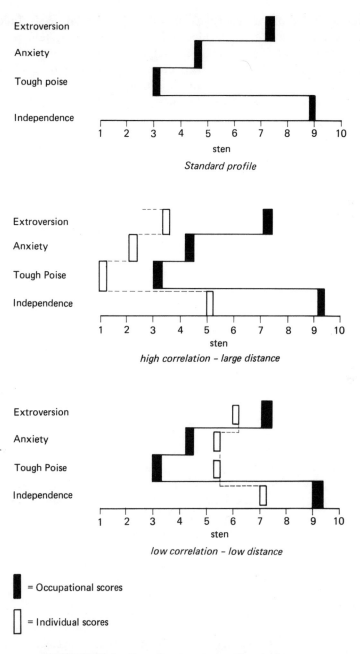

Standard profile

high correlation – large distance

low correlation – low distance

■ = Occupational scores

□ = Individual scores

FIGURE 11.1   *Complications in profile matching*

Evaluation and Other Aspects

requirements of five years ago rather than present-day needs. Indeed, the company may have decided to install a selection system in order to break away from the pattern set by its current employees. Of course, these problems can be overcome by including only 'ideal' or 'recent' employees in the sample which provide the basis for the standard profile but only the very largest organisation will have enough employees to be able to choose in this way.

MULTIPLE VACANCIES FOR ONE JOB

When there is only one vacancy the decision-making is quite straight-forward; the candidate with the highest combined mark derived from simple weighting or multiple regression or profile similarity is offered the job. However, if the company has a steady stream of vacancies and candidates the question becomes: will this particular candidate meet the standard, or should I wait for the next candidate? To answer this type of question with any certainty it will be necessary to compare the predictor mark with the criterion. The process is best demonstrated from an electronics assembly plant making (ULMA) fault detectors. The company administers a short battery of psychological tests and arrives at a score for each applicant. It employs all 20 people who apply for the job of ULMA fault-detector assemblers and follows up their performance six months after they have finished training. The work-study department has previously established that an efficient worker can assemble an average of 100 ULMA fault-detectors per hour. The data on the test scores and the job performance are cast into a scattergram as shown in Figure 11.2. The company finds that half of the applicants are satisfactory and reach efficient worker standard and it is only able to offer permanent positions to 10 of the ULMA assemblers – the remainder will be transferred to other jobs. By drawing a horizontal line at the Experienced Worker Standard (EWS) the firm can then draw a ruler horizontally across the page to determine the appropriate cutting point. In the example shown in Figure 11.2 the company should set a cutting score of 10 on the tests and employ only those who score 10 or more. This type of analysis is called quadrant analysis and it shows that using a cutting score of 10 on these tests would reduce below-standard workers to only 30 per cent in comparison with 50 per cent below standard when there is no selection. In this specific case a test score of 10 would provide an appropriate cutting point. It should be

noted that if the company was in a very favourable position and had
many applicants, it could use an even higher cutting point of, say 14,
and reduce the number of below-standard workers to only 17 per cent
(1 in 6).

An alternative approach is to plot a trend line which has as many
points above as below it (actually, the squares of the distances above
and below the line should cancel out exactly if the trend line is
perfect). The trend line can then be used to establish the test score
which is most likely to produce an EWS of 100. This score can then be
used as a cutting point.

Of course, decisions of this degree of precision can only be made
when there are both quantitative criterion scores and quantitative
predictor scores. In operative jobs this may be possible, but in a
situation where interviews are used for managerial selection, the
process is much more vague.

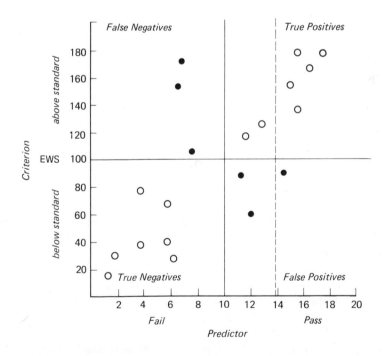

FIGURE 11.2 *Relating predictors to performance using a scattergram*

MULTIPLE VACANCIES FOR SEVERAL JOBS

Although deciding on cutting scores seems complex, it merely scratches the surface of the complexity which faces most selectors. A part of the over-simplification reflects a concentration upon recruitment when the situation actually involves both recruitment and placement. This is particularly true of large organisations. For example, an international accountancy organisation recruits over 100 graduates each year, and subjects them to a two-year management training programme. Of course individuals react to this programme in different ways: some find it challenging, others find the programme frustrating. Some of those who are challenged rise to the occasion, others simply rest on their laurels. Some of those who are frustrated work hard and overcome their frustration, others simple give up. The company needs hard-working, achievement-oriented accountants for those clients who are ambitious, organised and in the ascendancy. The company also needs relaxed, complacent, tolerant accountants for clients who are disorganised, or stolid. The problem is to select the right people and then place them in the appropriate situation. The process is thus much more complex. This complexity is probably best illustrated by Dunnette's (1963b) selection model. Dunnette's model is too imprecise to have a direct practical impact, but it is useful in reminding us that decisions are rarely as straightforward as they seem. A more statistical examination of some of these issues is given by Cronbach and Glesser (1965).

ESTIMATING THE VALUE OF SELECTION

Quadrant Analysis

Quadrant analysis is the simplest method of estimating the utility of a selection system and it is most useful with a predictor that has a clear pass/fail mark and a clear standard for the criterion. Criterion and predictor data are cast into a scattergram as in Figure 11.2 and a vertical line is drawn at the pass/fail mark while a horizontal line is drawn at the criterion standard. Simply counting the number of workers below standard and relating the number to the sample size gives the accuracy of selection without the predictor. In Figure 11.2 the chance level of success is 50 per cent. The next step is to count the number of passes (that is, those to the right of the pass mark). Then, the number to the right of the pass mark *and* above the criterion standard are counted and related to the number of passes. In this example, 70 per cent of those above the pass mark are also satisfactory workers. Consequently the use of the predictor has increased the percentage of acceptable workers by 20 per cent. Often it is more convenient to consider the *percentage improvement in selection* by relating the improvement to the baseline figure (that is, $20/50 \times 100 = 40\%$). It is worthwhile noting that the percentage improvement in selection is strongly influenced by the position of the pass/fail mark.

If the company in the example had many applicants it would be able to raise the pass mark to 14 and only one sixth of candidates would prove unsuccessful at the job and the percentage improvement in selection would be 66 per cent [$33/50 \times 100$). This example clearly demonstrates an important principle in selection: the usefulness of a selection method is strongly influenced by the number of applicants the company can afford to reject. A low *selection ratio* in which only a small proportion of applicants are offered jobs nearly always leads to improved efficiency of selection.

An example of quadrant analysis is given by Sneath *et al.* (1976) in which a large New York underwriting firm administered the Card Punch Operation Aptitude Test (CPOAT) to a sample of 41 operators. At the same time they collected information from their supervisors which enabled the company to classify the operators as above average or below average. The results they obtained is given in Figure 11.3.

Thus, without using the test 53 per cent ($21/40 \times 100$) of the company's workers were satisfactory. But by using the test 75 per cent of the workers were satisfactory ($15/20 \times 100$) and this represents an improvement in selection of 22 per cent. The correlation between test and criteria was 0.71.

Sneath's case study demonstrates that it is not necessary to plot a scattergram in order to calculate the efficiency of a selection device: it is possible to use simple frequency counts. It also demonstrates that the relationship between predictor and criteria can be expressed accurately as a correlation coefficient (however, it should be noted that in many cases the tetrachoric correlation, the *phi* coefficient or the point biserial correlation should be employed in preference to the more usual product moment correlation – see Guilford, 1965, p. 322ff).

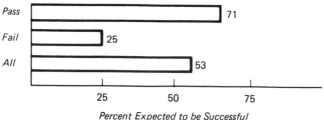

		Below standard	Above standard	Combined
	Pass	6	15	21
Predictor				
	Fail	15	5	20

Empirical Expectancy Chart

FIGURE 11.3   *CPOAT grades and efficiency of selection*
SOURCE Based on Sneath *et al.* (1976).

Expectancy Charts

The data from Sneath's case study can be expressed in another way:
75 per cent of candidates who pass the test can be expected to be
good operators whereas only 25 per cent of candidates who fail the
test can be expected to be good operators. On the basis of the
frequency counts an empirical expectancy chart may be constructed
and used as a basis for subsequent employment decisions. The use of
expectancy charts was pioneered by Lawshe and Bolda (1958) and
Lawshe *et al.* (1958).

Unfortunately, empirical expectancy charts are tedious to construct, they do not make the maximum use of the available data, and
due to sampling errors they sometimes produce anomalous results
(see Albright, Glennon and Smith, 1963, p. 93). These problems led
Lawshe and his co-workers to advocate the use of *theoretical expectancy* charts (which may be constructed from tables contained in
Appendix II). First it is necessary to obtain a correlation coefficient,
second, the selection ratio is computed, and finally, the table is used
to identify the proportion of applicants who pass the selection

procedure who would also be successful in the job. For example, in Sneath's case study a correlation of 0.71 was obtained between the score on the Card Punch Operator Aptitude Test and the evaluation by their superior. The company was satisfied with approximately 50 per cent of its employees. If the company used the test with a selection ratio of 50 per cent, then in theory it could expect that it would be satisfied with 75 per cent of its new employees (which is almost exactly what it obtained in practice). If the company selected only one applicant in five, it could expect to be satisfied with 90 cent of its new employees, whereas if it accepted nine out of ten applicants, it could expect to be satisfied with only 55 per cent of its new employees.

Expectancy Tables and the Dollar Value

Expectancy calculations may be tedious, but they are extremely important in deciding whether a selection system is worthwhile. For example, one pilot study of 100 policemen in a local police force indicated that there was a correlation of 0.33 between scores on the 16PF test and success in the two-year training programme. Seventy per cent of recruits successfully completed the course. To ensure a supply of 150 successful recruits each year, the police force needed to engage 215 cadets.

The question arose, would it be worthwhile to use the 16PF test when the initial set-up costs, including the training of 12 testers and supply of test materials, would be about £9000, and the recurrent annual cost would be about £9000 to screen about 2000 applicants per year? Expectancy tables can be used to answer this type of question. Turning to the section of the table where 70 per cent of employees are considered superior, it is possible to locate the theoretical expectancy for a correlation of 0.30 and a selection ratio of 10 per cent.

Using these parameters, 86 per cent of recruits could be expected to succeed if they were chosen on the basis of the 16PF test. Ony 175 applicants would be needed to ensure 150 qualified police men – a saving of 40 recruits per year.

Each wasted recruit costs £3000 and the saving of 40 recruits represents a total saving of £120 000 per year. In itself this would represent a return of over 600 per cent in the first year. This a conservative estimate since the correlation was rounded down and it was assumed most of the costs such as accommodation and instructors' time could not be deployed elsewhere. Furthermore, there was no correction for attenuation of the criteria or the restriction of range. When these factors are taken into account the saving rises to over £190 000 per year.

Another example of using expectancy tables to estimate the monetary value is given by a financial institution which was dissatisfied with the calibre of its assistant branch managers, and it estimated that in some areas less than 30 per cent of its assistant branch managers were successful. In a pilot study 99 assistant branch managers completed the 16PF test, the AH4 general intelligence test and the Rothwell-Miller Interest Test. Superiors' ratings were used as the criterion. A multiple regression analysis revealed that four scores (verbal intelligence, conscientiousness, assertiveness and imagination) produced a correlation of 0.61 with the supervisor's ratings. Of course, supervisors' ratings are an attenuated criterion, and there was also a small restriction of range since the concurrent method of validation was adopted. When these effects were taken into account the correlation rose to 0.70. After estimating a selection ratio of 0.5 the company was then able to draw up a table (see Table 11.1) for three hypothetical regions.

Thus for all regions, even those which were not initially giving concern, the use of the tests could be expected to reduce the number of unsatisfactory branch manages by 20 per cent. In a typical year the company would avoid hiring 44 unsuitable branch managers. If the costs of hiring an unsatisfactory manager are £2000 in terms of interviewers' and supervisors' time, training and salary costs of the recruit, the potential saving to the company is about £88 000 per year. The costs of installing the system would be about £3000 and the recurrent cost would be about £3000. Thus, even with the conservative estimates of the cost of hiring an unsatisfactory branch manager, the system should yield a return of about 1500 per cent.

TABLE 11.1   *Theoretical expectations of branch manager success*

Region	% of present em- ployees OK	% expected OK after testing	% Improvement
A	30	51	22
B	50	75	25
C	70	91	21

Calculations of this kind are clearly useful in making decisions whether to install a selection system. In order to make these calculations four pieces of information are needed and they are highlighted in Table 11.2.

Limitations of Expectancy Tables

The use of expectancy tables in computing the dollar value of any selection system provides an acceptable basis for most decisions and is the limit of what can be attained in most situations. However the approach has its limitations and the tables usually produce a conservative estimate of the value of a selection system.

The expectancy tables oversimplify the situation by dividing employees into successful and non-successful groups and a great deal of information is wasted by assuming that all unsuccessful recruits are worthless and that all successful recruits are equally productive. In fact there is often a wide range of productivity even in successful recruits. Another important disadvantage is the arbitrary nature of the decision to draw the line between success and failure. This

TABLE 11.2 *Information needed to calculate utility of selection*

1. *Validity of the selection device* – usually expressed in terms of a correlation coefficient. Generally, as validity increases, the utility of selection increases.

2. *Selection ratio* – the number of successful applicants divided by the total number of applicants. For example, if a firm interviewed 10 people and hired 9, the selection ratio would be 0.9. Generally, the lower the selection ratio, the greater the utility of selection. Even devices with low correlations of 0.2 can be useful when the selection ratio is less than 0.1

3. *Ratio of good performance to poor performance* – generally, selection methods are not much use when everyone can produce the same level of output. However, they are very useful when there is a vast difference between workers. As a rule of thumb, the best 15% of workers will produce 80% more of their labour costs than the poorest 15% (that is, the standard deviation of worker performance is usually about 40% of their labour costs).

4. The *number* of people hired per year and the average *length of service*.

decision has a strong influence on the final dollar value. For example, suppose an employer uses a selection device with a validity of 0.5 and a selection ratio of 0.2. If one manager judges that 50 per cent of employees are satisfactory, then the percentage improvement in selection will be 56 per cent (28/50). On the other hand, if another manager feels that only 30 per cent of employees are satisfactory the percentage improvement is 93 per cent (28/30).

Advanced Methods of Calculating Dollar Value

Naylor–Shine Table and Jarratt's Table

Naylor and Shine (1965) attempted to overcome these difficulties by presenting a new set of tables in which performance was assumed to be continuous and they calculated the percentage improvement in productivity for different combinations of validity, selection ratio and spread of performance. Ghiselli and Brown (1955) attempted to simplify the use of the tables by devising the nomograph shown in Figure 11.4.

In order to use the nomograph the selection ratio is located on the bottom axis and a line is projected up to the appropriate validity coefficient. The line is then projected horizontally to the scale giving the appropriate ratio of best to poorest worker and the percentage gain obtained.

Jarratt's (1948) table is slightly more complex since it requires knowledge of the standard deviation and the mean productivity of workers.

Both methods share several advantages: they are more precise and they avoid the often arbitrary decision about who is successful and who is unsuccessful by acknowledging the fact that productivity is a continuum rather than a dichotomy. A major disadvantage is that objective indices of productivity are not available for many jobs. But perhaps the main disadvantage of both the Naylor–Shine and Jarratt tables is that they finish just one stop short of the terminus. They do not calculate the monetary value of a selection system. Whilst percentage improvement in efficiency is much more useful in decision-making than the usual jargon of psychologists (correlations, t statistics, F statistics, and so on), most managers are used to making decisions based upon money estimates.

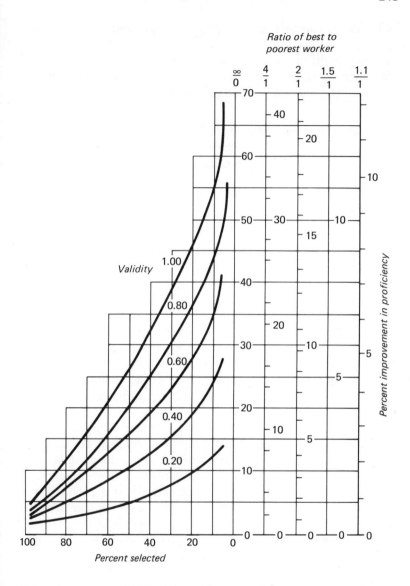

FIGURE 11.4   *Ghiselli-Brown nomograph for estimating improvement*
in productivity from selection

SOURCE   Ghiselli and Brown (1955).

Schmidt and Hunter's Decision Theoretic Equations

Building upon the work of earlier pioneers, Schmidt, Hunter and Pearlman (1982) provide equations which yield a direct measure of the monetary value of a selection system:

monetary value = average length of service of employees (years)
        × difference in job performance between selected
        v. non-selected employees (expressed as a z
        score)
        × the standard deviation of job performance in
        dollars of the unselected group

To obtain the net monetary value per employee it is then necessary to subtract the cost of the selecting of each individual. To establish the savings of the selection system for the company as a whole, it is then necessary to multiply the cost per individual by the number of those who will be selected. The formula, though simple, presents two major problems: it requires estimates of the average difference in performance between the selected group and the non-selected group expressed as a z score; and it requires an estimate of the standard deviation of the monetary value of non-selected employees.

In theory the first problem is relatively easy to overcome. Samples of selected and non-selected employees can be obtained and the average production for each group, together with the standard deviation of the unselected group can be calculated. The difference between the two averages is then divided by the standard deviation. In practice, however, it is almost impossible to convince employers of the need for this kind of study. Alternatively, it is probably more convenient to compute the difference from a correlation coefficient and using a slightly different formula (see Appendix I).

The second problem of estimating the standard deviation of the monetary value of unselected employees seemed difficult and almost intractable. Only a small number of studies have attempted the calculation and the procedure proved expensive and yielded estimates of uncertain accuracy. Recently, however, Hunter and Schmidt (1982) adopted a new approach. They attempted to estimate the worth of an individual to an organisation by asking supervisors to estimate the monetary value of the average employee – perhaps by estimating the cost of having an outside firm provide the products and services. They also asked supervisors to rate the value of a poor employee (15th percentile), and average employee (50th percentile) and a good employee (85th percentile). Hunter and Schmidt found that supervisors had little difficulty in making these judgements. Since the 85th and 15th percentile lie one standard deviation either side of the mean, it is a simple matter to calculate estimates of the standard deviation of the jobs and insert it into the appropriate formula. As a very general rule of thumb, Schmidt suggests that the standard deviation of the dollar value of employees is about 40 per cent of their wages.

Using these techniques Hunter and Schmidt attempted to assess the dollar value of using the Programmer Aptitude Test to select 600 computer programmers per year. A saving of at least $5.6 million was indicated. Bravely, Hunter and Schmidt went on to extrapolate these findings to the employment of programmers in the whole USA and concluded that, under the most conservative assumptions, a saving of $93 million is possible. They suggest that such a high level of gain is not atypical and that new selection procedures could save $600 per checkout clerk, $540 per adding-machine operative, $348 per production worker and $1020 per clerical worker, and $424 per nursing aid. Independent corroboration is offered by Arnold *et al.* (1982), who used a simple measure of strength, an arm dynamometer, to predict the productivity of steelworkers at Armco Inc. and the test had an average utility of $5000 per year for each employee selected.

During the fiscal year of 1979 the company hired 1853 entry-level workers; the average tenure of a new hire in the labour pool is about one year. Based on this information, the estimated yearly utility of the test would be £9.1 million.

It is apposite to finish this chapter with two quotations which underline the importance of choosing the correct method of assessing the utility of a selection device:

> In the past, the value of selection procedures has usually been estimated using statistics which do not directly convey economic value. These statistics include the validity coefficient, the increase in the percentage of 'successful' workers, expectancy tables, regression of job performance measures on test scores, etc. In general, organizational decision makers are less able to evaluate these statistics than statements made in terms of dollars. The

ability to state the value of selection methods in dollar impact on workforce output is, therefore, a powerful new tool for personnel psychologists. (Schmidt *et al.* 1982)

and that

Empirical studies that are available indicate much higher dollar values than psychologists have expected. (Hunter and Schmidt, 1982)

12   Bias in Selection

DISCRIMINATION AND TYPES OF BIAS

Discrimination is the essence of good selection: an employer tries to discriminate between the applicants who will be good workers and those who will be poor workers. Such discrimination is right and proper: it increases organisational efficiency, it conserves society's resources and it saves many individuals the stress and strain of struggling to cope with jobs beyond their capabilities. However, this discrimination is justified only when it is based upon the ability to do the job concerned. In practically all circumstances the decision should not be influenced by the sex, colour, creed or politics of the applicant. If these factors are allowed to influence decisions it can mean that less satisfactory candidates are hired with the inevitable organisational, individual and social consequences and it is usually termed 'bias'.

Bias can be divided into two kinds: direct and indirect. *Direct bias* is the most repugnant: it involves a conscious decision to exclude or impede applicants, usually on the grounds of race or sex. Direct bias is unethical and usually illegal and yet it is often hard to eradicate. Probably the best defence is for an organiation to have a widely-known and clearly-stated equal opportunities policy. Then the company should be prepared to take, and be seen to take, disciplinary action if, after proper investigation, an employee is shown to have violated the policy. Formally, two conditions apply when direct bias has occurred: the treatment is less favourable for the minority group; the reason for this less favourable treatment is the membership of the minority group.

Indirect bias is probably less repugnant but it can be equally potent in producing unfairness and injustice. Indirect bias is usually unintentional and arises when all groups are treated similarly but the effect is unfavourable to one particular group.

Sources of Indirect Bias

Indirect bias may arise in *job advertising*. For example, a company may have genuine equal opportunity policy but, by oversight, it may only advertise its vacancies in newspapers, magazines and media which are read exclusively by the white population. *Personnel specifications* are another possible source of bias because it is possible to include requirements which exclude large proportions of minority groups. However, such requirements are permissible only if they are necessary to the performance of the job. Pearn (undated) provides the following examples:

> An interesting case arose in the USA in the selection of police officers in which the height requirement effectively eliminating most female applicants. A job analysis was undertaken to determine the justifiability of the requirement. The study revealed that police offers had to be tall enough to fire the revolver across the roof of a police car ... As a result the minimum height requirement was lowered, and the proportion of women able to comply became greater. Because women are, on average, shorter than men, a smaller proportion could comply, even with the reduced requirement. However, the new height requirement was clearly and demonstrably job related and is within the law despite a degree of disproportionate impact against women.

Thus the touchstone for an unbiased requirement in a personnel specification is the requirement of the job itself. Any requirement which is discriminatory, must be job related. A third source of bias is the *procedure used to select* among the applicants who present themselves. So much attention has been given to this source of bias that it deserves a section of its own.

TYPES OF EVIDENCE OF BIASED SELECTION PROCEDURES

In spite of the fact that most people wish to abandon selection procedures which are biased, there is far less agreement upon what constitutes evidence of bias. Six main types of evidence may be offered:

1. Comments by unsuccessful candidates
2. Proportions engaged
3. Expert opinion
4. Experimental evidence
5. Internal consistency
6. Comparisons with subsequent performance

Comments by Unsuccessful Candidates

A great many, possibly the majority, of rejected candidates feel that they have been treated unfairly. Undoubtedly some of these candidates have received a poor deal. Undoubtedly, many of the other accusations are unjustified and arise from two major reasons. First, *rejected candidates may rationalise their experience* in order to maintain their self-pride. A second reason why the claims of rejected candidates need careful scrutiny is that *they often assume that everyone else's interviews are perfect*. Rejected candidates often support their claims of bias by pointing to inadequacies in the selection procedure such as interviewers who are inattentive. Whilst these allegations may be true, they do not amount to bias. Very few interviews are perfect. The interviews of successful candidates may be equally bizarre.

Thus, the accusations of rejected candidates provide very poor evidence of bias. Generally, action can only be taken where the occurrence of a specific and relevant irregularity is corroborated by independent evidence.

Proportions Engaged

Sometimes the proportions of majority and minority groups among successful applicants is put forward as evidence of bias. For example, if a company advertises for steelworkers and ultimately makes offers of employment to 90 men and only 10 women, this could be seen as bias since about 40 per cent of the workforce are women and the low proportion of engagements is the result of bias on the company's behalf. This type of reasoning led to the 'four-fifths rule' which is contained in the Uniform Guidelines (USA Government, 1978) on employee selection procedures. It says: 'A selection rate for any race, sex or ethnic group which is less than four-fifths (or 80 per cent) of the rate for the group with the highest rate will generally be regarded by the Federal enforcement agencies as evidence of adverse impact'. However, in the case of the steel workers, the accusation of bias against women is almost certainly false because very few women chose to apply. Indeed, if only five per cent of the *applicants* were women, an engagement rate of 10 per cent needs to be seen in an entirely different light. These complications are recognised by the Uniform Guidelines which states;

> Greater differences in selection rate may not constitute adverse impact where the differences are based on small numbers and are not statistically significant, or where special recruiting or other programs cause the pool of the minority or female candidates to be atypical of the normal pool of applicants from that group.

In order to meet this kind of situation a fair policy is sometimes defined as a system in which, 'the proportion of minority applicants who apply is similar to the proportion of minority applicants who are accepted'. In other words, if 10 per cent of the applicants were women, 10 per cent of those offered jobs should be women. This line of reasoning is more compelling and any company where the ratio of applicants to employment offers for minority groups is out of balance should look carefully at its selection procedures. Nevertheless, *on its own this type of information does not provide conclusive evidence of bias* because it involves the assumption that the level of ability in minority applicants and the level in the majority applicants is exactly equal.

In the real world local conditions may make this assumption untrue. For example, a light engineering firm in one of the valleys of South Wales expanded its production capacity and advertised for five production controllers. The firm happily accepted that men and women were equally suitable for the job. However, in spite of the fact that over 60 per cent of the applicants wer women, all five of the successful applicants were men.

Contrary to first impressions, in the context of that particular company at that particular time, the hiring decisions were almost certainly unbiased. Two companies in the locality had recently closed. One of them was a large knitwear factory which employed many women but on jobs which had little relevance to engineering trades. The other closure was a small car component factory which employed five male production controllers. Thus local conditions had produced a large pool of women applicants with little experience of the job and a small pool of male applicants with a great deal of experience of the job.

But, what is sauce for the goose is also sauce for the gander. If there are special circumstances where it is fair to employ a higher proportion of majority group applicants there must be circumstances where it is fair to employ a higher proportion of minority group applicants.

Expert Opinion

Another approach to establishing bias in a selection system is to ask experts to scrutinise the methods used and to arrive at an opinion. For example, if an equal opportunities commission suspected that a certain test is biased against a minority group, it could ask an expert psychologist, or even the test author, to look at the questions and pronounce upon their bias.

Past experience has shown that this is a very unsatisfactory type of evidence because experts rarely agree with each other and because their views may not be substantiated by scientific investigation. Little research in this area has involved measures which are used in selection. Efforts have largely concentrated upon the Wechsler Intelligence Scale for Children (WISC). The best documented example concerns Judge Grady's comments during a case in northern Illinois. Judge Grady personally examined the WISC test items and stated:

> It would have been helpful to the court if plaintiffs had produced the actual scoring sheets which would have shown the verbatim responses of the children. The production of that kind of evidence would have been far preferable to these almost casual recollections of (witnesses), the accuracy of which has to be taken on blind faith. (Koh, Abbatiello and McLoughlin, 1983; McLoughlin and Koh, 1982).

Because of the absence of empirical evidence, Judge Grady was forced to rely on his own views of cultural bias and decided that seven items of the WISC may possibly have been so culturally biased against black children, or at least sufficiently suspect, that their use was inappropriate. Judge Grady's views were supported by the test author's comments in a CBS program. Wechsler himself accepted the cultural bias hypothesis in relation to one question about children picking a fight (see Miele, 1979). However, subsequent analyses showed that there are no significant differences between the black and white groups in any of the seven disputed WISC items and indeed, two per cent more black children gave right answers to the 'fight' question, the bias of which was publicly conceded by Wechsler. A slightly different tack was taken by Sandoval and Miile (1980) who asked 100 volunteers to judge the bias of 30 test questions. Previous analysis had shown that half of these items were more difficult for Mexican Americans. The volunteers consisted of 38 blacks, 22 Mexican Americans and 40 Anglo-Americans. The results indicated that the volunteers were not able to determine accurately which items were more difficult for minority students and that there was no significant difference in accuracy between judges of the different ethnic background. Similar results have been reported by Jensen (1979) and Cole (1981), who claimed that judges were not able to determine accurately the cultural bias of items on a standardised test. Jensen's study is particularly interesting. His judges either a had PhD's in psychology or were advanced graduate students working for PhD's in psychology and the judges were black. Yet they too were unable to identify items which contained bias.

Experimental Evidence

Several investigators (for example, Haefner, 1977; McIntyre, Moberg and Posner, 1980) have tried to investigate the potential bias of selection methods using experimental techniques which control as many influences as precisely as possible. Typically, employers are sent applications for jobs. In the simplest form, the applications are identical except that the race and sex of the applicants are changed on some of the forms. Consequently, if the applicants from the majority group are given higher evaluations or receive more invitations for an interview, prejudice and bias are the only possible explanations for the results. In practice, the methods needs to be more complex because employers would be suspicious if they received a number of virtually identical applications. Consequently a series of different applications are used in a systematic way so that differences in the applications cancel each other out.

The method can also be used to investigate bias in interviews. A standard interview script is prepared and video-recorded. In some recordings the interviewee belongs to a minority group and in others the interviewee belongs to a majority group. Volunteers such as students or personnel officers then judge the recordings on the suitability of the applicant. Experimental evidence of this kind can be a powerful method of exploring bias but its results can be regarded as artificial because the judgement process in actual interviews may be quite different to the judgement process when watching videotapes of staged interviews.

Internal Consistency

Where a selection procedure has a number of component parts which can be scored independently, the relationship between the different parts can be used to detect bias. The situation is seen most clearly in tests but the principles apply to other measures. If test items are ranked in order of difficulty, biased items obtain different rankings from samples of majority and minority groups.

Comparison with Subsequent Performance

Probably the best definition of a fair selection system is that 'candidates who are equally likely to be successful in performing the job are equally likely to receive a job offer irrespective of their sex, colour, age or creed'. This implies a direct comparison with score on a selection measure and their competence at the job.

The simplest method of making this comparison is to use *quadrant analysis* as outlined in chapter 11. For example, suppose that a company has vacancies for widget-makers and it interviews 10 men and 10 women. Each interviewee is given a mark out of 10 on the basis of their interview performance and everyone who is interviewed is engaged. Then, three months later, after everyone has finished training and has settled down into the widget-making routine, the company collects data over a period of several weeks and works out the average number of widgets made per hour by each of the recruits. The company can compare interview performance with widget-making ability by drawing a scattergram (see Figure 12.1).

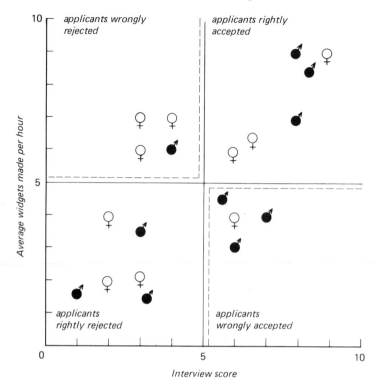

FIGURE 12.1   *Bias in selection using quadrant analysis*

Bias is most clearly shown in the top left and bottom right quadrants. The top left quarter contains the false negatives – the applicants who did badly at the interview but who turned out to be good employees. The bottom right contains the false positives – those who interviewed well but turned out to be poor employees. If selection is biased against women, there will be proportionately more women false negatives and proportionately more men false positives – in other words, selection will underestimate the performance of women and overestimate the performance of men. The diagram shows how the results might appear for a very biased set of interviews. *One* man who was able to do the job would have been wrongly rejected, whereas *three* women would have been wrongly rejected. This imbalance in the ratio of false negatives is direct evidence of sex bias. The fact that *some* women are wrongly rejected is neither here nor there: it is the higher proportion that matters. In practice the situation is more complex. Larger samples are needed and few employers would be prepared to employ everyone who applies: they would only hire those who were successful at the interview! Consequently, attention is usually confined to the false positives – the applicants who are wrongly accepted.

Regression analysis is more accurate and sophisticated than quadrant analysis. Instead of dividing the scattergram into quadrants a trend line can be fitted to the data either by eye or, preferably, by deriving a regression equation. The fairness of the regression line can then be inspected by looking at the distances from the regression line to the individuals on the scattergram. If the measure is fair the distances above the regression line will be cancelled out by the distances below the regression line for both the majority and minority groups.

It should be noted that, to be fair, a measure does not need to be equally accurate for both groups – it is the balance of the inaccuracies which matters (Bartlett and O'Leary, case IV, 1969). The regression approach probably has the widest support. Ledvinka, Markos and Ladd (1982) comment:

> The regression model is the one that seems to be implicit in the federal selection guidelines . . . it has also found some acceptance by the federal courts in title VII cases . . . In fact, most validation research now includes analysis of regression lines for minorities and non-minorities . . . that essentially tests for fairness as defined by the regression model.

In spite of the hegemony of the regression approach, three additional points must be noted. First, the short, non-statistical exposition contained in this chapter inevitably results in a great deal of oversimplification. More authorative expositions are given by Cleary and Hilton, 1968; Bartlett and O'Leary, 1969; Humphreys, 1973; and Jensen, 1974. Secondly, if fairness is defined in terms of equal prediction of ultimate job performance, then the way that the worker's competence is judged can be important. In an objective situation where all that matters is the number of objects a worker produces, there are few complications. But, as the earlier chapter on criteria implies, there are few jobs where this is the case and most validity studies depend upon the judgement of a superior. It is certainly possible for these criterion judgements to be biased either in favour or in detriment to a minority group. For example, Boem (1972) and Bray and Moses (1972) suggest that findings of bias are associated with the use of subjective criteria and that validity differences seldom occur when objective criteria are used. However, this possibility is less likely in the light of Schmidt, Berner and Hunter's (1973) investigation which concluded that when irrelevant factors are controlled, subjective criteria are no more likely to generate instances of single group validity than are more objective criterion measures. Third, when the regression model does find that a selection measure is biased against a minority group, what the are likely consequences? A company should try to use an alternative measure which is known to be fair. In practice it is hard to know in advance whether the new measure will be fairer than the old measure, and the best an organisation can do is to choose a selection system against which bias has not been proved. But the lack of proof may be due to two possibilities: the device may be genuinely more fair, or it may be that the new device is biased but the nature of the device makes bias more difficult to prove. For example, most psychological tests produce a score which can be directly related to performance and its bias can be subjected to statistical analysis.

Interviews on the other hand rarely yield a quantitative score and they may or may not be more biased. It is difficult to subject the vague bias of an interview to statistical analysis. If a measure is fair to the majority group but unfair to minorities another possibility emerges. The organisation could retain the measure for use with the majority group and devise an equally valid but different method for use with the minority group. While this strategem may be scientifical-ly acceptable, in practice its use is doubtful. The obvious differences in treatment of the majority and minority groups would *seem* to be unfair and would undoubtedly attract a great deal of criticism even though the different procedures were introduced with the best intentions. Finally, it should be noted that there are other models which assess bias according to the relationship between scores and performance. Ledvinka *et al.* (1982) identify:

1. Thorndike's (1971) constant ratio model
2. Cole's (1973) conditional probability model
3. the equal impact model

Of these rivals to the regression model, Thorndike's (1971) con-stant ratio model has received the greatest attention. Thorndike holds that in a fair selection procedure the pass marks on a test should be set so that the proportions of applications passing the test should be the same as the proportions of the groups who will satisfy the criteria for good workers. Suppose, for example, a company finds that 30 per cent of its successful workers are from a minority group but, when a single pass mark is used for all groups, only 20 per cent of the successful candidates are from the minority groups. In these situations, Thorndike would advocate lowering the pass mark for the minority group until 30 per cent of those who are successful are from a minority group. This procedure attempts to eliminate unfairness in a situation where the two groups differ much more at the selection stage than in actual performance on the job and it is particularly relevant when the validity of the selection device is low. Thorndike's method is in essence a sophisticated quota system, but like all quota systems it shares the disadvantages that the average performance of those selected is reduced. Hunter and Schmidt (1976) comment:

> If lowered performance is met by increased rates of expulsion and firing, then the institution is relatively unaffected but (1) the quotas are undone and (2) there is considerable anguish for those selected who didn't make it. On the other hand, if the institution tries to adjust to the candidates selected by quotas there may be great cost and inefficiency.

BIAS OF SPECIFIC PREDICTORS

The previous section has sought to establish a sound conceptual basis for the definition of bias so that empirical evidence of bias can be evaluated on a rational basis as follows.

Bias of Tests

Racial Bias of Tests

Many of the investigations under this heading have not been concerned with bias *per se*, but with the rather different topic of *differential validity*. Differential validity exists when a test or other measure is valid for the majority group but not for the minority group and vice-versa. Differential validity is always important from the viewpoint of accurate selection, but it is only partially relevant to bias in selection. There are circumstances where using a test which is valid for whites and not valid for blacks is, racially, quite fair. Bartlett and O'Leary (1969) examine six possible types of differential validity and find four of them to be fair.

Concern about the consequences of differential validity escalated during the 1960s in response to highly publicised court cases such as the Motorola case and psychologists such as Berdie (1971) suggested that tests have been misused because psychologists have failed to take account of the differences in validity that tests have for different populations. Subsequent analysis and research have indicated that such fears of differential validity are confounded. A classic analysis by Boem (1972) examined 160 validity coefficients derived from diverse samples of medical technicians, craftsmen, clerical workers, administrators, welders, and so on, and found only 33 examples of single-group validity and further concluded that these instances of single-group validity appear to be related to the use of ratings as criteria and to the use of small samples. Gael and Grant (1972) examined the validity of tests used for the selection of telephone service representatives and concluded that the validity coefficients for black and white applicants were comparable and that common test standards could be used to evaluate minority and non-minority job applicants. Ruch (1972) also reanalysed studies of differential validity.

The empirical finding that differential validity is rare was extended by conceptual developments. Schmidt and Hunter (1978) point out that many of the studies of differential validity have used very small samples – especially for the minority groups. Consequently, the correlations based on these small samples are very unstable and fluctuate within a wide range. It follows that many of the low correlations for minority groups which give rise to apparent differential validity, are merely random fluctuations of correlations similar to those obtained for the majority group (Schmidt, Berner and Hunter, 1973; Hunter and Schmidt, 1978). In an extremely rigorous analysis of 866 validity studies comparing blacks and whites, involving control over statistical artifacts and a combined sample size of 185 487 data points, Hunter, Schmidt and Hunter (1979) conclude that *there is no apparent evidence of differential validity*. Furthermore, they could find no evidence to support the hypothesis that differential validity is more likely to arise when subjective criteria are used. In order to avoid the artifacts introduced by the use of small samples, investigators should clearly consult tables giving appropriate sample sizes for investigations of this kind (for example, Trattner and O'Leary, 1980).

Unfortunately, the fact that differential validity rarely exists does not completely settle the question of racial bias in tests. Validity coefficients rely essentially upon correlations and correlations merely indicate that the pattern of the results are similar: there may be absolute differences. Since the absence of differential validity can co-exist with certain types of bias, alternative types of evidence must be considered.

Earlier in this chapter, it was noted that the internal consistency of a test can be used as evidence of bias. Jensen (1977) undertook an internal consistency analysis of the Wonderlic Personnel Test, which is used in industry as a measure of intelligence. He compared the rank order of the questions of the test, according to the percentage of each group passing each question, the assumption being that if some of the items were unfair to blacks, they would appear much lower down the list. On the basis of the results he concluded that the Wonderlic shows very little evidence of cultural bias.

Probably the best type of evidence of bias is to regress test scores against criterion data. A number of studies have employed this strategy. Ruch (1972) re-analysed 20 validity studies to check regression coefficients for blacks and whites and he found that 64 per cent of the regressions did not show any significant differences compared with the 86 per cent (or slightly less) which would be expected to be free from significant differences by chance alone. A re-analysis by Jensen (1980) indicated that there was rarely any difference in either the slope or the standard error of the regression but there was a significant and consistent bias for the intercepts. He goes on to note that the white intercept is usually higher than that for blacks and consequently if the regression equation for whites is used to predict the criterion measure for blacks, the average performance of the blacks will be overpredicted.

A landmark study was conducted by Campbell *et al.* (1973). The six-year study involved 1400 government workers employed in jobs where there were objective criteria and sufficient numbers of blacks to provide adequate samples. Again it was found that the minority group's performance is overpredicted when the formulae for a majority group is used. These are not isolated results. Similar findings have also been obtained by Guinn, Tupes and Alley (1970); Foley (1971) and Thomas (1975). In a slightly different context of college selection Linn (1973) reviewed the regressions equations used for selection in 22 racially-integrated colleges. He found that the college performance of blacks was overpredicted in 18 cases and in no college was their performance underpredicted.

Sex Bias of Tests

There is much less information concerning the sex bias of tests. In terms of differential *validity* it has been consistently found that validity coefficients for women are nearly always slightly higher than the validity coefficients for men. Initially this finding emerged from studies in educational settings (for example, Seashore, 1962; Stanley, 1967). More recently, Schmitt, Mellon and Bylenga (1978) collected 6219 validity pairs which had been published in three leading journals. Their analysis supported the earlier contention that the validity coefficients of females were higher than those for males but the differences were small. The analysis permitted an examination of coefficients collected in employment settings rather than educational settings. In employment settings, however, it was found that the validity coefficients of males tended to be higher by 0.038. Of course, this difference is very small and may be an artifact of small sample sizes in the 135 studies including in the sub-analysis.

Arnold *et al.* (1982) used physical tests such as lifting 34kg bags, shovelling slag, climbing on a ladder and carrying 23kg bags to predict success as steelworkers. Again, they found higher validities for females. They also undertook a *regression analysis* and noted that a combined regression line would result in a slight bias against men. Few other examples of a regression analysis of sex bias are available but a study by Bickel, Hammel and O'Connell (1975) showed that, contrary to first impressions, there was a small but statistically significant selection bias *in favour of women* at the University of California in Berkeley.

Tests and Bias against Older or Handicapped People

Very little research has been conducted into the age bias of tests even though a prima-facie case could be made out that older applicants would produce lower performance in tests than on job performance. The situation concerning bias against handicapped people is even more confused since so much would depend upon the nature of the handicap. For example, there seems no reason why intelligence tests should be biased against epileptics, but they may be biased against people with defective vision or motor co-ordination. Consequently, separate studies would be needed for each type of handicap and the difficulties in obtaining adequate samples are quite formidable.

Bias of Interviews and Application Blanks

Interviews are essentially interactive occasions which result in subjective judgements about an applicant's suitability. In theory interviews could be more prone to conscious and subconscious bias than tests. In practice, findings concerning interview bias are not easily organised into a logical sequence. Although a regression approach is technically feasible – the regression approach has not been widely used. Since interview judgements are usually global judgements, the internal consistency approach is not possible and most investigators have, therefore, been forced to use the experimental approach.

In a typical investigation, standard descriptions of candidates are produced. Sometimes they are given a black identity, sometimes a male identity and sometimes a female identity. They are then mailed to a potential employer and differences in the responses are noted. Because the descriptions are standard except for the racial and sex identity, any differences which emerge are evidence of bias. In practice, the methodology is often more complicated in order to ensure that the descriptions are equivalent and to ensure that employers do not detect the purpose of the applications. Often student volunteers are used as judges instead of actual employers. More recently, specially prepared videotapes of interviews have been used rather than relying upon written resumes. This type of methodology has two main disadvantages. First, the artificial nature of the studies might produce results which are inaccurate, and second, it is not entirely clear whether interviews or applications blanks are being examined for evidence of bias.

Racial Bias of Interviews and Application Blanks

Reilly and Chao (1982) attempted to bring together evidence of bias in interviews and application blanks. They indicate that decisions based on biodata could be expected to be biased because many personal history and background data are related to gender, age and race. Moreover, the choice of items for a selection system using biodata, might favour items which are valid but work at the direct expense of minority groups. Pace and Schoenfeldt (1977) found, for example, that having a Detroit address was negatively correlated with a certain criterion. But, since more blacks lived in the city than in the suburbs, this particular item was likely to have had an adverse impact. However, after reviewing 11 studies of application blanks, Reilly and Chao (1982) conclude that where two groups differ only slightly in their performance on criteria, biodata may result in minimal adverse impact.

Interviews might also be expected to give rise to bias since the subjective impressions of the interviewer are often decisive. After reviewing 12 studies Reilly and Chao conclude, 'Nor is there any evidence that interviews will have less adverse impact than tests.'

Probably the best study investigating the bias of résumés is by McIntyre *et al.* (1980). They mailed résumés to a carefully constructed sample of companies. They then compared responses and found 86 instances of black favouritism and 52 instances of white favouritism. In other words, there was evidence of bias in favour of black applicants. More detailed analysis indicated that black applicants are the beneficiary of favouritism in every region of the USA except the West, in every job category sampled except those applying for electrical engineering positions and in organisations of all sizes sampled. This is not an isolated result. Other investigators (Wexley and Nemeroff, 1974; Rand and Wexley, 1975; and Haefner, 1977) have found little evidence of unfavourable evaluations being given to black candidates. Newman (1978) found a definite trend for larger companies to discriminate in favour of blacks.

Sex Bias of Interviews and Application Blanks

There is fairly strong evidence that interviews and application blanks can be used in a way that is biased against women (Reilly and Chao, 1982). A review by Arvey (1979) showed that there is a consistent tendency for females to be given lower evaluations then men even when they have similar or identical qualifications. This is particularly true when the jobs are considered to be masculine in nature. Haefner (1977) showed that males tended to be given half a grade more on a five-point grading scale. McIntyre *et al.* (1980) also found that employers preferred male applicants over females and on average took 2.6 days longer to reply to speculative applications made by women.

Interviews differ from most other methods of selection because physical attractiveness may be taken into account. Heilman and Saruwatari (1979) and Heilman (1980) investigated the possible bias of attractiveness by asking 45 college students to evaluate application forms and photographs of men and women applicants for either a clerical or management position. Male candidates who were 'attractive' always tended to obtain higher evaluations, but with female candidates the situation was more complex. When attractive women were applying for clerical jobs, they obtained higher ratings, but when attractive women were applying for managerial jobs, they obtained lower ratings than the unattractive women. There is evidence that the sex bias is strongly influenced by the context – especially the proportion of women applicants. Heilman (1980) suggests that when less than 25 per cent of the applicants were women, there is a greater level of bias against women. A further contextual factor is the type of interviewer. It is surprising that no authoritative study could be located which attempted to establish whether female interviewers also give lower ratings to female interviewees. A final contextual influence is the personality of the interviewer. Work by Simas and McCarrey (1979) suggests that 'high authoritarian' selectors were more likely to offer jobs to men, and this was true for both male and female personnel officers.

Age and Handicap Bias of Interviews

The age bias of the interview and application blank has received relatively little attention, but from the material available there appears to be a strong, pervasive bias against older workers. Haefner (1977), using a set of carefully controlled stimuli, compared the racial, sex and age bias of 286 employers in Illinois. He found that the age bias was roughly the same size as the sex bias (half a scale point on a five-point scale), and whilst this bias would not make much difference to the evaluations of highly competent applicants, it could make a substantial difference to barely competent applicants. Rosen and Jerdee (1976) examined the stereotypes of undergraduate students towards 60-year-old workers and found that they were rated lower on performance capacity and potential for development, but higher on stability.

There is also a paucity of information concerning bias against handicapped people. Arvey's (1979) review supported the notion that handicapped applicants are usually given credit for higher motivation but they are less likely to be given job offers. Stone and Sawatzki (1980) produced taped interviews of applicants who had a psychiatric disability or a physical disability or no disability, and applicants who had had two nervous breakdowns were less likely to be offered jobs.

Bias of Peer Evaluations

Reilly and Chao (1982) could locate no studies specifically relating to the fairness of peer evaluations. However, they found some studies concerning the average ratings given by peers to different ethnic groups. As we have seen earlier in this chapter, a difference in average scores does not necessarily imply bias. Two points emerge from the studies. First, special training programmes and situations may reduce or perhaps even eliminate racial prejudice. However racial bias is generally to be expected. Secondly, bias in peer evaluations can work both ways. Members of a given race tend to evaluate their same race peers higher.

Amazingly there appears to be no evidence concerning the potential sex bias involved in peer ratings.

Bias of Self-Assessment

The general tendency of the evidence collected by Reilly and Chao is that blacks tend to give themselves higher ratings than whites, but these differences were not always significant. However, one study found that the majority group tended to give themselves higher ratings on typing ability and that these estimates were more valid than the lower estimates of the minority group.

Bias of References

References, like interview judgements, offer a great deal of scope for both direct and indirect bias, but Reilly and Chao could only find one empirical investigation of the phenomena. They report that 1.9 per cent of black applicants received negative references compared to 0.9% of white applicants who received negative references. Because the sample sizes were large, these differences were statistically significant, but the practical significance was negligable since the acceptance rate for blacks was 99 per cent the acceptance rate for whites. In terms of predictive validity reference checks were marginally valid for both black and white groups.

WIDER ASPECTS OF AFFIRMATIVE ACTION

It is appropriate at the end of a chapter on bias in selection to widen the focus and consider additional aspects of affirmative action.

The first wider issue concerns the influence of company policy. Rosen and Merich (1979) asked 78 administrators in local government to evaluate résumés of male and female applicants and to suggest appropriate starting salaries. Two organisational policies were simulated, a strong commitment to fair employment and, mere lip service to equal opportunities. The results indicated that the strength of the policy made little difference to general preferences but a strong policy resulted in a reduction of the starting salaries thought appropriate for females.

The second wider issue concerns the cost of affirmative action. Usually the costs to an organisation and its customers are difficult to quantify. However, Arnold *et al.* (1982) attempted to calculate the cost of a policy of ensuring that 20 per cent of employment offers for steelworkers were made to women. Using the techniques outlined in the chapter on utility, they were able to estimate that the cost of the policy was approximately $2.8 million during one fiscal year. The calculations serve to remind us that affirmative action policies have their costs. Unfortunately the calculations do not provide an answer to the controversy surrounding affirmative action because the benefits remain unquantified.

The final point concerns the impact of affirmative action upon individuals. Chacko (1982) investigated the perceptions of 55 women managers. The results showed that women who perceived they had been selected because of their sex had less organisational commitment, less satisfaction with their work, with supervisors, and their co-workers, and experienced more role conflict and ambiguity than women who felt that sex was not an important factor in their selection.

13   Some Remaining Issues

So far this book has dealt with a variety of issues within the general area of personnel selection. Previous chapters have provided information on the preparatory work needed for any efficient selection system, including conducting job analyses, the preparation of personnel specifications and the development of criterion measures. Different types of selection methods (for example, interviews and psychological tests) have also been dealt with in some detail and general issues such as the validity, utility and fairness of selection procedures have been covered.

Some concepts and research findings of prime relevance to the selection process have not yet been covered at an appropriate level of detail, either because they are of general relevance to the whole process of selection or because they require an understanding of material covered in earlier chapters. This chapter deals with these remaining issues.

ASSESSMENT CENTRES

In almost all selection situations it is not sensible to base decisions on one predictor only (for example, an interview) or even on one type of predictor only (for example, a battery of psychological tests). When several predictors are used together the fundamental aim should be to ensure that the predictors provide information on different aspects of candidates' performance. In other words predictors should not duplicate each other (it is pointless to measure the same factor twice), but they should complement each other. For example, a group discussion exercise might provide information concerning a managerial candidate's interpersonal skills, and psychological tests could be used to provide information on intelligence and aptitudes.

One popular and successful method of managerial selection and placement that makes use of many different predictors is the assessment centre approach.

The assessment centre method involves getting groups of candidates together (often about 6 to 8 people) and involving them in a variety of tests, interviews, and work-sample exercises. Candidates are generally assessed by senior managers plus, sometimes, a consultant psychologist. The candidates may be either candidates for initial selection to an organisation or existing employees where future promotion and development within the organisation are being assessed; though the two types of candidate are not normally mixed within the same group. Assessment centres extend for a period of say, two or three days, though they may be as long as a week or as short as one day.

Detailed information on the research base for assessment centres and the development and use of assessment centre procedures can be found in Ungerson (1974), Moses and Byham (1977) and Thornton and Byham (1982).

The fundamental building block of an assessment centre is the development of a set of dimensions that are thought to be indicative of managerial potential for the jobs and organisation in question. These dimensions are derived from a comprehensive study of jobs under examination, usually employing a job analysis technique (see Chapter 2), interviews with experienced managers and a study of dimensions found to be successful in other assessment centre programmes. The dimensions typically arrived at include factors such as, oral communication skill, leadership, problem analysis, planning and organisation.

Assessment centres vary in the number of different dimensions that are evaluated (anything from about 7 to 26). One very influential assessment programme, American Telephone and Telegraph company (AT and T) uses between 8 and 25 dimensions depending on the level being assessed (Crooks, 1977). A published catalogue of assessment centre dimensions (Development Dimensions, 1975) contains a list of 26 representative dimensions commonly employed by organisations.

Jeswald (1977) provides some criteria that might be helpful in arriving at a final list of assessment dimensions. He emphasises, for example, that assessment dimensions should be defined in behavioural terms. 'For example "oral communication skills" can be defined in terms of eye contact, enunciation, voice modulation, gestures, etc. Certain other concepts, such as "character" or "maturity" may be too vague to permit reliable observation' (p. 59).

During an assessment-centre evaluation, candidates are assessed on the basis of their performance on several tests and exercises and each test is designed to examine specific dimensions. Exercises used in assessment centres include interviews, in-tray (in-basket) exercises, group discussions, role-plays (for example, manager-subordinate interviews), simulated decision-making and judgement exercises and pencil-and-paper psychological tests. Table 13.1 provides examples of the dimensions assessed by two of the exercises in an assessment centre designed for potential first-list managers.

TABLE 13.1   *Dimensions assessed by two assessment centre exercises*

Background Interview

Background interviews are conducted with each candidate by assessors who are specially trained. The interviews are primarily to assess the following dimensions:

Oral communication skill	Initiative
Oral presentation skill	Independence
Written communication skill	Planning and organisation
Stress tolerance	Delegation and control
Career ambition	Problem analysis
Leadership	Judgement
Sensitivity	Decisiveness
Flexibility	Reading and understanding
Tenacity	

In-basket Exercise

The in-basket exercise simulates the problems a newly-appointed foreman might encounter. The in-basket contains 14 items and takes one and a half hours to complete. During the assessment day each participant is interviewed for one hour relative to his or her performance on the in-basket.

The following dimensions are assessed from the in-basket performance:

Oral communication skill	Planning and organisation
Written communication skill	Delegation and control
Stress tolerance	Problem analysis
Leadership	Judgement
Sensitivity	Decisiveness
Flexibility	Reading and understanding
Initiative	

SOURCE   Crooks (1977).

Figure 13.1 provides an illustration of how the information derived from an assessment centre might be utilised.

The basis of most (if not all) assessment centre designs is the identification of a key set of assessment dimensions. This method for designing assessment centres has been attacked by Sackett and Dreher (1982, 1984) (see also Neidig and Neidig, 1984). Sackett and Dreher (1984, p. 188) summarise the current approach as follows: 'Through

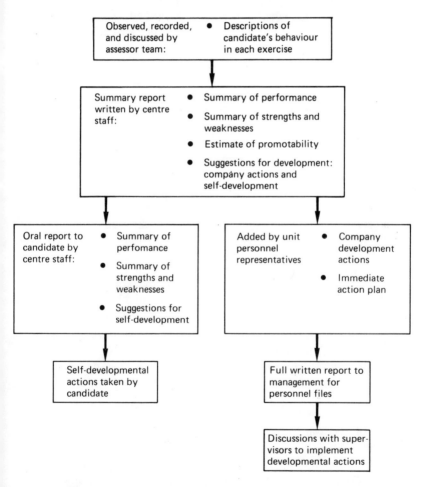

FIGURE 13.1 *The flow of assessment centre information*
SOURCE Jeswald (1977).

observation of behaviour in a variety of exercises which simulate important job functions, evaluation of the extent to which candidates possess each of a series of personal characteristics is made pooling information obtained by multiple assessors.'
These evaluations are thus integrated to form an over-all evaluation. Sackett and Dreher (1984) go on to argue that utilising a set of global assessment dimensions and producing assessment on these dimensions based on an aggregate over a number of different exercises may be inappropriate. They suggest (p. 190) an alternative where: 'Critical managerial roles are identified and exercises designed to simulate these roles. Effectiveness in each exercise, or role, is evaluated.' Effectiveness of behaviour is assessed on each exercise – *not* on a set of global dimensions.

In other words the building block of the assessment centre is the specific exercise *not* the assessment dimension.

Most organisations using assessment centres recognise that a considerable amount of effort should go into the training of assessors for assessment centre programmes. Although there is no clear concensus on the format, content and duration of this training some useful discussion of the issues can be found in Byham (1977) and Frank and Whipple (1978). Useful guidance on training people to rate and assess others can also be found in Latham and Wexley (1981). Fay and Latham (1982) provide an illustration of the benefits that training can have in reducing errors for various different types of rating scales. On the basis of their own work and existing literature they provide suggestions on the objectives that a rating training programme should seek. These include the acceptance by trainee assessors of the following points:

(a) That performance related dimensions are often correlated (this has often been found to be the case for assessment centre dimensions). In other words a person who is good at one thing is often good at others.

(b) That ratings that show a high proportion of positive scores are not necessarily an indication of leniency error.

(c) Ratings should not necessarily form a normal distribution with most people scoring in the middle of the range and equal numbers above and below the middle, with few very high or low scores.

(d)   It is not *necessarily* an error when a ratee is given the same score on many scales.

Benefits, Limitations and Validity

The use of assessment centres is widespread in the United States, and similar techniques have been in use for some time in the United Kingdom (particularly in the Armed Services and Civil Service). A survey in the early 1970s (Gill and Thakur 1983) revealed that of a sample of 360 UK organisations only 17 were using or considering using assessment centres. There seems to be considerable current interest in the technique (for example, Jones 1981; Dulewicz and Fletcher, 1982) and although there is little hard evidence, some preliminary research (Robertson and Makin, in press) suggests that usage is now higher. One reason for the general acceptability of assessment centres is the strong base of research evidence in their favour. Despite their general popularity assessment centres have drawbacks. Holdsworth (1975, p. 20), for instance, expresses the following view:

> There are only two snags of any real importance. The method requires a lot of skill and expertise, and is costly. Standard packages are available but the advantage gained by the realism of the exercise situations is largely lost unless they are tailored to the particular organisation, and the system as a whole needs to be adapted to the individual company's requirements and existing procedures. Whether a standard package is bought or a consultant commissioned to design a tailor made system, an initial cost of £3000–£5000 is likely to be involved. The actual running costs of the programme will also be quite high: senior management (assessor) time, candidate time, continued presence of a consultant or full-time psychologist (optional but desirable), travel and accommodation. However, if the results achieved by some companies can be repeated, this investment would be amply rewarded.

In terms of validity, the evidence concerning assessement centres demonstrates that they can produce impressive validities and validity coefficients of +0.5 are not uncommon (see Huck, 1973; Klimoski and Strickland, 1977). Klimoski and Strickland do, however, sound a note of warning about assessment centres. Essentially they argue that assessment centres may not identify true ability and expertise in the job but simply be a good means of identifying people who will be well regarded by their superiors (perhaps because they resemble them) and will therefore achieve rapid promotion, salary increases and so on. This does not necessarily mean that they are the most competent people. Klimoski and Strickland also raise a number of other cautions concerning the validity of assessment centres and suggest further research needs.

It is also worth noting that with only a few exceptions (for example, Huck and Bray, 1976) the research on assessment centre validity is based on entirely male samples. Ritchie and Moses (1983) have recently produced data based on a seven-year longitudinal study which goes some way towards remedying this extreme imbalance:

> Assessment centre predictions of the potential of 1,097 women managers were found to be significantly related to career progress 7 years later. In addition, comparisons of specific dimension ratings made in this assessment center and those made for men in the Management Progress Study were conducted. Similar rating distributions of potential for men and women were noted. Also, substantial similarities were found in the relationships between specific dimension ratings and progress of men and women. It appears increasingly clear that differences in managerial potential are far more attributable to individual rather than sex differences.

FAKING AND DISTORTION

Some selection methods require the candidate to provide information of one sort or another so that decisions may be taken concerning their suitability. Quite frequently there is some opportunity for candidates to present false or misleading impressions or information about themselves. Some selection methods are more open to this sort of contamination than others. Tests of intellectual ability, or aptitude and skill, or ability-based work-sample tests may be rather difficult to fake. Pencil-and-paper assessments of personality and biographical information obtained at interviews, through application forms or biodata questionnaires seem to provide more opportunity for faking or distortion on the part of candidates. Golstein (1971) examined information provided on application forms by candidates for employ-ment and checked this against information provided by previous employers. In general the data indicated a substantial number of discrepancies between the employee's application form and the data provided by previous employers. It is of course possible that the previous employers' information, rather than the candidates was wrong. Goldstein notes, however, that the simplest explanation seems to point to bias on the part of the applicant.

The largest amount of agreement occurred on the topic of previous position held. The categories where discrepancies were largest were the duration of previous employment and the previous salary earned. Eighteen out of 25 applicants, where salary could be compared, over-stated their salary. Thirty-nine out of 46 applicants over-stated the amount of time spent in their previous job. Goldstein notes that in interviews, too, the responses with the most inaccurate information were duration of employment and salary earned.

In interview situations, faking or distortion of responses is clearly possible. Blum and Naylor (1968) suggest that the interview produces face-to-face pressure that might cause respondents to stretch the truth.

The possibility of misleading information being given at interviews may not be too troublesome since interviews are certainly not the best method for collecting 'factual' information. For other selection methods, notably biodata and pencil-and-paper psychological tests, faking or lying may be a more severe problem. In addition to Goldstein's work other studies have shown that responses to biographical questionnairies and similar self-report measures such as application forms can be distorted. When there is distortion the general tendency is for the respondent's scores to change towards their perception of what represents a 'good' score. Klein and Owens (1965) asked students to fill out a biographical questionnaire as if they were applying for a job for which the employer wanted a truly creative research scientist. Zalinski and Abrahams (1979) conducted a similar study but in their research senior students in psychology were asked to fill in an interest inventory that could be used to 'determine how similar you are to successful psychologists' (p. 164). The students were also told that such inventories have been used as selection instruments in applicant screening programmes. Such information, given to students who were reasonably committed to a career in psychology, presumably produced circumstances rather like a real selection situation.

Significantly, in both studies the respondents were able to fake their scores in such a way that they produced a score that was more like an *objectively-derived* score for creative scientists and psychologists respectively. In other words their faking was reasonably accurate. It should be remembered that both of these studies were of simulated rather than real selection situations. Some comfort concerning the occurrence of faking in *real* situations can be drawn from previous research. This research has indicated that students in artificial situations fake more than industrial applicants. Also some studies have found little evidence of faking in selection situations when compared with non-selection situations (for a brief review see Schrader and Osburn, 1977). Zalinski and Abrahams (1979, p. 162) note that:

> In general, research on faking under simulated conditions has demonstrated that subjects, can when so instructed, significantly increase scores on selection-relevant scales. Investigations in which the effects of faking in an actual selection setting could be reliably assessed, indicate that less distortion may occur in real-life settings than are typically shown in simulated faking studies (Campbell, 1971). However it is clear that additional research in actual selection settings is seriously needed. The fact that few studies have been reported for real-life settings is probably attributable to the difficulties of designing such research.

As a result of their research results both Schrader and Osburn (1977) and Zalinski and Abrahams (1979) provide suggestions on how faking might be minimised in real-life selection situations. Zalinski and Abrahams suggest that when a questionnaire is used, that it is not advisable to use only the job-relevant scales of the questionnaire – but that all of the questionnaire items should be used. Schrader and Osburn suggest that instructions to candidates indicating that a 'lie-scale' might be embedded in the questionnaire might reduce the likelihood of faking to a considerable extent. Presumably, although they do not state this explicitly, it docs not matter whether or not there really is a lie-scale contained in the biodata questionnaire.

Lie-scales

Many pencil-and-paper measures of personality include scales that are described as lie-scales, for example, the Eysenck Personality

Inventory (EPI) (Eysenck and Eysenck, 1963). Some forms of the 16PF can be scored for motivational distortion. Despite the names given to such scales (lie-scales, faking-good/bad, and so on) there is some uncertainty about whether they do actually indicate the truthfulness of a candidate's responses. It has been suggested that such scales provide an indication of the extent to which respondents attempt to produce socially-desirable responses although there is some uncertainty concerning this also. Elliot (1981) provides a review of this material.

What seems clear is that real-life applicants return higher scores on lie-scales than similar applicants who are not being selected for employment (see Elliott, 1981).

Despite this clear finding the interpretation of a high lie-scale score from a candidate is difficult. A high lie-scale score cannot be taken as a clear indication that the candidate has lied or is an habitual liar. McKerracher and Watson (1968), for example, found that pathological liars in a hospital for disturbed offenders scored lower on a lie-scale than other patients. This and other evidence of uncertainty concerning the meaning of lie-scale scores does not mean that they are worthless, but such scores need to be interpreted carefully. Elliot (1981, p. 10), who provides some empirical information and a useful discussion of lie-scales in the selection context, quotes Rotter (1960); 'What we call faking is only our recognition of the fact that the subject is taking the test with a different purpose or goal than the experimenter wants him to have'.

ORGANISATIONAL ISSUES

Material presented so far in this book has examined many aspects of the personnel selection process and some attention has been given to the nature of the organisations in which employees work (for example, chapter 6). Several authors, notably Argyris (1976, p. 154) have been critical of the amount of attention that personnel selection specialists pay to organisational factors:

What is the primary environment within which the individual interacts or within which the individuals are embedded? The organisation. Where is the environment – the organisation – in the model used by industrial psychologists who select, place and train individuals for organisations? The answer is, I believe, in a black box between the predictor variables and the criterion variables. Why? Because given the emphasis on prediction, the paradigm used in selection and placement must assume that the organisational environment is relatively static and benign and, therefore, need not be known.

Organisations come in a variety of sizes and many organisations are too small to conduct a predictive or concurrent validity study that involves collecting data from large numbers of candidates. As far as small organisations are concerned, the strategies that seem most appropriate involve the use of either content validation, synthetic validation or validity generalisation. The concepts and procedures involved here are described fully in chapter 6. In brief, content validity involves ensuring by detailed job analysis, that the selection instruments used provides adequate measurement of the operations, and skills that are relevant to job success. Synthetic validity was introduced by Lawshe (1952) in a specific attempt to devise a method of value to small firms. It involves the following steps, (i) job analysis, to estimate the extent to which jobs require a certain characteristic, (ii) applying this measure and calculating an average score for all jobs, (iii) relating average scores to requirements. Validity generalisation (Schmidt and Hunter (1977); Callender and Osburn, 1982; Burke, 1984) is a procedure where existing empirical work concerning test validities for specific jobs is used as a basis for inferring the *expected* validity if tests are used for other jobs within the same job family. Detailed job analysis is required to establish the degree of correspondence between the jobs in question (see chapter 2).

A common thread linking all of these strategies for developing selection procedures is that comprehensive job analysis data needs to be obtained in order to be certain that the relationship between predictor and criterion measures is as anticipated.

An interesting practical example of the use of a content-validation procedure in a small firm is provided by Robinson (1981). Mossholder and Arvey (1984) provide a comprehensive review of synthetic validity and Schmidt, Hunter and Caplan (1981) provide an illustration of the use of validity generalisation procedures.

As Argyris argues, several issues relating to the nature of organisations and the views that one holds about how they develop and function are of considerable importance to the personnel selection process.

TABLE 13.2 *Criterion variables used in some assessment centre validation studies*

1966	Management level, salary, and salary progress	Psychologists	AT&T
1967	Ratings, ranking and number of promotions	Mixed*	AT&T
1968	Special performance review	Managers	AT&T
1969	Increase in responsibility	Managers	IBM
1969	Salary standing	Managers	IBM
1970	Ratings, salary progress, and number of promotions	Mixed	SOHIO
1970	Ratings (timing of criterion measures varied)	Mixed	SOHIO
1970	Interview with superior	Managers	Union Carbide
1972	Promotions and demotions	Managers	IBM
1972	Ratings, but obtained concurrent with assessment centre	Managers	Various
1972	Ratings, but obtained concurrent with assessment centre	Managers	Hospital
1973	Ratings, but obtained concurrent with assessment centre	Managers	Roben and Har
1974	Ratings, but obtained concurrent with assessment centre	Managers	State Government
1976	Management level achieved	Managers	AT&T

TABLE 13.2 *cont'd*

1975	Salary growth	–	SOHIO
1975	Ratings, but obtained concurrent with assessment centre	Managers	–
1976	Rating and ranking	Managers	AT&T

SOURCE After Klimoski and Strickland (1977).

One crucial issue concerns the nature of criterion variables selected by the organisation to validate predictors used in the selection process. It must be remembered that predictors cannot be proved to be valid *per se*. They can be shown to be accurate predictors of various criterion measures (production quantity/quality, abseentism, turnover, rate of promotion, salary progress, and so on). If these criterion measures are important components of individual and organisational success, then it is sensible to use the relevant predictors for selection purposes. What Argyris, amongst others, argues is that sometimes selection specialists lose sight of the fact that predictors are validated against *specific* criteria. More significantly these predictors may not be the only, nor the best indicators of individual success and value to the organisation as a whole.

These points are important and should be taken into account when selection decisions are made. One implication is that considerable further thought and research effort needs to go into the development of a more comprehensive set of criterion variables than those traditionally in use – although this does not imply that current criteria are either unimportant or irrelevant.

Klimoski and Strickland (1977), for example, have examined the criterion variables used in a variety of studies on assessment centres (see Table 13.2) and note that, though at first glance the list appears to be diverse, criteria are generally of what have been described as the status quo variety:

They suggest some possibilities for alternative criteria (p. 358):

If we wish to move away from the status quo, then, we need criteria other than advancement. While we do not have the answers, some possibilities present themselves: nominations of individuals on *value to the organisation* or estimates of replacement cost; measures of management objectives achieved; critical contributions to the organisation, such as sales or output; peer or *subordinate ratings*; or some combination of these or other criteria (see Lawler and Rhode, 1976), for some innovative solutions to the problem of establishing the value of people in organisations). Perhaps assessment centers do have superior validity for these criteria as well; the evidence simply is not available, and it should be.

A grasp of the nature of the organisation is important to the potential employee as well as to the designers of a selection system. Wherever possible it is sensible to provide the employee with a clear understanding of the nature of the organisation. This might be done, for example, by providing job or employment preview information, brochures, visits and films.

Appendix I   Some Useful Formulae

1   FORMULAE FOR STANDARD DEVIATIONS

1.1 $\sigma = \sqrt{\dfrac{\Sigma x^2}{N}}$
   general formula for standard deviation of a population

1.2 $\sigma = \sqrt{\dfrac{\Sigma x^2}{N-1}}$
   standard deviation of a population calculated from sample size N

where x = deviation from mean
      N = sample size

1.3 $\sigma = \dfrac{1}{N} \sqrt{N\Sigma X^2 - (\Sigma X)^2}$
   standard deviation computed without knowledge of deviations

where X = scores
      N = sample size

2   FORMULAE FOR CORRELATIONS

2.1 $r_{xy} = \dfrac{\Sigma xy}{N\sigma_x\sigma_y}$
   basic formula for product moment correlation

where x and y are scores

2.2 $\quad r_{xy} = \dfrac{N\Sigma XY - (\Sigma X)(\Sigma Y)}{\sqrt{[N\Sigma X^2 - (\Sigma X)^2][N\Sigma Y^2 - (\Sigma Y^2)]}}$

formula for computing product moment correlation from original data

where X and Y are original scores

2.3 $\quad rho = 1 - \dfrac{6\Sigma D^2}{N(N^2-1)}$

basic formula for rank order correlation

where D are differences in ranks

2.4 $\quad r_b = \dfrac{M_p - M_q}{\sigma_t} \times \dfrac{pq}{y}$

Bi-serial coefficient of correlation used when one variable is reduced to two categories

where:

M_p = mean value of higher group
M_q = mean value for lower group
p = proportion of cases in higher group
q = proportion of cases in lower group
y = ordinate of normal curve at division p/q
σ_t = standard deviation of total sample

2.5 $\quad r_b = \dfrac{M_p - M_t}{\sigma_t} \times \dfrac{p}{y}$

alternative bi-serial formulae

2.6 $\quad r_{pbi} = \dfrac{M_p - M_q}{\sigma_t} \sqrt{pq}$

point bi-serial coefficient used when one of the variables is a genuine dichotomy

2.8 $\quad r_{pbi} = \dfrac{M_p - M_t}{\sigma_t} \sqrt{\dfrac{p}{y}}$

alternative point bi-serial formula

2.9 $\quad r_{cos-pi} = \text{COS}\left(\dfrac{180° \sqrt{bc}}{\sqrt{ad} + \sqrt{bc}}\right)$

tetrachoric correlation used when both variables are reduced to a dichotomy.

where a,b,c,d, are respective frequencies
in a 2 × 2 contingency table.

3 FORMULAE FOR CORRECTING (PRODUCT MOMENT) CORRELATIONS

3.1 $r_{xyw} = \dfrac{r_{xy}}{\sqrt{r_{yy}}}$

correction for atte-
nuation of *criterion*

where:

$r_{xy\infty}$ = corrected correlation
r_{xy} = original correlation
r_{yy} = reliability of criterion (or estimate of)

3.2 $r_{tt} = \dfrac{2r_{hh}}{1 + r_{hh}}$

Spearman–Brown
Correction for split-
half reliability

where:

r_{tt} = corrected correlation
r_{hh} = original correlation based on half of the questions

3.3 $R = \dfrac{r(\Sigma/\sigma)}{\sqrt{1 - r^2 + r^2\,(\Sigma^2/\sigma^2)}}$

correction for restric-
tion of range of *pre-
dictor* (for example,
test)

where:

R = corrected correlation
r = original correlation
σ = standard deviation in restricted sample
Σ = standard deviation in population

3.4 $R = \sqrt{1 - \left(\dfrac{\sigma^2}{\Sigma^2}\right)(1 - r^2)}$

correction for restric-
tion of range of *criter-
ion*

same notation as 3.3

4 FORMULAE FOR PROFILE MATCHING

$$4.1 \quad r_p = \frac{4K - \Sigma w_j d_j^2}{4K + \Sigma w_j d_j^2}$$

formula for comparing two group profiles where weights are attached to components

where:

K = median χ square for number of scores in profile
wj = weight to be given to a score (usually based on standard deviation of jth score)
dj = difference between two groups in jth score

$$4.2 \quad rp = \frac{(4K^1 + \Sigma D^2) - \Sigma d^2}{(4K^1 + \Sigma D^2) - \Sigma d^2}$$

formula for comparing an individual profile with a group profile

5 FORMULAE FOR EVALUATING TEST UTILITY

$$5.1 \quad k = \sqrt{1 - r^2}$$

Coefficient of alienation (degree of lack of relationships)

$$5.2 \quad E = 100 \, (1 - \sqrt{1 - r^2})$$

Index of forecasting efficiency (percentage reduction in error by prediction)

$$5.3 \quad d = r^2 \times 100$$

Coefficient of determination (percentage of variance accounted for)

$$5.4 \quad \Delta \bar{U} = d_t SD_y$$

Utility of selection per individual in first year

where:

d_t = difference in job performance in standard deviation units

SD_y = standard deviation in job peformance in cash terms for unselected group

5.5 $\quad \Delta U = Td_t\, SD_y$

Utility of selection per individual over T years.

5.6 $\quad \Delta U = TNd_tSD_y - NC$

Utility of selection for N individuals over T years taking cost of selecting each individual into account

where N = number of individuals
C = cost of selection

5.8 $\quad r = \dfrac{t}{\sqrt{t^2 + (N_t - 2)}}$

estimation of point biserial correlation from t statistic

where:

N_t = total number in study.

5.9 $\quad d = \dfrac{1}{\sqrt{pq}} \sqrt{\dfrac{N_t - 2}{N_t}} \cdot \dfrac{r}{\sqrt{1 - r^2}}$

Formulae for estimation of d (difference in job performance in standard score units between selected and unselected group) where:

p = proportional size of larger sample
q = proportional size of smaller sample
N = total number in study

5.10 $\Delta\bar{U} = r_{xy} \, SD_y \, \theta/p - C/p$ formula for utility of selection per year for one selectee

where:

r_{xy} = correlation between predictor and criterion
SD_y = standard deviation in cash value of job performance of unselected group
θ = ordinate at point of cut corresponding to p or normal curve with *mean* = 0, *sd* = 1
p = proportion selected
C = costs of selecting one applicant

SOURCES

Formulae 1.1–2.9, 3.2, 5.1–5.3: Guilford, 1965.
Formulae 3.1, 3.3, 3.4 Guion, 1965
Formulae 4.1–4.3: Cattell *et al.* 1970
Formulae 5.4–5.10. Schmidt, Hunter and Pearlman, 1982

Appendix II: Theoretical Expectancy Tables

Appendix II

TABLE F *Theoretical expectancies where 30 per cent are 'superior'*

		Predictor categories†			
r	A	B	C	D	E
.15	38	32	30	28	22
	38	35	33	32	30
.20	40	34	29	26	21
	40	37	34	32	30
.25	43	35	29	24	19
	43	39	36	33	30
.30	46	35	29	24	16
	46	40	37	33	30
.35	49	36	29	22	14
	49	42	38	34	30
.40	51	37	28	21	12
	51	44	39	34	30
.45	55	38	28	20	10
	55	46	40	35	30
.50	58	38	27	18	09
	58	48	41	35	30
.55	61	39	27	17	07
	61	50	42	36	30
.60	64	40	26	15	05
	64	52	43	36	30
.65	68	41	25	13	04
	68	54	44	37	30
.70	72	42	23	11	03
	72	57	46	37	30
.75	76	43	22	09	02
	76	59	47	37	30
.80	80	44	20	06	01
	80	62	48	37	30
.85	85	45	17	04	–
	85	65	49	37	30

*This table and the four tables which follow it, are taken from Lawshe, C. H., Bolda, R. A., Brune, R. L. and Auclair, G. (1958) 'Expectancy charts II: their theoretical development', *Personnel Psychology* 11, 545–59. (Used by permission.)

†Predictor category code: First row, individual expectancies, A—highest 20%, B—second 20%, C—middle 20%, D—fourth 20%, E—lowest 20%. Second row, institutional expectancies, A—upper 20%, B—upper 40%, C—upper 60%, D—upper 80%, E—all.

TABLE G *Theoretical expectancies where 40 per cent are 'superior'**

			Predictor categories		
r	A	B	C	D	E
.15	48	44	40	36	32
	48	46	44	42	40
.20	51	45	40	35	30
	51	48	45	43	40
.25	54	44	40	34	28
	54	49	46	43	40
.30	57	46	40	33	24
	57	51	47	44	40
.35	60	47	39	32	22
	60	53	49	45	40
.40	63	48	39	31	19
	63	56	50	45	40
.45	66	49	39	29	17
	66	58	51	46	40
.50	69	50	39	28	14
	69	60	53	46	40
.55	72	53	38	26	12
	72	62	54	47	40
.60	75	53	38	24	10
	75	64	55	48	40
.65	79	55	37	22	08
	79	67	57	48	40
.70	82	58	36	19	06
	82	69	58	49	40
.75	86	59	35	17	04
	86	72	60	49	40
.80	89	61	34	14	02
	89	75	61	49	40
.85	93	64	32	10	01
	93	79	63	50	40

*See footnotes to Table F.

TABLE H *Theoretical expectancies where 50 per cent are 'superior'**

			Predictor categories		
r	A	B	C	D	E
.15	58	54	50	46	42
	58	56	54	52	50
.20	61	55	50	45	39
	61	58	55	53	50
.25	64	56	50	44	36
	64	60	56	54	50
.30	67	57	50	43	33
	67	62	58	54	50
.35	70	58	50	42	30
	70	64	59	55	50
.40	73	59	50	41	28
	73	66	61	56	50
.45	75	60	50	40	25
	75	68	62	56	50
.50	78	62	50	38	22
	78	70	63	57	50
.55	81	64	50	36	19
	81	72	65	58	50
.60	84	65	50	35	16
	84	75	66	59	50
.65	87	67	50	33	13
	87	77	68	59	50
.70	90	70	50	30	10
	90	80	70	60	50
.75	92	72	50	28	08
	92	82	72	61	50
.80	95	75	50	25	05
	95	85	73	61	50
.85	97	80	50	20	03
	97	88	76	62	50

*See footnotes to Table F.

TABLE I *Theoretical expectancies where 60 per cent are 'superior'*

			Predictor categories		
r	A	B	C	D	E
.15	68	64	60	57	52
	68	66	64	62	60
.20	71	63	60	56	48
	71	67	65	63	60
.25	73	65	60	55	48
	73	69	66	63	60
.30	76	66	61	54	44
	76	71	68	64	60
.35	78	68	61	53	40
	78	73	69	65	60
.40	81	69	61	52	37
	81	75	70	66	60
.45	83	71	61	51	34
	83	77	72·	66	60
.50	86	72	62	50	31
	86	79	73	67	60
.55	88	74	62	48	28
	88	81	75	68	60
.60	90	76	62	47	25
	90	83	76	69	60
.65	92	78	63	45	21
	92	85	78	70	60
.70	94	80	64	43	18
	94	87	80	71	60
.75	96	83	65	42	14
	96	90	81	71	60
.80	98	86	66	39	11
	98	92	83	72	60
.85	99	90	68	36	07
	100	97	88	74	60

*See footnotes to Table F.

TABLE J *Theoretical expectancies where 70 per cent are 'superior'**

		Predictor categories			
r	A	B	C	D	E
.15	77	73	69	69	62
	77	75	73	72	70
.20	79	75	70	67	59
	79	77	75	73	70
.25	81	75	71	65	58
	81	78	76	73	70
.30	84	76	71	65	54
	84	80	77	74	70
.35	86	78	71	64	52
	86	82	78	75	70
.40	88	79	72	63	49
	88	83	79	75	70
.45	90	80	72	63	46
	90	85	81	76	70
.50	91	82	73	62	42
	91	87	82	77	70
.55	93	83	73	61	39
	93	88	83	78	70
.60	95	85	74	60	36
	95	90	85	79	70
.65	96	87	75	59	32
	96	92	86	80	70
.70	97	89	77	58	29
	97	93	88	80	70
.75	98	91	78	57	25
	98	95	89	81	70
.80	99	94	80	56	20
	99	97	91	82	70
.85	100	96	83	55	16
	100	98	93	84	70

*See footnotes to Table F.

Bibliography

Abrahams, N. M. and Alf, E. (1972a) 'Pratfalls in moderator research', *Journal of Applied Psychology*, 56, 3, 245–51.

Abrahams, N. M. and Alf, E. (1972b) 'Reply to Dunnette's "Comments on Abrahams and Alf's 'Pratfalls in moderator research'"', *Journal of Applied Psychology*, 56, 3, 257–61.

Adams, S. (1950) 'Does face validity exist?' *Journal of Educational and Psychological Measurement*, 10, 320–28.

Adkins, D. C. (1974) *Test Construction* (Columbus, Ohio: Merrill).

Albright, L. E., Glennon, J. R. and Smith, W. J. (1963) *The Use of Psychological Tests in Industry* (Copenhagen: Munksgaard).

Albright, L. E., Smith, W. J. and Glennon, J. R. (1959) 'A follow up on some "invalid" Tests for selecting salesmen', *Personnel Psychology*, 12, 105–12.

Algera, J. A. (1983) 'Objective and task characteristics as determinants of reactions by task performers', *Journal of Occupational Psychology*, 56, 95–107.

American Psychological Association (1954) *Technical Recommendations for Psychological Tests and Diagnostic Techniques* (Washington DC: A.P.A.).

American Psychological Association (1966) *Standards for Educational and Psychological Tests and Manuals* (Washinton, DC: A.P.A.).

American Psychological Association (1974) *Standards for Educational and Psychological Tests* (Washington DC: A.P.A.) (quoted by Anastasi, 1982).

American Psychological Association (1981) 'Ethical principles of psychologists', *American Psychologist*, 36, 633–8.

Anastasi, A. (1982) *Psychological Testing* (New York: Macmillan).

Anstey, E. (1977) 'A 30-year follow up of the CSSB procedure, with lessons for the future', *Journal of Occupational Psychology*, 50, 149–59.

Argyris, C. (1976) 'Problems and new directions for industrial psychology', In M. D. Dunnette (ed.) *Handbook of Industrial and Organizational Psychology* (Chicago: Rand McNally).

Arnold, J. D., Rauschenberger, J. M., Soubel, W. G. and Guion, R. M. (1982) 'Validation and utility of a strength test for selecting steelworkers', *Journal of Applied Psychology*, 67, 5, 588–604.

Arvey, R. D. (1979) *Fairness in selecting employees* (Reading, Mass: Addison-Wesley, 1979).

Arvey, R. D. and Campion, J. E. (1982) 'The employment interview: a summary and review of recent literature', *Personnel Psychology*, 35, 281–322.

Ash, P. (1960) 'Validity information exchange, No. 13–07', *Personnel Psychology*, 13, 456.

Asher, J. J. (1972) 'The biographical item: can it be improved?' *Personnel Psychology*, 25, 251–69.

Asher, J. J. and Sciarrino, J. A. (1974) 'Realistic work sample tests: A review', *Personnel Psychology*, 27, 519–33.

Baehr, M. and Williams, G. B. (1967) 'Underlying dimensions of personal background data and their relationship to occupational classification', *Journal of Applied Psychology*, 51, 481–90.

Baier, D. E. and Dugan, R. D. (1956) 'Tests and performance in a sales organization', *Personnel Psychology*, 9, 17–26.

Bandura, A. (1977) *Social Learning Theory* (Englewood Cliffs, New Jersey: Prentice-Hall).

Barlett, C. J. and O'Leary, B. S. (1969) 'A differential prediction model to moderate the effects of heterogeneous groups in personnel selection and classification', *Personnel Psychology*, 22, 1–17.

Bass, B. M. (1952) 'Ultimate criteria of organizational worth', *Personnel Psychology*, 5, 157–74.

Bass, B. M. (1954) 'The leaderless group discussion', *Psychological Bulletin*, 51, 465–92.

Bass, B. M. (1957) 'Reducing leniency in merit ratings', *Personnel Psychology*, 9, 359–69.

Bass, B. M. (1962) 'Further evidence on the dynamic character of criteria', *Personnel Psychology*, 15, 93–7.

Bechtoldt, H. P. (1959) 'Construct validity: a critique', *American Psychologist*, 1959, 619–29.

Beck, J. E. and Cox, C. J. (1980) *Advances in Management Education* (London: Wiley).

Behrend, H. (1953) 'Absence and turnover in a changing economic climate', *Occupational Psychology*, 27, 69–79.

Bem, D. J. (1972) 'Self perception theory', in L. Berkowitz (ed.) *Advances in Experimental Social Psychology, vol. 6* (New York: Academic Press).

Bender, J. M. (1973) 'What is typical of assessment centres', *Personnel Psychology*, July/August, 50–7.

Bennett, G. K., Seashore, H. G. and Wesman, A. (1974) *Differential Aptitude Tests* (New York: Psychological Corporation).

Berdie, F. S. (1971) 'What test questions are likely to offend the general public', *Journal of Educational and Psychological Measurement*, 8, 2, 87–93.

Bernadin, H. J., Albares, K. M. and Cranny, C. J. (1976), 'A recomparison of behavioural expectation scales to summated scales', *Journal of Applied Psychology*, 61, 564–70.

Betz, N. E. and Weiss, D. J. (1975) *Simulation Studies of Two Stage Ability Testing*, Research report 74–4, psychometric methods program (Minneapolis: University of Minnesota, 1974).

Bickel, P. J., Hammel, E. A. and O'Connel, J. W. (1975) 'Sex bias in graduate admissions: data from Berkeley', *Science*, 187, 398–404.

Bilodeau, E. A. (1966) *Acquisition of Skill* (London: Academic Press).

Birt, J. A. (1968) 'The effect of the consistency of job inventory information on simulated airmen assignment', unpublished Ph.D. thesis, Lafayette, Indiana: Purdue University (quoted by McCormick, 1976).

Blum, M. L. and Naylor, J. C. (1968) *Industrial Psychology: its Theoretical and Social Foundation* (New York: Harper and Row).

Boem, V. R. (1972) 'Negro-white differences in validity of employment and training selection procedure', *Journal of Applied Psychology*, 56, 33–9.

Bolsher, B. T. and Springbett, B. M. (1961) 'The reaction of interviewers to favorable and unfavorable information', *Journal of Applied Psychology*, 45, 95–103.

Boshoff, A. B. (1969) 'A comparison of three methods for the evaluation of managerial positions', *Psychologica Africana*, 12, 212–21.

Bray, D. W. and Campbell, R. J. (1968) 'Selection of salesmen by means of an assessment centre', *Journal of Applied Psychology*, 52, 36–41.

Bray, D. W. and Grant, D. L. (1966) 'The assessment center in the measurement of potential for business management', *Psychological Monographs*, 80.

Bray, D. W. and Moses, J. L. (1972) 'Personnel selection', *Annual Review of Psychology*, 23, 545–76.

Breakwell, B. G. M., Foot, H. and Gilmour, R. (1982) (eds) *Social Psychology: A Practical Manual* (London: British Psychological Society and Macmillan Press).

British Institute of Management and Institute of Personnel Management (1980) *Selecting Managers: How British Industry Recruits* (London: BIM, IPM).

British Psychological Society (1980a) 'Notes for guidance in planning short courses in psychological testing', *Bulletin of the British Psychological Society*, 33, 244–9.

British Psychological Society (1980b) 'Technical recommendations for psychological tests', *Bulletin of the British Psychological Society*, 33, 161–4.

Browning, R. C. (1968) 'Validity of reference ratings from previous employers', *Personnel Psychology*, 21, 389–93.

Burke, M. J. (1984) 'Validity generalization: a review and critique of the correlation model', *Journal of Applied Psychology*, 37, 93–115.

Burns, T. (1957) 'Management in action', *Operational Research Quarterly*, 8, 45–60.

Byham, W. C. (1977) 'Application of the assessment center method', in J. L. Moses and W. C. Byham (1977) *Applying the Assessment Center Method* (New York: Pergamon).

Callender, J. C. and Osburn, H. G. (1982) 'Another view of progress in validity generalization: Reply to Schmidt, Hunter, and Pearlman', *Journal of Applied Psychology*, 67, 846–52.

Campbell, D. P. (1971) *Handbook for the Strong Vocational Interest Blank* (Stanford: Stanford University Press).

Campbell, D. P. (1977) *Handbook for the Strong Campbell Interest Inventory* (Stanford: Stanford University Press).

Campbell, D. T. and Fiske, D. W. (1959) 'Convergent and discriminant validation by the multitrait-multimethod matrix', *Psychological Bulletin*, 56, 2.

Campbell, J. P. (1976) 'Psychometric theory', in Dunnette, M. D. (ed.)

Handbook of Industrial and Organizational Psychology (Chicago: Rand-McNally).

Campbell, J. T., Crooks, L. A., Mahoney, A. M. and Rock, D. A. (1973) *An Investigation of Sources of Bias in the Prediction of Job Performance – a Six Year Study*, ETS report PR–73–37 (Princetown, New Jersey: Educational Testing Service).

Campion, J. E. (1972) 'Work sampling for personnel selection', *Journal of Applied Psychology*, 56, 40–4.

Carlson , R. E. (1967) 'Selection interview decisions: the relative influence of appearance and factual written information on an interviewer's final rating', *Journal of Applied Psychology*, 51, 461–8.

Carlson, R. E., Thayer, P. W., Mayfield, E. C. and Peterson, D. A. (1971) 'Improvements in the selection interview', *Personnel Journal*, 50, 268–75.

Carroll (1959) 'Review of the DAT', in O. K. Buros (ed.) *Fifth Mental Measurement Yearbook* (Highland Park, N. J.: Gryphan Press).

Carroll, S. J. and Nash, A. N. (1972) 'Effectiveness of a forced choice reference check', *Personnel Administration*, March–April, 42–6.

Cascio, W. F. and Phillips, N. F. (1979) 'Performance testing: a rose among thorns?' *Personnel Psychology*, 32, 751–66.

Cattell, R. B. (1957) *Personality and Motivation Structure and Measurement.* (New York: Harcourt, Brace and World).

Cattell, R. B. (1965) *The Scientific Analysis of Personality* (Harmondsworth: Penguin).

Cattell, R. B., Eber, H. W. and Tasuoka, H. M. (1970) *Handbook for the Sixteen Personality Factor Questionnaire* (Windsor: National Foundation for Educational Research).

Cederblom, D. and Lounsbury, J. W. (1980) 'An investigation of user acceptance of peer evaluation', *Personnel Psychology*, 33, 567–79.

Chacko, T. I. (1982) 'Women and equal employment opportunity: some unintended effects', *Journal of Applied Psychology*, 67, 1, 119–123.

Champagne, J. E. and McCormick, E. J. (1964) *An Investigation of the Use of Worker-Oriented Job Variables in Job Evaluation* (Lafayette, Indiana: Occupational Research Centre, Purdue University.

Christal, R. E. (1969) 'Collecting analysing and reporting information describing jobs and occupations', Comments by the Chairman and Proceedings of 19 Division of Military Psychology Symposium (Washington DC: American Psychological Association).

Cleary, T. A. and Hilton, T. L. (1968) 'An investigation of item bias', *Educational and Psychological Measurement*, 28, 61–75.

Cole, N. S. (1973) 'Bias in selection', *Journal of Educational Measurement*, 10, 237–55.

Cole, N. S. (1981) 'Bias in testing', *American Psychologist*, 36, 10, 1067–77.

Coombs, C. H. and Salter, G. A. (1949) 'A factorial approach to job families', *Psychometrika*, 14, 33–42.

Cox, J. W. (undated) *Cox Mechanical Test Ml* (Altrincham, Cheshire: Human Factors).

Cronbach, L. J. (1951) 'Coefficient alpha and the internal structure of tests', *Psychometrika*, 16, 297–334.

Cronbach, L. J. (1970) *Essential of Psychological Testing* (New York: Harper & Row).

Cronbach, L. J. and Glesser, G. C. (1965) *Psychological Tests and Personnel Decisions* (Urbana: University of Illinois Press).

Cronbach, L. J. and Meehl, P. E. (1955) 'Construct validity in psychological tests', *Psychological Bulletin*, 52, 4, 281–302.

Crooks, L. A. (1977) 'The selection and development of assessment center techniques', in J. L. Moses and W. C. Byham, *Applying the Assessment Center Method* (New York: Pergamon).

Cureton, E. E. (1971) 'The stability coefficient', *Educational and Psychological Measurement*, 31, 45–55.

Cureton, E. E., Cook, J. A., Fischer, R. T., Laser, S. A., Rockwell, N. J., and Simmons, J. W. (1973) 'Length of test and standard error of measurement', *Educational and Psychological Measurement*, 33, 63–8.

Daniels, A. W. and Otis, J. L. (1950) 'A method for analysing employment interviews', *Personnel Psychology*, 3, 425–44.

Davey, D. M. and Harris, M. (1982) *Judging People* (London: McGraw-Hill).

Dean, R. A. and Wanous, J. P. (1984) 'Effects of realistic job previews on hiring bank tellers', *Journal of Applied Psychology*, 69, 61–8.

Decker, P. J. (1982) 'The enhancement of behavior modeling training of supervisory skills by the inclusion of retention processes', *Personnel Psychology*, 35, 323–32.

De Nisi, A. S. and Shaw, J. B. (1977) 'Investigations of the use of self reports of abilities', *Journal of Applied Psychology*, 62, 641–4.

Deubert, L. W., Smith, M. C., Downs, S., Jenkins, L. C. B. and Berry, D. C. (1975) 'The selection of dental students: A pilot study of an assessment of manual ability by practical tests', *British Dental Journal*, 139, 357–61.

Development Dimensions (1975) *Catalogue of Assessment and Development Exercises* (Pittsburgh: Development Dimension).

Dipboye, R. L., Fontelle, G. A. and Garner, K. (1984) 'Effects of previewing the application on interview process and outcomes', *Journal of Applied Psychology*, 69, 118–28.

Division of Occupational Psychology (1983) 'Code of professional conduct', in *Register of Members of the Division of Occupational Psychology of the British Psychological Society* (Leicester: British Psychological Society).

Downey, J. E. (1919) *Graphology and the Psychology of Handwriting* (Baltimore: Warwick & York).

Downs, S. (1968) 'Selecting the older trainee: A pilot study of trainability tests', *National Institute of Industrial Psychology Bulletin*, 19–26.

Downs, S. (1973) 'Trainability assessments: sewing machininsts', *Research Paper SL6* (Cambridge, England: Industrial Training Research Unit).

Downs, S. (1977) 'Trainability testing: A practical approach to selection', *Training Information Paper No. 11* (London: Her Majesty's Stationery Office).

Downs, S., Farr, R. M. and Colbeck, L. (1978) 'Self appraisal: A convergence of selection and guidance', *Journal of Occupational Psychology*, 51, 271–8.

Dreger, R. M. and Miller, K. S. (1968) 'Comparative psychological studies of whites and negroes in the United States: 1959–65, *Psychological Bulletin Monograph Supplement*, part 2, September, 1–58.

Dulewicz, V. and Fletcher, C. (1982) 'The relationship between previous experience, intelligence and background characteristics of participants and their performance in an assessment centre', *Journal of Occupational Psychology*, 55, 197–207.

Dunnette, M. D. (1962) 'Personnel Management', *Annual Review of Psychology*, 13, 285–314.

Dunnette, M. D. (1963a) 'A note on the criterion', *Journal of Applied Psychology*, 47, 251–4.

Dunnette, M. D. (1963b) 'A modified model for selection research', *Journal of Applied Psychology*, 47, 317–23.

Dunnette, M. D. (1972) 'Comments on Abrahams and Alf's "Pratfalls in moderator research"', *Journal of Applied Psychology*, 56, 3, 252–6.

Ebel, R. L. (1975) 'Prediction? Validation? Construct validity?' paper presented at *Content Validity II Conference, Bowling Green State University*, 1975 (quoted by Guion, 1977).

Eberhardt, B. J. and Muchinsky, P. M. (1982) 'An empirical investigation of the factor stability of Owen's Biographical Questionnaire', *Journal of Applied Psychology*, 67, 138–45.

Edwards, A. L. (1957) *Techniques of Attitude Scale Construction* (New York: Appleton Century Crofts).

Edwards, B. J. (1975) 'Application forms', in B. Ungerson (ed.) *Recruitment Handbook* (London: Gower).

Ekpo-Ufot, A. (1979) 'Self-perceived task relevant abilities, rated job performance and complaining behavior of junior employees in a government ministry', *Journal of Applied Psychology*, 64, 429–34.

Elliot, A. G. P. (1981) 'Some implications of lie scale scores in real-life selection', *Journal of Occupational Psychology*, 54, 9–16.

Equal Employment Opportunity Commission (1978) *Uniform Guidelines for Employee Selection Procedures* (Washington, DC: Equal Employment Opportunity Commission).

Eysenck, H. J. (1960, 1970 new edn) *The Structure of Human Personality* (London: Routledge & Kegan Paul).

Eysenck, H. J. (1973) *The Inequality of Man* (London: Temple Smith).

Eysenck, S. B. G. and Eysenck, H. J. (1963) 'An experimental investigation of desirability response set in a personality questionnaire', *Life Sciences*, 5, 343–55.

Eysenck, H. J. and Nias, D. K. B. (1982) *Astrology: Science or Superstition?* (London: Temple Smith).

Fay, C. H. and Latham, G. P. (1982) 'Effects of training and rating scales on rating errors', *Personnel Psychology*, 35, 105–16.

Fine, S. A. (1986) 'Job analysis', in Buk, R. *Performance Assessment* (Baltimere: The Johns Hopkins University Press).

Fine, S. A. and Elsner, E. J. (1980) *Performance Appraisal in the Department of Housing and Urban Development: a Functional Job Analysis Approach* (Washington, DC: Advanced Resources Research Organization).

Fine, S. A. and Wiley, W. W. (1977) *An Introduction to Job Analysis*

(Kalamazoo, Michigan, North-east: Upjohn Institute for Employment Research).

Flanagan, J. C. (1954) 'The critica' ·incident technique', *Psychological Bulletin*, 51, 327–58.

Flanagan, J. C. (1960) *Flanagan Industrial Tests* (Chicago: Science Research Associates).

Flanagan, J. C. and Burns, R. K. (1955) 'The employee performance record: a new appraisal and development tool', *Harvard Business Review*, 33, 5, 95–102.

Fleishman, E. A. (1966) 'Human abilities and the acquisition of skill', in E. A. Bilodeau, *Acquisition of Skill* (London: Academic Press).

Fleishman, E. A. and Hogan, J. C. (1978) *A Taxonomic Method for Assessing the Physical Requirements of Jobs: the Physical Abilities Analysis Approach* (Washington DC: Advanced Research Resources Organization).

Foley, P. P. (1971) *Validity of the Officer Qualification Test for Minority Group Applicants to Officer Candidate School* (Washington DC: Naval Personnel Research and Development Laboratory).

Forbes, R. J. and Jackson, P. R. (1980) 'Non-verbal behaviour and the outcome of selection interviews', *Journal of Occupational Psychology*, 53, 65–72.

Fordham, K. G. (1975) 'Job advertising', in B. Ungerson (ed.) *Recruitment Handbook* (London: Gower).

Fox, J. B. and Scott, J. R. (1943) 'Absenteeism: management's problem', *Business Research Studies, no. 29*, Harvard University, Bureau of Business Research, 30, no. 4.

Frank, F. D. and Whipple, D. (1978) 'An assessor certification program: based on simulation of the assessor job', *Journal of Assessment Center Technology*, 1, Spring.

Frederiksen, N. and Gilbert, A. C. F. (1960) 'Replication of a study of differential predictability', *Educational and Psychological Measurement*, 20, 4, 759–67.

Frederiksen, N. and Melville, D. S. (1954) 'Differential predictability in the use of test scores', *Educational and Psychological Measurement*, 14, 647–56.

Frederiksen, N., Saunders, D. R. and Wand, B. (1957) 'The 'in-basket test', *Psychological Monographs: General and Applied*, 71, Whole no. 483.

Gael, S. and Grant, D. L. (1972) 'Employment test validation for minority and non-minority telephone company service representatives', *Journal of Applied Psychology*, 56, 2, 135–9.

Gardener, K. E. and Williams, A. P. O. (1973) 'A twenty-five year, follow-up of an extended interview procedure in the Royal Navy: Part 1', *Occupational Psychology*, 47, 1–13.

Gauquelin, M. (1978) *Cosmic Influences on Human Behavior* (2nd edn.) (New York: AST).

Gauquelin, M. (1980) *Spheres of Destiny* (London: Dent).

Gauquelin, M., Gauquelin, F. and Eysenck, S. B. G. (1979). 'Personality and position of the planets at birth: an empirical study', *British Journal of Social and Clinical Psychology*, 18, 71–5.

Getzels, J. W. and Jackson, P. W. (1962) *Creativity and Intelligence* (London: Wiley).

Ghiselli, E. E. (1956) 'Dimensional problems of criteria', *Journal of Applied Psychology*, 40, 1–4.

Ghiselli, E. E. (1960) 'The prediction of predictability', *Educational and Psychological Measurement*, 20, 1, 3–8.

Ghiselli, E. E. (1966) *The Validity of Occupational Aptitude Tests* (New York: Wiley).

Ghiselli, E. E. (1973) 'The validity of aptitude tests in personnel selection', *Personnel Psychology*, 26, 461–77.

Ghiselli, E. E. and Brown, C. W. (1955) *Personnel and Industrial Psychology* (New York: McGraw-Hill).

Gill, R. W. T. (1979) 'The in-tray (in-basket) exercise as a measure of management potential', *Journal of Occupational Psychology*, 52, 185–97.

Gill, D., Ungerson, B. and Thakur, M. (1973) *Performance Appraisal in Perspective: A survey of current practice* (London: Institute of Personnel Management).

Glickman, A. S. (1956) 'The naval knowledge test', *Journal of Applied Psychology*, 40, 389–92.

Goldstein, A. P. and Sorcher, M. (1974) *Changing Supervisory Behaviour* (New York: Pergamon Press).

Goldstein, I. L. (1971) 'The application blank: How honest are the responses?' *Journal of Applied Psychology*, 55, 491–2.

Gordon, M. E. and Cohen, S. L. (1973) 'Training behavior as a predictor of trainability', *Personnel Psychology*, 26, 261–72.

Gordon, M. E. and Kleiman, L. S. (1976) 'The prediction of trainability using a work-sample test and an aptitude test: A direct comparison', *Personnel Psychology*, 29, 243–53.

Grant, D. L. and Bray, D. W. (1966) 'The assessment center in the measurement of potential for business management', *Psychological Monographs*, 80, Whole no. 625.

Grigg, A. E., 1948 'A farm knowledge test', *Journal of Applied Psychology*, 32, 452–5.

Guilford, J. P. (1959) *Personality* (New York: McGraw-Hill).

Guilford, J. P. (1965) *Fundamental Statistics in Psychology and Education* (New York: McGraw-Hill).

Guilford, J. P. (1967) *The Nature of Human Intelligence* (New York: McGraw-Hill).

Guinn, N., Tupes, E. C. and Alley, W. E. (1950) *Cultural Subgroup Differences in the Relationships between Air Force Aptitude Composites and Training Criteria*, Technical Report, no. 70–35 (Brooks Air Force Base, Texas: Air Force Human Resources Laboratory).

Guion, R. M. (1965) *Personnel Testing* (New York: McGraw-Hill).

Guion, R. M. (1977) 'Content validity – the source of my discontent', *Applied Psychological Measurement*, 1, 1, 1–10.

Guion, R. M. (1978) '"Content Validity" in moderation', *Personnel Psychology*, 31, 205–13.

Gulliksen, H. (1950) *Theory of Mental Tests* (New York: Wiley).

Haefner, J. E. (1977) 'Race, age, sex and competence as factors in employer selection of the disadvantaged', *Journal of Applied Psychology*, 62, 2, 199–202.

Hambleton, R. K., Swaminathan, H., Cook, L. L. Eignor, D. R. And Gifford, J. A. (1978) Developments in latent trait theory: models, technical issues, and applications', *Review of Educational Research*, 48, 4, 467–510.

Hakel, P. M., Dobmay, J. and Dunnette, M. D. (1970) *Checklists for Describing Job Applicants* (Minnesota: University of Minnesota, Industrial Relations Center).

Hartley, C., Brecht, M., Pagerey, P., Weeks, G., Chapanis, A. and Hoecker, D. (1977) Subjective time estimates of work tasks by office workers', *Journal of Occupational Psychology*, 50, 23–36.

Harvey, O. L. (1934) 'The measurement of handwriting considered as a form of expressive movement', *Character and Personality* 2, 310–21.

Heilman, M. E. (1980) 'The impact of situational factors on personnel decisions concerning women. Varying the sex composition of the applicant pool', *Organizational Behavior and Human Performance*, 26, 386–96.

Heilman, M. E. and Saruwatari, L. R. (1979) 'When beauty is beastly: the effects of appearance and sex on evaluations of job applicants for managerial and non managerial jobs', *Organizational Behavior And Human Performance*, 23, 360–72.

Heim, A. W. (1967) *AH4 Group Test of General Intelligence* (Slough: National Foundation for Educational Research).

Heim, A. W. (1968) *Manual for the A5 Group Test of High-grade Intelligence* (Slough: National Foundation for Educational Research).

Heim, A. W., Watts, K. P. and Simmonds, V. (1970) *Manual for the AH6 Group Tests of High-Level Intelligence* (Slough: National Foundation for Educational Research).

Heneman, H. G. (1974) 'Comparisons of self and superior ratings of managerial performance', *Journal of Applied Psychology*, 59, 638–42.

Henry, J. (ed.) *Criterion Conference* (Pirehurst, North Carolina: Richardson Foundation).

Herriot, P. (1981) 'Towards an attributional theory of the selection interview', *Journal of Occupational Psychology*, 54, 165–73.

Herriot, P. and Rothwell, C. (1981) 'Organizational choice and decision theory. Effects of employers' literature and selection interview', *Journal of Occupational Psychology*, 54, 17–31.

Hinricks, R. (1964) 'Communications activity of industrial research personnel', *Personnel Psychology*, 17, 193–204.

Hodgkiss, J. (1979) *Differential Aptitude Tests: British Manual* (Slough: National Foundation for Educational Research).

Holdsworth, R. E. (1975) 'Identifying management potential', *British Institute of Management Survey Report No. 27* (London: BIM).

Holland, J. L. (1959) 'A theory of vocational choice', *Journal of Counselling Psychology*, 6, 35–44.

Hollandsworth, J. G., Kazelskis, R., Stevens, J. and Dressel, M. E. (1979) 'Relative contributions of verbal, articulative and non verbal communication to employment decisions in the job interview setting', *Personnel Psychology*, 32, 359–67.

Hollingsworth, H. L. (1929) *Vocational Psychology and Character Analysis* (New York: Appleton Century Crofts).

Horn, J. L. and Knapp, J. R. (1974) 'On the subjective character of the empirical base of the structure of intellect model', *Psychological Bulletin*.

Howard, G. S. and Dailey, P. R. (1979) 'Response-shift bias: a source of contamination of self report measures', *Journal of Applied Psychology*, 64, 144–50.

Howard, G. S., Dailey, P. R. and Gulanick, N. A. (1979) 'The feasibility of informed pretests in attenuating response shift bias', *Applied Psychological Measurement*, 3, 481–94.

Huck, J. R. (1973) 'Assessment centers: a review of the external and internal validities', *Personnel Psychology*, 26, 191–212.

Huck, J. R. and Bray, D. W. (1976) 'Management assessment center evaluations and subsequent job performance of white and black females', *Personnel Psychology*, 29, 13–30.

Hulin, C. L. (1962) 'The measurement of executive success', *Journal of Applied Psychology*, 46, 303–6.

Humphreys, L. G. (1973) 'Statistical definitions of test validity for minority groups', *Journal of Applied Psychology*, 58, 1, 1–4.

Hunter, J. E. and Schmidt, F. L. (1976) 'A critical analysis of the statistical and ethical implications of various definitions of "test bias"', *Psychological Bulletin*, 83, 1053–71.

Hunter, J. E. and Schmidt, F. L. (1978) 'Differential and single group validity of employment tests by race: a critical analysis of three recent studies', *Journal of Applied Psychology*, 63, 1, 1–11.

Hunter, J. E. and Schmidt, F. L. (1982) 'Fitting people to jobs: the impact of personnel selection on national productivity' in M. D. Dunnette and E. Fleishman (eds) *Human Performance and Productivity* (Hillsdale, New Jersey: Lawrence Eribaum).

Hunter, J. E., Schmidt, F. L. and Hunter, R. (1979) 'Differential validity of employment tests by race: a comprehensive review and analysis', *Psychological Bulletin*, 86, 4, 721–35.

Ilgen, D. R. and Seely, W. (1974) 'Realistic expectations as an aid in reducing voluntary resignations', *Journal of Applied Psychology*, 59, 452–5.

Jansen, A. (1973) *Validation of Graphological Judgements* (Paris: Mouton).

Jarratt, R. F. (1948) 'Percent increase in output of selected personnel as an index of test efficiency', *Journal of Applied Psychology*, 32, 135–45.

Jenkins, J. G. (1946) 'Validity for what?' *Journal of Consulting Psychology*, 10, 93–8.

Jensen, A. R. (1974) 'How biased are culture-loaded tests?' *Genetic Psychology Monographs*, 90, 185–244.

Jensen, A. R. (1977) 'An examination of culture bias in the Wonderlic Personnel test', *Intelligence*, 1, 51–64.

Jensen, A. R. (1980) *Bias in Mental Testing* (London: Methuen).

Jeswald, T. A. (1977) 'Issues in establishing an assessment center', in Moses, J. L. and Byham, W. C. *Applying the Assessment Center Method* (New York: Pergamon).

Jones, A. (1981) 'Inter-rater reliability in the assessment of group exercises at a UK assessment centre', *Journal of Occupational Psychology*, 54, 79–86.

Jones, M. H. (1950) 'The adequacy of employee selection reports', *Journal of Applied Psychology*, 34, 219–24.

Kagan, J. and Lesser, G. S. (1961) (eds) *Contemporary Issues in Thematic Apperception Methods* (Springfield, Illinois: Charles C. Thomas).

Kane, J. J. and Lawler, E. E. (1978) 'Methods of peer assessment', *Psychological Bulletin*, 85, 555–86.

Kelley, H. H. and Michela, J. L. (1980) 'Attribution theory and research', *Annual Review of Psychology*, 31, 457–501.

Kelly, G. A. (1955) *The Psychology of Personal Constructs* (New York: Norton).

Keenan, A. (1976) 'Effects of non-verbal behaviour of interviewers on candidates' performance', *Journal of Occupational Psychology*, 49, 171–6.

Keenan, A. and Wedderburn, A. A. I. (1980) 'Putting the boot on the other foot: candidates' descriptions of interviewers', *Journal of Occupational Psychology*, 53, 81–9.

Kerr, W. A., Koppelmeir, G. and Sullivan, J. J. (1951) 'Absenteeism, turnover and morale in a metals fabrication factory', *Occupational Psychology*, 25, 50–5.

Kesselman, G. A. and Lopez, F. E. (1979) 'The impact of job analysis on employment test validation for minority and non-minority accounting personnel', *Personnel Psychology*, 32, 91–108.

Kilcross, M. C. (1976) *A Review of Research in Tailored Testing*. Report no. 9/76 (Farnborough, Hants: APRE, Royal Aircraft Establishment).

Kirchner, W. K. and Dunnette, M. D. (1957) 'Applying the weighted application blank technique to a variety of office jobs', *Journal of Applied Psychology*, 41, 206–8.

Klein, S. P. and Owens, W. A. (1965) 'Faking of a scored life history blank as a function of criterion objectivity', *Journal of Applied Psychology*, 49, 452–4.

Klemmer, E. T. and Snyder, F. W. (1972) 'Measurement of time spent communicating', *Journal of Communication*, 22, 142–58.

Klimoski, R. J. and Rafaeli, A. (1983) 'Inferring personal qualities through handwriting analysis', *Journal of Occupational Psychology*, 56, 191–202.

Klimoski, R. J. and Strickland, W. J. (1977) 'Assessment centers – valid or merely prescient?' *Personnel Psychology*, 30, 353–61.

Koh, T. E., Abbatiello, A. and McLoughlin, C. S. (1983) *Cultural Bias in WISC Subtest Items: a response to Judge Grady's Suggestions in Relation to the PASE case*, Mimeographed notes (6007 N. Sheridan Road, Chicago, Illinois, 60660).

Krug, R. E. (1961) 'Personnel selection', in B. von H. Gilmer (ed.) *Industrial Psychology* (New York: McGraw-Hill).

Kuder, G. F. (1960) *Administrators Manual for the Kuder Preference Record* (Chicago: Science Research Associates).

Kuder, G. F. and Richardson, M. W. (1937) 'The theory of estimation of test reliability', *Psychometrika* 2, 151–60.

Landy, F. J. (1976) 'The validity of the interview in police officer selection', *Journal of Applied Psychology*, 61, 193–8.

Landy, F. J. and Trumbo, D. A. (1980) *Psychology of Work Behavior* (Homewood, Illinois: Dorsey Press).

302   Bibliography

Latham, G. P. and Saari, L. M. (1979) 'Application of social learning theory to trained supervisors through behavioural modeling', *Journal of Applied Psychology*, 64, 239–46.
Latham, G. P., Saari, L. M., Pursell, E. D. and Campion, M. A. (1980) 'The situational interview', *Journal of Applied Psychology*, 65, 422–47.
Latham, G. P. and Wexley, K. N. (1981) *Increasing Productivity Through Performance Appraisal* (Reading, Mass: Addison-Wesley).
Lawler, E. E. and Rhode, J. G. (1976) *Information and Control in Organizations* (Pacific Palisades: Goodyear Publishing Company).
Lawshe, C. H. (1952) 'What can industrial psychology do for small business employee selection?', *Personnel Psychology*, 5, 31–4.
Lawshe, C. H. and Bolda, R. A. (1958) 'Expectancy charts I: their use and empirical development', *Personnel Psychology*, 11, 353–65.
Lawshe, C. H. and Schucker, R. E. (1959) 'The relative efficiency of four weighting methods in multiple prediction', *Educational Psychological Measurement*, 19, 103–14.
Lawshe, C. H., Bolda, R. A., Brune, R. L. and Auclair, G. (1958) 'Expectancy charts II: their theoretical development', *Personnel Psychology*, 11, 545–60.
Ledvinka, J., Markos, V. H. and Ladd, R. T. (1982) 'Long-range impact of fair selection standards on minority employment', *Journal of Applied Psychology*, 67, 1, 18–36.
Lefcourt, H. M. (1976) *Locus of Control: Current Trends in Theory and Research* (Hilldale, New Jersey: Erlbaum).
Lemke, E. A. and Kirchner, J. H. (1971) 'Multivariate study of handwriting, intelligence and personality correlates', *Journal of Personality Assessment*, 35, 584–92.
Lent, R. H., Aurback, H. A. and Levin, L. S. (1971a) 'Research design and validity assessment', *Personnel Psychology*, 24, 247–74.
Lent, R. H., Aurback, H. A. and Levin, L. S. (1971b) 'Predictors, criteria, and significant results', *Personnel Psychology*, 24, 519–33.
Leonard, R. L. (1976) 'Cognitive complexity and the similarity – attraction paradigm', *Journal of Research in Personality*, 10, 83–8.
Levine, A. S. and Zachert, V. (1951) 'Use of biographical inventory in the Air Force classification program', *Journal of Applied Psychology*, 35, 241–4.
Levine, E. L., Ash, R. A. and Bennet, A. (1980) 'Exploratory comparative study of four job analysis methods', *Journal of Applied Psychology*, 524–35.
Levine, E. L., Flory, A. and Ashe, R. A. (1977) 'Self asessment in personnel selection', *Journal of Applied Psychology*, 52, 428–35.
Lewin, A. Y. and Zwany, A. (1976) 'Peer nominations: a model, a literature critique and paradigm for research', *Personnel Psychology*, 29, 423–47.
Lewis, C. (1980) 'Investigating the employment interview: a consideration of counselling skills', *Journal of Occupational Psychology*, 53, 111–16.
Linn, R. L. (1973) 'Fair test use in selection', *Review of Educational Research*, 43, 139–61.
Locke, E. A. (1976) 'Nature and causes of job satisfaction', in Dunnette, M. D. (ed.) *Handbook of Industrial and Organizational Psychology* (Chicago: Rand–McNally).

Loewenthal, K. (1975) 'Handwriting and self-presentation', *Journal of Social Psychology*, 96, 267–70.

Loewenthal, K. (1982) 'Handwriting as a guide to character', in D. M. Davey and M. Harris, *Judging People* (London: McGraw-Hill).

Lord, F. M. (1971) 'The self-scoring flexilevel test', *Journal of educational Measurement*, 8, 147–51.

Lord, F. M. and Novick, M. R. (1968) *Statistical Theories of Mental Test Scores* (New York: Addison-Wesley).

Lumsden, J. (1976) 'Test theory', *Annual Review of Psychology*, 27, 254–80.

Lumsden, J. and Ross, J. (1973) 'Validity as theoretical equivalence', *Australian Journal of Psychology*, 25, 3, 191–7.

Luntz, C. (1962) *Vocational Guidance by Astrology* (Saint Paul, Minnesota: Llewellyn Public).

McCall, M. W., Morrison, A. and Hannan, R. L. (1978) *Studies of Managerial Work: Results and Methods* (Greenboro, North Carolina: Centre for Creative Leadership).

McClelland, D. C. (1963) *The Achievement Motive* (New York: Appleton-Century-Crofts).

McClelland, D. C. (1976) *The Achieving Society* (New York: Irvington).

McClelland, D. C. and Bradburn, N. M. (1957) *N Achievement and Managerial Success*, paper, Harvard (quoted in McClelland, 1976).

McClelland, J. N. and Rhodes, F. (1969) 'Prediction of job success for hospital aides and orderlies from MMPI scores and personal history data', *Journal of Applied Psychology*, 53, 49–54.

McCormick, E. J. (1959) 'The development of processes for indirect or synthetic validity, III. Application of job analysis to indirect validity', *Personnel Psychology*, 12, 402–13.

McCormick, E. J. (1976) 'Job and task analysis', in M. D. Dunnette (ed.) *Handbook of Industrial and Organizational Psychology* (Chicago: Rand-McNally).

McCormick, E. H. and Asquith, R. H. (1960) *An Analysis of Work Patterns of CIC Personnel for CUA–59 Class Ships* (Washington, DC: The Clifton Corporation).

McCormick, E. J., Cunningham, J. W. and Gordon, G. C. (1967) 'Job dimensions based on factorial analysis of worker oriented job variables', *Personnel Psychology*, 20, 417–30.

McCormick, E. J., Cunningham, J. W. and Thornton, G. C. (1972) 'The prediction of job requirements by a structured job analysis procedure', *Personnel Psychology*, 26, 431–40.

McCormick, E. J., Finn, R. H. and Scheips, C. D. (1957) 'Patterns of job requirements', *Journal of Applied Psychology*, 41, 358–64.

McCormick, E. J. Jeaneret, P. R. and Mecham, R. C. (1972) 'A study of job characteristics and job dimensions based on the Position Analysis Questionnaire (PAQ)', *Journal of Applied Psychology*, 56, 347–68.

McCormick, E. H. and Tiffin, J. (1974) *Industrial Psychology* (Englewood Cliffs: Prentice-Hall).

MacIntyre, S., Moberg, D. J. and Posner, B. Z. (1980) 'Preferential treatment in pre selection decisions according to sex and race', *Academy of Management Journal*, 23, 4, 738–49.

McKerracher, D. W. and Watson, R. A. (1968) 'The Eysenck Personality Inventory in male and female subnormal psychopaths in a special security hospital', *British Journal of Social and Clinical Psychology*, 7, 295–302.

Macleod, S. (1982) 'Applied astrology: an intuitive approach', in D. M. Davey and M. Harris *Judging People* (London: McGraw-Hill).

McLoughlin, C. S. and Koh, T. H. (1982) 'Testing intelligence: a decision suitable for the psychologist', *Bulletin of the British Psychological Society*, 35, 308–11.

Madden, J. M., Hazel, J. T. and Christal, R. E. (1964) *Worker and Supervisor Agreement Concerning the Worker Job Description* (US Air Force Personnel Research Laboratory) Technical report 64–10.

Makin, P. J. and Robertson, I. T. (1983) 'Self assessment, realistic job previews and occupational decisions', *Personnel Review*, 12, 21–5.

Marquardt, L. D. and McCormick, E. J. (1972) *Attribute Rating Profiles of the Job Elements of the Position Analysis Questionnaire* (Lafayette, Indiana: Department of Psychological Sciences, Purdue University) Contract NR 151 231.

Marquardt, L. D. and McCormick, E. J. (1974) *The Utility of Job Dimensions based on Form B of the Position Analysis Questionnaire in a Job Component Validation Model* (Lafayette, Indiana: Occupational Research Centre, Department of Psychological Sciences, Purdue University) Report no. 5.

Marshall, G. (1964) *Predicting Executive Achievement* (unpublished DBA thesis, Harvard).

Mayfield, E. C., Brown, S. H. and Hamstra, B. W. (1980) 'Selection interviewing in the life insurance industry: an update of reearch and practice', *Personnel Psychology*, 33, 725–39.

Mayo, J., White, O. and Eysenck, H. J. (1977) 'An empirical study of the relation between astrological factors and personality', *Journal of Social Psychology*, 105, 229–36.

Mecham, R. C. (1970) *'The Synthetic Prediction of Personnel Test Requirements and Job Evaluation Points using the Position Analysis Questionnaire* (Ph. D thesis, Lafayette, Indiana: Purdue University).

Mecham, R. C. and McCormick, E. J. (1969) *The Rated attribute requirements of job elements in the Position Analysis Questionnaire* (Lafayette, Indiana: Occupational Research Centre, Purdue University) Report no. 1.

Meehl, P. E. (1954) *Clinical vs. Statistical Prediction* (Minneapolis: University of Minnesota Press).

Mehrabian, A. (1965) 'Communication length as an index of communicator attitude', *Psychological Reports* 17, 519–22.

Messick, S. (1974) *The Standard Problem: Meaning and Values in Measurement and Evaluation*, Presidential address to Division of Measurement and Evaluation APA, New Orleans, August 1974, reported by Guion (1977).

Meyer, H. H. (1961) *An Exploratory Study of the Executive Position Description Questionnaire in the Jewel Tea Company Inc.*, Conference on executive study (quoted by Prien and Ronan, 1971).

Meyerson, P., Prien, E. . and Vick, T. (1965) 'Differentiating positions using an executive position questionnaire', *Journal of Industrial Psychology*, 3, 3, 19–23.

Meyer, H. H. and Bertotti, J. M. (1956) 'Uses and misuses of tests in selecting key personnel', *Personnel*, 277–85.

Miele, F. (1979) 'Cultural bias in the WISC', *Intelligence*, 3, 149–64.

Mintz, A. and Blum, M. L. (1949) 'A re-examination of accident proneness concept', *Journal of Applied Psychology*, 33, 195–211.

Mintzberg, H. H. (1973) *The Nature of Managerial Work* (New York: Harper & Row).

Mischel, W. (1968) *Personality Assessment* (New York: Wiley).

Mischel, W. (1977) 'Self control and the self in T. Mischel (ed.) *The Self-psychological and philosophical issues* (Totowa, NJ: Rowman & Littlefield).

Monahan, C. J. and Muchinsky, P. M. (1983) 'Three decades of personnel selection research', *Journal of Occupational Psychology*, 56, 3, 215–25.

Morrisby, J. R. (1955) *Manual for the Differential Test Battery* (Slough: National Foundation for Educational Research).

Morse, J. E. and Archer, W. B. (1967) *Procedural Guide for Conducting Occupational Surveys in the United States Air Force* PRL–TR–67–11 (Lackland Air Force Base: Personnel Research Laboratory, Aerospace Division).

Mosel, J. L. and Cozan, L. W. (1952) 'The accuracy of application blank work histories', *Journal of Applied Psychology*, 36, 365–9.

Mosel, J. N. and Goheen, H. W. (1959) 'The employment recommendation questionnaire: III validity of different types of references', *Personnel Psychology*, 12, 469–77.

Moses, J. L. and Byham, W. C. (1977) *Applying the Assessment Center Method* (New York: Pergamon).

Moss, D. (1984) *In-basket Performance and Cognitive Complexity* (Unpublished M.Sc. dissertation, University of Manchester Institute of Science and Technology).

Mossholder, K. W. and Arvey, R. D. (1984) 'Synthetic validity: a conceptual and comparative review', *Journal of Applied Psychology*, 69, 322–33.

Muchinsky, P. M. (1979) 'The use of reference reports in personnel selection: a review and evaluation', *Journal of Occupational Psychology*, 52, 287–97.

Muesser, R. E. (1953) 'The weather and other factors influencing employee punctuality', *Journal of Applied Psychology*, 37, 329–37.

Munroe Frazer, J. (1966) *Employment Interviewing* (London: MacDonald & Evans).

Murray, H. A. *et al.* (1938) *Explorations in Personality* (London: Oxford University Press).

Naylor, J. C. and Shine, L. C. (1965) 'A table for determining the increase in mean criterion score obtained by using a selection device', *Journal of Industrial Psychology*, 3, 33–42.

Neidig, R. D. and Neidig, P. J. (1984) 'Multiple assessment center exercises and job relatedness', *Journal of Applied Psychology*, 69, 182–6.

Neiner, A. G. and Owens, W. A. (1982) 'Relationships between two sets of biodata with 7 years separation', *Journal of Applied Psychology*, 67, 146–50.

Newman, J. M. (1978) 'Discrimination recruitment: an empirical analysis',

Industrial and Labour Relations Review, 32, 15–23.

Nias, D. K. B. (1982) 'Astrology: Fact or fiction?' in D. Mackenzie Davey and M. Harris, *Judging People* (London: McGraw-Hill).

Orr, D. B. (1960) 'A new method of clustering jobs', *Journal of Applied Psychology*, 44, 44–9.

Owens, W. A. (1971) A quasi-actuarial basis for individual assessment. American Psychologist, 26, 992–999.

Owens, W. A. (1976) 'Background data', in M. D. Dunnette (ed.) *Handbook of Industrial and Organisational Psychology* (Chicago: Rand–McNally).

Owens, W. A. and Schoenfeld (1979) 'Towards a classification of persons', *Journal of Applied Psychology*, 64, 569–607.

Pace, L. A. and Schoenfeldt, L. F. (1977) 'Legal concerns in the use of weighted applications', *Personnel Psychology*, 30, 159–66.

Palmer, G. J. and McCormick, E. J. A. (1961) 'A factor analysis of job activities', *Journal of Applied Psychology*, 45, 289–94.

Palormo, J. M. (1973) *Computer Programmer Aptitude Battery* (Chicago: Science Research Associates).

Parker, D. and Parker, J. (1975) *The Compleat Astrologer* (London: Mitchell Beazley).

Parry, M. E. (1968) 'Ability of psychologists to estimate validities of personnel tests', *Personnel Psychology*, 21, 139–47.

Patterson, J. (1976) *Interpreting Handwriting* (New York: McKay).

Pearlman, K. (1980) 'Job families: a review and discussion of their implications for personnel selection', *Psychological Bulletin*, 87, 1, 1–29.

Pearn, M. A. (undated) *The Fair Use of Selection Tests* (Slough: National Foundation for Educational Research.

Pervin, L. A. (1980) *Personality: theory assessment and research*, 3rd edn (Chichester: John Wiley).

Phares, E. J. (1976) *Locus of control and personality* (Morristown, New Jersey: General Learning Press).

Pollock, J. and Lake, T. (1983) *What Do You Want to Know about Job Candidates* (London: Centre for Professional Employment Counselling, 37 Jermyn Street).

Popovich, P. and Wanous, J. P. (1982) 'The realistic job preview as persuasive communication', *Academy of Management Review*, 7, 570–8.

Prien, E. P. (1977) 'The function of job analysis in content validation', *Personnel Psychology*, 30, 167–74.

Prien, E. P., Barrett, G. V. and Suwtlik, B. (1965) 'Use of questionnaires in job evaluation', *Journal of Industrial Psychology*, 3, 91–4.

Prien, E. P. and Ronan, W. W. (1971) 'Job analysis: a review of research findings', *Personnel Psychology*, 24, 371–96.

Primoff, E. S. (1975) *How to Prepare and Conduct Job Element Examinations*, GPO No. 029–000–00131–6 (Washington, DC: US Government Printing Office) Primoff, E. S. (1980) 'The use of self assessments in examining', *Personnel Psychology*, 33, 283–90.

Psychological Corporation (1944) *General Clerical Test* (New York: Psychological Corporation).

Rafaeli, A. and Klimoski, R. J. (1983) 'Predicting sales success through handwriting analysis: an evaluation of the effects of training and handwritten sample content', *Journal of Applied Psychology*, 68, 212–17.

Rand, T. M. and Wexley, K. M. (1975) 'Demonstration of the effect "similar to me" in simulated employment interviews', *Psychological Reports*, 36, 535–44.

Raven, J. L. (1960) *Guide to the Standard Progressive Matrices* (London: H. K. Lewis).

Rawls, D. and Rawls, J. R. (1968) 'Personality characteristics and personal history data of successful and less successful executives', *Psychological Reports*, 23, 1032–4.

Reilly, R. R., Blood, M. R., Brown, B. M. and Maletsa, C. A. (1981) 'The effects of realistic job previews: a study and discussion of the literature', *Personnel Psychology*, 34, 823–4.

Reilly, R. R. and Chao, G.T. (1982) 'Validity and fairness of some alternative employee selection procedures', *Personnel Psychology*, 35, 1–62.

Richards, S. A. and Jafee, C. L. (1972) 'Blacks supervising whites: a study of interracial difficulties in working together in a simulated organisation', *Journal of Applied Psychology*, 56, 234–40.

Ritchie, R. J. and Moses, J. L. (1983) 'Assessment center correlates of women's advancement into middle management: a 7-year longitudinal analysis', *Journal of Applied Psychology*, 68, 227–31.

Robertson, I. T. and Downs, S. (1979) 'Learning and the prediction of performance: development of trainability testing in the United Kingdom', *Journal of Applied Psychology*, 64, 42–50.

Robertson, I. T. and Kandola, R. S. (1982) 'Work sample tests: validity, adverse impact and applicant reaction', *Journal of Occupational Psychology*, 55, 171–83.

Robertson, I. T. and Makin, P. J. (in press) 'Management selection in Britain: a survey and critique', *Journal of Occupational Psychology*.

Robertson, I. T. and Mindel, R. M. (1980) 'A study of trainability testing', Journal of Occupational Psychology, 53, 131–8.

Robinson, D. D. (1981) 'Content oriented personnel selection in a small business setting', *Personnel Psychology*, 34, 77–87.

Rodger, A. (undated) *The Seven Point Plan* (London: National Institute of Industrial Psychology).

Rosen, B. and Jerdee, T. H. (1976) 'The nature of job-related age stereotypes', *Journal of Applied Psychology*, 61, 2, 180–3.

Rosen, B. and Merich, M. F. (1979) 'Influence of strong vs weak fair employment policies and applicants' sex on selection and salary recommendations in management simulations', *Journal of Applied Psychology*, 64, 435–9.

Rosensteel, R. K. (1953) *A Validation of a Test Battery and Biographical Data for Machine Operator Trainees* (M.Sc. Thesis, Bowling Green State University).

Rosenthal, D. and Lines, R. (1972) 'Handwriting as a correlate of extraversion', *Journal of Personality Assessment*, 42, 45–8.

Ross, L. (1977) 'The intuitive psychologist and his short comings: distortion in the attribution process', *Advances in Experimental Social Psychology*, 10, 174–220.

Rothstein, M. and Jackson, D. N. (1980) 'Decision making in the employment interview: An experimental approach', *Journal of Applied Psychology*, 65, 271–83.

Rotter, J. B. (1960) 'Some implications of a social learning theory for the prediction of goal directed behaviour from testing procedures', *Psychological Review*, 67, 301–16.

Rotter, J. B. (1966) 'Generalized expectancies for internal versus external control of reinforcement', *Psychological Monographs*, 80, 1, 609.

Ruch, W. W. (1972) *A Reanalysis of Published Differential Validity Studies*. Paper presented at American Psychological Association meeting Honolulu, September (quoted by Jensen, A. R. 1980).

Rundquist, E. A. (1969) 'The prediction ceiling', *Personnel Psychology*, 22, 109–16.

Runnymede Trust (British Psychological Society Joint Working Party on Employment Assessment and Racial Discrimination) (1980) *Discriminating Fairly: A Guide to Fair Selection* (London: Runnymede Trust/British Psychological Society).

Rusmore, J. T. (1967) 'Identification of aptitudes associated with two criteria of management. Success for twenty theoretically defined jobs' in Henry (ed.) *Criterion Conference* (Pirehurst, North Carolina: Richardson Foundation) quoted in Prien (1977).

Sackett, P. R. and Dreher, G. F. (1982) 'Constructs and assessment center dimensions: Some troubling empirical findings', *Journal of Applied Psychology*, 67, 401–10.

Sackett, P. R. and Dreher, G. F. (1984) 'Situation specificity of behaviour and assessment center validation strategies: A rejoinder to Neidig and Neidig', *Journal of Applied Psychology*, 69, 187–90.

Sandoval, J. and Miille, M. P. W. (1980) 'Accuracy of judgements of WISC–R item difficulty for minority groups', *Journal of Consulting and Clinical Psychology*, 48, 2, 249–53.

Saville, P. and Holdsworth, R. (1983) *Management Interest Inventory* (Esher, Surrey: Saville–Holdsworth).

Saville, P. and Holdsworth, R. (1984) *Occupational Personality Questionnaire*, (Esher Green, Surrey: Saville Holdsworth).

Sawyer, J. (1966) 'Measurement and prediction, clinical and statistical', *Psychological Bulletin*, 66, 178–200.

Schmidt, F. L., Berner, J. G. and Hunter, J. E. (1973) 'Racial differences in validity of employment tests. *Journal of Applied Psychology*, 58, 1, 5–9.

Schmidt, F. L., Greenthal, A. C., Hunter, J. E., Berner, J. G. and Seaton, F. W. (1977) 'Job samples vs paper and pencil trades and technical tests: Adverse impact and examine attitudes', *Personnel Psychology*, 30, 187–97.

Schmidt, F. L. and Hunter, J. E. (1977) 'Development of a general solution to the problem of validity generalization', *Journal of Applied Psychology*, 62, 529–40.

Schmidt, F. L. and Hunter, J. E. (1978) 'Moderator research and the law of small numbers', *Personnel Psychology*, 31, 215–29.

Schmidt, F. L., Hunter, J. E. and Caplan, J. R. (1981) 'Validity generalization results for two groups in the petroleum industry', *Journal of Applied Psychology*, 66, 261–73.

Schmidt, F. L., Hunter, J. E. and Pearlman, K. (1981) 'Task differences as moderators of aptitude test validity in selection: a red herring', *Journal of Applied Psychology*, 66, 2, 166–185.

Schmidt, F. L., Hunter, J. E. and Pearlman, K. (1982) 'Assessing the economic impact of personnel programs on workforce productivity', *Journal of Applied Psychology*, 35, 333–47.

Schmidt, F. L., Hunter, J. E. and Urry, V. W. (1976) 'Statistical power in criterion-related validation studies', *Journal of Applied Psychology*, 61, 4, 473–85.

Schmitt, N. (1976) 'Social and situational determinants of interview decisions: implications for the employment interview' *Personnel Psychology*, 29, 79–101.

Schmitt, N. and Fine, S. A. (1983) 'Inter-rater reliability of judgements of functional levels and skill requirements of jobs based on written task statements', *Journal of Occupational Psychology*, 56, 121–7.

Schmitt, N., Gooding R. Z., Noe, R. A. and Kirsch, M. (1984) 'Meta-analyses of validity studies published between 1964 and 1982 and the investigation of study characteristics', *Personnel Psychology* 37, 407–22.

Schmitt, N., Mellon, P. M. and Bylenga, (1978) 'Sex differences in validity for academic and employment criteria', *Journal of Applied Psychology*, 63, 2, 145–50.

Schrader, A. D. and Osburn, H. G. (1977) 'Biodata taking: effects of induced subtlety and position specificity', *Personnel Psychology*, 30, 395–404.

Schwab, D. P. and Heneman, H. G. (1969) 'Relationship between interview structure and interview reliability in an employment situation', *Journal of Applied Psychology*, 53, 214–17.

Schwab, D., Heneman, H. G. and DeCottis (1975) 'Behaviorally anchored rating scales: a review of the literature', *Personnel Psychology*, 28, 549–62.

Science Research Associates (1980) *Catalogue of Tests for Business and Industry* (Chicago: Science Research Associates).

Seashore, H. G. (1962) 'Women are more predictable than men', *Journal of Counselling Psychology*, 9, 261–70.

Sharma, J. M. and Vardhan (1975) 'Graphology – what handwriting can tell you about an applicant', *Personnel*, 52, 57–63.

Shaw, J. B. and McCormick, E. J. (1976) *The Prediction of Job Ability Requirements Using Attribute Data Based upon the Position Analysis Questionnaire*, Report prepared for USA. Office of Naval Research – contract no. N000 14 76 CO274 (Purdue: Department of Psychological Sciences, Purdue University).

Siegal, A. I. (1983) 'The miniature job training and evaluation approach: additional findings', *Personnel Psychology*, 36, 41–56.

Siegal, A. I. and Bergman, B. A. (1975) 'A job learning approach to performance prediction', *Personnel Psychology*, 28, 325–39.

Simas, K. and McCarrey, M. (1979) 'Impact of recruiter authoritarianism and applicant sex on evaluation and selection decisions in a recruitment interview analogue study', *Journal of Applied Psychology*, 64, 483–91.

Simpson, D. and Saville, P. (1975) *British Reliability and Validity Data on the Computer Programmer Aptitude Battery* (Slough: National Foundation for

Educational Research).

Smith, J. M. (1980) 'Applications and uses of repertory grids in management education' in J. E. Beck and C. J. Cox, *Advances in Management Education* (London: Wiley).

Smith, J. M. (1981) *Are There Four Fatal Flaws in the 30 year CSSB follow up?* Paper read at the Annual Occupational Psychology Conference of the British Psychological Society, University of Sussex.

Smith, J. M. (1982) 'Selection interviewing: a four-step approach', in J. Breakwell, H. Foot and R. Gilmour (eds) *Social Psychology: A Practical Manual* (London: British Psychological Society and Macmillan Press).

Smith, J. M. (1984) *Survey Item Bank* (Bradford: MCB Publications).

Smith, J. M., Hartley, J. and Stewart, B. J. M. (1978) 'A case study of repertory grids used in vocational guidance', *Journal of Occupational Psychology*, 51, 1, 97–104.

Smith, J. M. and Stewart, B. J. M. (1977) 'Repertory grids: a flexible tool for establishing the content and structure of a manager's thoughts', *Management Bibliographies and Reviews, vol. 3*, edited by Ashton, D. (Bradford: MCB Publications).

Smith, J. M., Beck, J., Cooper, C. L., Cox, C., Ottatway, R. and Talbot, R. (1982) *Introducing Organizational Behaviour* (London: Macmillan).

Smith, P. L. (1976) 'The problem of criteria', in M. D. Dunnette (ed.) *Handbook of Industrial and Organizational Psychology* (Chicago: Rand-McNally).

Smith, P. L. and Kendall, L. M. (1963) 'Retranslation of expectations: an approach to the construction of unambiguous anchors for rating scales', *Journal of Applied Psychology*, 47, 149–55.

Sneath, F., Thakur, M. and Medjuck, B. (1976) *Testing People at Work* (London: Institute of Personnel Management).

Sonneman, U. and Kerman, J. P. (1962) 'Handwriting analysis – A valid Selection Tool?' *Personnel Psychology*, 39, 8–14.

Sparks, C. P. (1970) 'Validity of psychological tests', *Personnel Psychology*, 23, 39–46.

Sparrow, J., Patrick, J., Spurgeon, P. and Barwell, F. (1982) 'The use of job component analysis related aptitudes in personnel selection', *Journal of Occupational Psychology*, 55, 3, 157–64.

Spearman, C. (1927) *The Abilities of Man* (London: Macmillan).

Springbett, B. M. (1958) 'Factors affecting the final decision in an employment interview', *Canadian Journal of Psychology*, 12, 13–22.

Stanley, J. C. (1967) 'Further evidence via analysis of variance that women are more predictable academically than men', *Ontario Journal of Educational Research*, 10, 49–56.

Stark, S. (1959) 'Research criteria of executive success', *Journal of Business*, 32, 1–14.

Stewart, R. (1967) *Managers and their jobs* (London: Macmillan).

Stone, C. L. and Sawatzki, B. (1980) 'Hiring bias and the disabled interview: effects of manipulating work history and disability information of the disabled job applicant', *Journal of Vocational Behavior*, 16, 96–104.

Strauss, G. and Sayles, L. R. (1980) *Personnel: the Human Problems of Management* (Englewood Cliffs: Prentice-Hall).

Strong, E. K. (1951) 'Permanence of interest scores over 22 years', *Journal of Applied Psychology*, 35, 89–92.

Tavernier, G. (1973) *Design of Personnel Systems and Records* (London: Gower).

Taylor, J. B. (1968) 'Rating scales as measures of clinical judgement: a method for increasing scale reliabiability and sensitivity', *Educational and Psychological Measurement*, 28, 747–66.

Tenopyr, M. L. (1977) 'Content-construct confusion', *Personnel Psychology*, 30, 47–54.

Tenopyr, M. L. and Oeltjen, P. D. (1982) 'Personnel selection and classification', *Annual Review of Psychology*, 33, 582–618.

Thomas, P. J. (1975) *Racial Differences in the Prediction of Class 'A' School Grades*, Technical Bulletin NPRDC–TR–75–39 (San Diego: California Navy Personnel Research and Development Centre).

Thomson, H. A. (1970) 'Comparison of predictor and criterion judgements of managerial performance using the multi-trait – multi-method approach', *Journal of Applied Psychology*, 54, 6, 496–502.

Thorndike, R. L. (1949) *Personnel Selection: Test and Measurement Techniques* (New York: Wiley).

Thorndike, R. L. (1971) 'Concepts of culture fairness', *Journal of Educational Measurement*, 8, 2, 63–70.

Thornton, G. C. and Byham, W. C. (1982) *Assessment Centers and Managerial Performance* (New York: Academic Press).

Thurstone, L. L. (1938) *Primary Mental Abilities* (Chicago: University of Chicago Press).

Thurstone, L. L. and Thurstone, T. G. (1941) *Factorial Studies of Intelligence* (Chicago: University of Chicago Press).

Thurstone, T. G. and Thurstone, L. L. (1952) *Thurstone Test of Mental Alertness* (Henley on Thames: Science Research Associates).

Tiffin J. and Phelan, R. F. (1953) 'Use of the Kuder Preference Record to predict turnover in an industrial plant', *Personnel Psychology*, 6, 195–204.

Tomkins, S. S. (1961) in J. Kagan and G. S. Lesser (eds) *Contemporary Issues in Thematic Apperception Methods* (Springfield, Illinois: Charles C. Thomas).

Trattner, M. H. (1963) 'Comparison of three methods for assembling aptitude test batteries', *Personnel Psychology* 16, 221–32.

Trattner, M. H., Fine, S. A. and Kubis, J. F. (1955) 'A comparison of worker requirement ratings made by reading job descriptions and by direct observation', *Personnel Psychology*, 8, 183–94.

Trattner, M. H. and O'Leary, B. S. (1980) 'Sample sizes for specified statistical power in testing for differential validity', *Journal of Applied Psychology*, 65, 2, 127–34.

Uhrbrock, R. S. (1961) '2000 scaled items', *Personnel Psychology*, 3, 285–316.

Ulrich, L. and Trumbo, D. (1965) 'The selection interview since 1949; *Psychological Bulletin*, 53, 100–116.

Ungerson, B. (1974) 'Assessment centres a review of research findings', *Personnel Review*, 3, 4–13.

Urry, V. W. (1977) 'Tailored testing: a successful application of latent trait theory', *Journal of Educational Measurement*, 14, 2, 181–96.

USA Government (1978) *Uniform Guidelines on Employee Selection Procedures*, Federal Register, 43, no. 166, 38296–38309.

Valenzi, E. and Andrews, I. R. (1973) 'Individual differences in the decision process of employment interviewers', *Journal of Applied Psychology*, 58, 49–53.

Vernon, P. E. (1960) *The Structure of Human Abilities* (London: Methuen).

Vernon, P. E. (1969) *Intelligence and Cultural Environment* (London: Methuen).

Vincent, M. D. (1974) *Vincent Mechanical Diagrams Test* (Slough: National Foundation for Educational Research).

Wainer, H. and Thissen, D. (1981) 'Graphical data analysis', *Annual Review of Psychology*, 32, 191–241.

Wallace, S. R. (1974) 'How high the validity', *Personnel Psychology*, 27, 397–407.

Walner, T. (1975) 'Hypotheses of handwriting psychology and their verification', *Professional Psychology*, 6, 8–16.

Wanous, J. P. (1977) 'Organizational entry: newcomers moving from outside to inside', *Psychological Bulletin*, 84, 601–18.

Wechsler, D. (1955) *Wechsler Adult Intelligence Scale* (New York: Psychological Corporation).

Weiss, D. J. and Davis, R. V. (1960) 'An objective validation of factual interview data', *Journal of Applied Psychology*, 44, 381–5.

Wernimont, P. F. and Campbell, J. P. (1968) 'Signs, samples and criteria', *Journal of Applied Psychology*, 52, 372–6.

West, L. and Bolanovich, D. J. (1963) 'Evaluation of typewriting proficiency: preliminary test development', *Journal of Applied Psychology*, 47, 403–7.

Wexley, K. N. and Nemerof, H., F. W. (1974) 'The effects of racial prejudice, race of applicant and biographical similarity on interviewer evaluations of job applicants', *Journal of Social and Behavioral Sciences*, 20, 66–78.

Wexley, K. N. and Silverman, S. B. (1978) 'An examination of differences between managerial effectiveness and response patterns on a structured job analysis questionnare', *Journal of Applied Psychology*, 63, 5, 646–9.

Whitlock, G. H., Clouse, R. J. and Spencer, W. F. (1963) 'Predicting accident proneness', *Personnel Psychology*, 16, 35–44.

Wiens, A. N., Jackson, R. H., Manaugh, T. S. and Matarazzo, J. D. (1969) 'Communication length as an index of communicator attitude: A replication', *Journal of Applied Psychology*, 53, 264–6.

Wietz, J. and Nuckols, R. C. (1953) 'A validation study of "How Supervise"', *Journal of Applied Psychology*, 37, 7–8.

Wing, A. M. and Baddely, A. D. (1978) 'A simple measure of handwriting as an index of stress', *Bulletin of the Psychonomic Society*, II, 245–6.

Winter, D. G. and Stewart, A. J. (1977) 'Power motive reliability as a function of retest instructions', *Journal of Consulting Clinical Psychology*, 45, 436–40.

Wollowick, H. B. and McNamara, W. J. (1969) 'Relationships of the components of an assessment center to management success', *Journal of Applied Psychology*, 53, 348–52.

Wonderlic, E. F. (1959) *Wonderlic Personnel Test* (PO Box 7, Northfield, Illinois: E. F. Wonderlic).

Youngman, R., Ostoby, J. D., Monk, J. D. and Heywood, J. (1978) *Analysing Jobs* (Farnborough, Hants: Gower Press).

Zalinski, J. S. and Abrahams, N. M. (1979) 'The effects of item context in faking personnel selection inventories', *Personnel Psychology*, 32, 161–6.

Zdep, S. M. and Weaver, H. B. (1967) The graphoanalytic approach to selecting life insurance salesmen', *Journal of Applied Psychology*, 51, 295–9.

Zedeck, S., Tziner, A., and Middlestat, S. E. (1983) 'Interview validity and reliability: an individual analysis approach', *Personnel Psychology*, 36, 355–70.

Zepp, M., Belenky, A. and Rosen, T. (1977) *Reliability of Functional Job Analysis Statements* (Washington DC: Sidney, A. Time Associates).

Index

Page numbers followed by 'F' and 'T' indicate, respectively, Figures and Tables.

314